Introduction to Media Literacy

SAGE | 50 YEARS

SAGE was founded in 1965 by Sara Miller McCune to support the dissemination of usable knowledge by publishing innovative and high-quality research and teaching content. Today, we publish more than 850 journals, including those of more than 300 learned societies, more than 800 new books per year, and a growing range of library products including archives, data, case studies, reports, and video. SAGE remains majority-owned by our founder, and after Sara's lifetime will become owned by a charitable trust that secures our continued independence.

Los Angeles | London | New Delhi | Singapore | Washington DC

Introduction to Media Literacy

W. James Potter

University of California, Santa Barbara

Los Angeles | London | New Delhi
Singapore | Washington DC

Los Angeles | London | New Delhi
Singapore | Washington DC

FOR INFORMATION:

SAGE Publications, Inc.
2455 Teller Road
Thousand Oaks, California 91320
E-mail: order@sagepub.com

SAGE Publications Ltd.
1 Oliver's Yard
55 City Road
London EC1Y 1SP
United Kingdom

SAGE Publications India Pvt. Ltd.
B 1/I 1 Mohan Cooperative Industrial Area
Mathura Road, New Delhi 110 044
India

SAGE Publications Asia-Pacific Pte. Ltd.
3 Church Street
#10-04 Samsung Hub
Singapore 049483

Copyright © 2016 by W. James Potter

ISBN 978-1-4833-7958-6

Acquisitions Editor: Matthew Byrnie
Associate Editor: Natalie Konopinski
eLearning Editor: Gabrielle Piccininni
Editorial Assistant: Janae Masnovi
Production Editor: Laura Barrett
Copy Editor: Megan Markanich
Typesetter: C&M Digitals (P) Ltd.
Proofreader: Jeff Bryant
Indexer: Teddy Diggs
Cover Designer: Gail Buschman
Marketing Manager: Ashlee Blunk

15 16 17 18 19 10 9 8 7 6 5 4 3 2 1

BRIEF CONTENTS

DETAILED TABLE OF CONTENTS

CHAPTER 8 • Mass Media Effects 143

CHAPTER 9 • Springboard 165

The topic of media literacy is huge. If you do a Google search for "media literacy" you will get over 16 million hits for websites. If you were to spend one minute looking at each of these websites for 24 hours a day with no breaks, it would take you more than 30 years to get to all of them. Clearly, there is too much for anyone to read and absorb. This situation is likely to leave you asking: What is the core essence of media literacy?

I asked myself this question about 25 years ago when I was designing my mass media courses and wanted to take a media literacy approach rather than a traditional academic approach of simply presenting a long list of facts. The mass media were a different phenomenon than other college subjects such as a foreign language, a historical period, or a type of math. The mass media are so integrated into everyone's everyday life that we all take them for granted. Also, the media were so current and changing that it was hard to pin teach some facts that were going to last for a long time. Thus I needed a different approach to teaching such a dynamic everyday phenomenon. Because the mass media were so much a part of everyone's lives, I needed to present the information in a practical way rather in an academic theory-based way. I needed to find a way to show students that there was a lot they were taking for granted so I needed to sensitize them to many things that were happening every day in their lives. This led to me asking questions such as: What do students need to know about how the mass media are affecting them? What do they need to know about the content? What do they need to know about the media industries? Finding information to answer these questions was not difficult, because even then there was so much published about the mass media. The challenge lay in making decisions about what was most important. So I took a couple years getting my notes ready to teach these courses. I eventually refashioned my notes into a book which was published in 1994. After the seventh edition came out in the winter of 2013, my editor suggested that I also write a more introductory version, and so I began working on this book—*An Introduction to Media Literacy*.

What distinguishes this book from *Media Literacy*, is that it is much shorter (by about half) and more practical in its approach, that is, it presents less information about the media industries, their content, their audiences and their effects. Instead the focus is much more on the essential facts that students need to know then translating those ideas into exercises that students can use to develop their understanding of media literacy.

This book will show you this media literacy perspective and set you on a path to exercise more power to use the media to achieve your own goals rather than letting the media use you to achieve their goals.

ORGANIZATION OF THE BOOK

This book is composed of 9 chapters and four issues appendices. The 9 chapters will provide you with the essentials of media literacy that you can use to develop your own perspective on media literacy, then use that perspective to debate the four issues presented in the appendices.

In Chapter 1, I show you why developing media literacy is such an important thing to do. Chapter 2 presents what I call the "media literacy approach." The next six chapters provide basic information about the four knowledge facets of media literacy: Media industries, audiences, content, and effects. Chapter 3 helps you see the media industries from a historical perspective so that you can appreciate the challenges they have overcome to arrive at their current status, then Chapter 4 shows you why understanding the economic perspective is so important to media literacy. Chapter 5 focuses on the audience from the industry's perspective then Chapter 6 examines the audience from the individual's perspective. Chapter 7 analyzes media content and shows that all types of content rest on a foundation of "one-step remove" reality. Chapter 8 will help you expand your vision about what constitutes a media effect. Finally, Chapter 9 summarizes the book's most important ideas by presenting you with a dozen guidelines that you can use in your everyday lives to increase your media literacy.

Each of these 9 chapter begins with a highlighting of the key ideas that structure that chapter. The text in the chapter then explains those ideas in enough detail to prepare you for the concluding section, which helps you to use the information in the chapter to think in a more media literate manner. Most chapters present exercises to help you think more deeply about the perspectives presented in the chapter and to use the information in your own lives. At the end of each chapter is a list of places you can go to get more information on the chapter topic and to keep up to date as we move forward into the future.

I have included four appendices—each focusing on a different media issue. The encountering of these issues can be incorporated at various places as you proceed through the chapters or can be saved to the end of the course after you have transformed the information throughout all 9 chapters into your own knowledge structure on media literacy. Each appendix begins with a statement about how that issue represents a debate or a controversy. I then briefly lay out the argument that people typically use when addressing the issue. Next I present a description of the situation, which is a set of facts that people typically use as evidence for the controversy and information they site in support of their position. The heart of each appendix is the analysis section, where I show you how to dig below the surface of the issue layer by layer to reveal its complexity. Because space is limited in each appendix, I cannot a complete analysis that reveals all the layers and all the complexity of each issue, but what I do present can be used as a model of how to proceed when continuing with your own analysis of the issue.

HOW TO GET THE MOST OUT OF THIS BOOK

The first challenge we all face when confronting a new body of information is motivation. We ask ourselves: Why should I expend all the effort to learn this? How will learning this help me enough to make all that effort worthwhile?

Our initial answers to these questions are likely to make us feel that learning about media literacy is not worth the effort because we feel that we already know a lot about the media. We are familiar with a large number of websites, apps, recording artists, and celebrities. We are already able to access a wide range of entertainment and information, so why would we need to learn a lot more about the media?

This book will show you the answer to that question. By presenting you with some key insights about things you don't know about the mass media, you will be able to expand your perspective into new areas. Your growing perspective will allow you to exercise more control over your media exposures so that you can get more value from those messages.

When you read each of these chapters, be strategic. Begin with the list of **Learning Objectives** to alert you to the purposes of the chapter. Also, answer the **Test Your Knowledge** questions at the beginning of the chapter; your answers will let you know where the strengths and weaknesses are in your existing knowledge structures. Next, use what you have learned from the chapter objectives and your answers to the knowledge questions to formulate your own list of questions, which will then be your reading strategy.

Now you are ready to read the chapter actively. By *actively*, I mean don't just scan the words and sentences; instead, keep your list of questions in your mind and focus on those parts of the chapter that provide answers to your strategic questions. When you have finished reading the chapter, close the book and see if you can articulate the key ideas from that chapter. Check your recall by opening the book and looking at the list of **Key Ideas** I have provided at the end of that chapter. Can you remember only a random mass of facts, or can you envision an organized set of knowledge structured by your questions?

If all of your questions were not answered in the chapter, then continue reading on the topic beginning with the **Further Reading** suggestions presented at the end of most chapters. Also, you might want to update yourself with fresher information so check out the **Keeping Up To Date** suggestions. With many aspects of the mass media, information changes quickly. As I wrote this book, I tried to site the most current facts possible, but by the time you read the book, some of those facts and figures may have gone out of date.

Because media literacy is much more about using information instead of simply memorizing facts, each chapter offers two features to help you internalize the ideas in the chapter. The **Applying Skills** questions give you opportunities to employ each of the seven media literacy skills by engaging more fully with the ideas in the text. Also, the **Applying Media Literacy** feature presents you with extended exercises that take you step-by-step through a process of using the information from the text in a way that makes it relevant for your own experiences.

Finally, you will get more out of each chapter if you try to incorporate the information you are learning into your own experience. Do not get caught in the trap of thinking that it is sufficient to memorize the facts in each chapter and then stop thinking about the material. Simply memorizing facts will not help you increase your media literacy much. Instead, you need to *internalize* the information by drawing it into your own experiences. Continually ask yourself, "How does this new information fit in with what I already know?" "Can I find an example of this in my own life?" and "How can I *apply* this when I deal with the media?" The more you try to apply what you learn in this book, the more you will be internalizing the information and thus making it more a natural part of the way you think.

ANCILLARIES

edge.sagepub.com/potterintro

SAGE edge offers a robust online environment featuring an impressive array of tools and resources for review, study, and further exploration, keeping both instructors and students on the cutting edge of teaching and learning. SAGE edge content is open access and available on demand. Learning and teaching has never been easier!

SAGE edge for Students provides a personalized approach to help students accomplish their coursework goals in an easy-to-use learning environment.

- Mobile-friendly **eFlashcards** strengthen understanding of key terms and concepts

- Mobile-friendly practice **quizzes** allow for independent assessment by students of their mastery of course material

- A customized online **action plan** includes tips and feedback on progress through the course and materials, which allows students to individualize their learning experience

- **Learning objectives** that reinforce the most important material

- Carefully selected chapter-by-chapter **video and multimedia content** which enhance classroom-based explorations of key topics

- Chapter-specific **study questions** are designed to help reinforce key concepts in each chapter for self-review

- EXCLUSIVE! Access to full-text **SAGE journal articles** that have been carefully selected to support and expand on the concepts presented in each chapter

SAGE edge for Instructors, supports teaching by making it easy to integrate quality content and create a rich learning environment for students.

- **Test banks** provide a diverse range of pre-written options as well as the opportunity to edit any question and/or insert personalized questions to effectively assess students' progress and understanding

- Editable, chapter-specific **PowerPoint® slides** offer complete flexibility for creating a multimedia presentation for the course

- EXCLUSIVE! Access to full-text **SAGE journal articles** have been carefully selected to support and expand on the concepts presented in each chapter to encourage students to think critically

- **Chapter activities** for individual or group projects provide lively and stimulating ideas for use in and out of class reinforce active learning.

- **Lecture notes** summarize key concepts by chapter to ease preparation for lectures and class discussions

- Chapter-specific **discussion questions** help launch classroom interaction by prompting students to engage with the material and by reinforcing important content

TO CONCLUDE

This book is an introduction. It is designed to show you the big picture so you can get started efficiently on increasing your own media literacy. It is important to get started now. The world is rapidly changing because of newer information technologies that allow you to create and share you own messages in addition to accessing all kinds of information on just about any conceivable topic.

I hope you will have fun reading this book. And I hope it will expose you to new perspectives from which you can perceive much more about the media. If it does, you will be gaining new insights about your old habits and interpretations. If this happens, I hope you will share your new insights and "war stories" with me. Much of this book has been written to reflect some of the problems and insights my students have had in the media literacy courses I have taught. I have learned much from them. I'd like to learn even more from you. So let me know what you think and send me a message at wjpotter@comm.ucsb.edu.

See you on the journey!

ACKNOWLEDGMENTS

Thank you Matt Byrnie for suggesting that I write *Introduction to Media Literacy* to serve the needs of a different audience than my *Media Literacy* book, which is now going into its eighth edition and has been translated into six languages over the past two decades. And thank you Matt and Natalie Konopinski, Development Editor, for steering me through the very challenging task of cutting the size of *Media Literacy* in half, while not losing any of the key ideas; for helping me translate those ideas into more practical expression without disregarding the rigorous base of research; and for helping me write a book that would appeal to an audience interested in media literacy but wanting a different approach than I had been providing up to this point.

I thank the following reviewers for their thoughtful contributions and the manuscript: Teresa Bergman, University of the Pacific; Michael A. Cavanagh, East Carolina University; Lori Dann, Eastfield College; Tom Grier, Winona State University; Rachel Alicia Griffin, Southern Illinois University Carbondale; Rachael Hanel, Minnesota State University, Mankato; Nina Huntemann, Suffolk University; Frank Nevius, Western Oregon University; Michael Plugh, Fordham University; Jeff Shires, Purdue University North Central; Beatriz Wallace, Duke University; Ken Wolfe, University of Missouri–St. Louis; Catherine Wright, George Mason University; Jingsi Christina Wu, Hofstra University.

I also thank the many other talented people at SAGE that made this book possible. I am especially grateful for Matt's Editorial Assistant Janae Masnovi who did the photo research; for Gabrielle Piccininni, the e-Learning Editor, who created the many digital ancillaries that go along with this book; and for Ashlee Blunk, Marketing Manager. Last but not definitely not least, I thank two people who did the detailed work that readers often take for granted but who are responsible for the quality of how the book looks and the words sound—Production Editor Laura Barrett and Copyeditor Megan Markanich.

ABOUT THE AUTHOR

W. James Potter, professor at the University of California, Santa Barbara, holds one PhD in communication studies and another in instructional technology. He has been teaching media courses for more than two decades at Indiana University; Florida State University; University of California, Los Angeles (UCLA); Stanford University; and Western Michigan University. He has served as editor of the *Journal of Broadcasting & Electronic Media* and is the author of well over 100 scholarly articles and over two dozen books, including *Media Literacy* (now in its 8th edition), *Media Effects, The 11 Myths of Media Violence, Becoming a Strategic Thinker: Developing Skills for Success, On Media Violence, Theory of Media Literacy: A Cognitive Approach*, and *How to Publish Your Communication Research* (with Alison Alexander).

▸ Media literacy strengthens your ability to exercise control over the vast array of messages you encounter through daily media exposure.

Test Your Knowledge: True or False

Before reading this chapter, think about which of the following statements you believe to be **true** and which you believe to be **false**.

1. There is now so much information in our culture that people are cutting back on their time with the media.

2. We should avoid media as much as possible in order to protect ourselves from its harmful effects.

3. Automatic routines have far more disadvantages than advantages.

4. The best way to become more media literate is to stop encountering the media unconsciously and to instead consciously process each message.

Answers can be found on page 247.

1

WHY INCREASE MEDIA LITERACY?

OUR MESSAGE-SATURATED CULTURE

Our culture is saturated with a flood of information. Most of this information is delivered by media **messages** that aggressively compete for our attention. Hollywood releases more than 700 hours of feature films each year, which adds to its base of more than 100,000 hours of films they have already released in previous years. Commercial TV stations generate about 48 million hours of video messages every year worldwide, and radio stations send out 65.5 million hours of original programming each year. In addition, users of a video platform such as YouTube upload more than 100 hours of new video *every minute of every day* (YouTube, 2014). We now have more than 140 million book titles in existence, and another 1,500 new book titles are published throughout the world each day. Then there is the World Wide Web—or Internet—which is so huge that no one knows how big it really is. Google started indexing web pages about a decade ago and has now cataloged more than 13.4 billion pages (de Kunder, 2013), which is a truly large number. However, Google has barely scratched the surface of the web, because these 13.4 billion pages have been estimated to be only 1% of all webpages (Sponder, 2012).

Growth Is Accelerating

Not only are we already saturated with media messages but the rate of production of media messages is growing at an

Learning Objectives

After reading this chapter, you will be able to do the following:

1. Identify how our culture is saturated with a constant flow of information from the media.

2. Recognize how you have been navigating through this flood of information unconsciously with automatic routines that determine what gets filtered into your attention.

3. Describe the ways in which our mental programming is influenced by parents, institutions, everyday experience, and the mass media.

4. Analyze your own media exposure and product buying habits.

5. Develop a well-informed skepticism about how the media have been shaping your automatic routines to achieve their goals, often at the expense of you achieving your own personal goals.

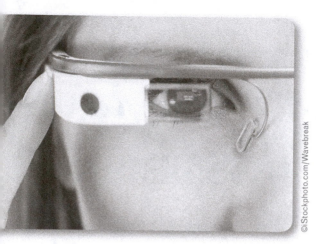
©iStockphoto.com/Wavebreak

▶ Google Glass projects information directly into the wearer's view with its Internet-connected glasses.

accelerating pace. More information has been generated in the last two years than the sum total of all information throughout all recorded history up until two years ago (Silver, 2012). And the rate continues to accelerate!

Why is so much information being produced? One reason is that there are now more people producing information and sharing it than ever before. Half of all the scientists who have ever lived are alive today and producing information. Also, the number of people in this country who identify themselves as musicians has more than doubled in the past four decades, the number of artists have tripled, and the number of authors has increased fivefold (U.S. Bureau of the Census, 2013).

Another reason is that the technology now exists to provide easy-to-use platforms to create and share messages. For example, until recently if you wanted to produce a recording of a song and share it with a large audience, you had to hire musicians and rent a recording studio. Next, you had to make copies of the song (usually a vinyl disc, cassette, or CD) and then go around to record stores to persuade those managers to stock your album. Then you had to persuade program managers at radio stations to play your song so audiences would hear it and want to buy it. Now all you need is a computer with some easy-to-use software (like GarageBand) to produce a recording of your song with high production values; then you upload it to one of many music-sharing platforms. You can also be a videographer, a journalist, a fiction writer, a photographer, or even a video game designer as a hobby and make your messages easily available to millions of people, just like professional artists. Or you could generate and share smaller scale messages such as e-mails and tweets. There are now 2 billion Internet users worldwide, and they send and receive 300 billion e-mail messages each day; Twitter has 500 million tweets per day; and Facebook reports that 100 million photos are uploaded each and every day (Pingdom, 2014).

High Degree of Exposure

Over the last three decades, every new survey of media use has shown that people on average have been increasing their exposure time every year. In your lifetime, much of the increase in media exposure has been from video games and computer usage, which was typically engaged at the same time as other media use, especially listening to music or watching TV (Roberts & Foehr, 2008). Now the fastest growing area of media exposure is with social media, which is increasing at a rate of 37% a year on computers and 63% a year on mobile devices (Nielsenwire, 2012). It is clear that the media are an extremely important part of our everyday lives.

Coping

How do we try to keep up with all this information? One way to cope is to multitask. A recent study of media use found that the average young person (8 to 18) was exposed to about 8 hours of media messages but accomplished this exposure in less than 6 hours per day, which indicates a considerable amount of multitasking (Roberts & Foehr, 2008). With multitasking, a person can listen to recorded music, text friends, and watch video on a pop-up window all at the same time and thus experience 3 hours of media exposure for each hour of clock time.

▶ Social media is the fastest growth area for media exposure, and users consume most of it on mobile devices.

Multitasking, however, is not a good enough strategy for helping us keep up with the flood of information. Remember the figure of 13.4 billion webpages that Google has indexed thus far? If you wanted to check out all these pages and you started reading one every minute of every hour of every day with no breaks, it would take you more than 25 centuries to get through all those pages! Even if you multitasked by viewing five Internet pages simultaneously, it would still take you five centuries to read them all. And that is just Internet pages. While multitasking helps increase our exposure, it is not a good enough strategy to help us get out ahead of the information glut.

AUTOMATIC ROUTINES

The powerful tool that the human mind uses to navigate through all this chaos is the **automatic routine,** which is a sequence of behaviors that we learn from experience then apply again and again with little effort. Once you have learned a sequence—such as tying your shoes, brushing your teeth, driving to school, or playing a song on the guitar—you can perform that task over and over again with very little effort compared to the effort it took you to learn it in the first place. Think of the process of learning to do something as the recording of instructions in our minds, much like how computer programmers write lines of code that tell the computer what to do. Once that code is written, it can later be loaded into our minds and run automatically to guide us through that task with very little conscious thought or effort.

We have developed automatic routines to help us filter out almost all mass media messages and filter in only a tiny fraction of those messages. Thus, we encounter almost all media messages in a state of **automaticity**—that is, we put our minds on "automatic pilot" where our minds automatically filter out almost all message options. I realize that this might sound strange, but think about it. We cannot possibly consider every possible message and consciously decide whether to pay attention to it or not. There are too many messages to consider. So our minds have developed automatic routines that guide this filtering process very quickly and efficiently so we don't have to spend much, if any, mental effort.

▶ Search engines help users sift through billions of webpages for information but may still leave an overwhelming number of options that create a feeling of "information overload."

©iStockphoto.com/Yongyuan Dai

To illustrate this automatic processing, consider what you do when you go to the supermarket to buy food. Let's say you walk into the store with a list of 12 items you need to buy, and 15 minutes later you walk out of the store with your 12 items. In this scenario, how many decisions have you made? The temptation is to say 12 decisions, because you needed to have made a decision to buy each of your 12 items. But what about all the items you decided *not to buy?* The average supermarket today has about 40,000 items on its shelves. So you actually made 40,000 decisions in the relatively short time you were in the supermarket—12 decisions to buy a product and 39,988 decisions not to buy a product. How did you accomplish such an involved task in such a short period of time? You relied on automatic routines that reside in your unconscious mind and reveal themselves to you as your buying habits.

Our culture is a grand supermarket of media messages. Those messages are everywhere whether we realize it or not, except that there are far more messages in our culture than there are products in any supermarket. In our everyday lives—such as when we enter a supermarket—we load an automatic program into our mind that tells it what to look for and ignore the rest. Automatic processing guides most—but certainly not all—of our media exposures. With automatic processing, we encounter a great many media messages without paying much attention to them; thus, we have the feeling that we are filtering them out because we are not paying conscious attention to them. Every once in a while something in a message or in our environment triggers our awareness of a particular message and we pay attention to it, but most messages get filtered out unconsciously.

Advantages and Disadvantages

While there are major advantages to automatic processing, there are also some serious disadvantages. To illustrate these advantages and disadvantages of our automatic processing, think of how you use Internet search engines (like Google, Bing, Yahoo, Ask). Search engines are great tools to help us sort through all the information available on the Internet and alert us to particular sites that will provide the most useful information for our needs. By typing in a few key words, we can direct the search engine to navigate through the huge mass of information to find just the bits we want. For example, if you Google *information overload*, you will get 7.3 million results in .07 seconds. While this Google search is helpful in going from 13.4 billion indexed pages down to 7.3 million pages—a filtering out of 99.95% of all webpages considered—it still leaves us with 7.3 million choices about which sites to access. But Google doesn't stop at this point; it continues filtering by ranking those 7.3 million pages and displaying only the top choices on the first screen of results it presents to you. How does it do this enormous amount of filtering? It uses its special algorithm that factors in three things in its rankings: popularity of sites as determined by how many visits a site gets from other people, suitability of the site for you as estimated by your history of searching an Internet usage (data gathered by Google), and payments from sites who want to buy a higher ranking. This algorithm makes for a wonderfully efficient search experience—going from 7.3 million relevant sites down to the "top 20." But does the algorithm deliver to you the sites with the most credible information? No, because the filtering algorithm is dominated by a concern over popularity, rather than other criteria such as credibility, most insightful information, or most current information. To understand the value of the algorithm, we must understand how well the criteria used by the algorithm matches our own criteria for the value of the search to us.

© Jupiterimages/Creatas/Thinkstock

▶ How is shopping in a supermarket similar to consuming media content?

We cannot avoid using automatic routines; they are essential to our mental well-being. However, it is possible to rely too much on these automatic routines. When this occurs, we get into a rut of paying attention only to the same kinds of messages over and over. This limits our range of experience. When we rely too much on automatic routines for filtering, we are in danger of narrowing down our world rather than growing and expanding our experiences. To illustrate this, let's return to the previously given supermarket example. Let's say you are very health conscious. Had you been less concerned with efficiency when you went into the supermarket, you would have considered a wider range of products and read their labels for ingredients. Not all low-fat products have the same fat content; not all products with vitamins added have the same vitamins or the same proportions. Or perhaps you are very price conscious. Had you been less concerned with efficiency, you would have considered a wider variety of competing products and looked more carefully at the unit pricing, so you could get more value for your money. When we are *too* concerned with efficiency, we lose opportunities to expand our experience and to put ourselves in a position to make better decisions that can make us healthier, wealthier, and happier.

Programming Automatic Routines

Because these automatic routines are learned, they are guided by a sequence of memories. Think of these sequences of memories like mental programs that are continually running in the back of your mind—that is, your subconscious. These mental programs are like computer programs. Your computer relies on many programs to do all sorts of things automatically so that you do not have to program it from scratch every day. Likewise, your human mind relies on many mental programs to guide you through all kinds of routines each day—thus, freeing you up to think about other things.

This brings us to an important question: Who has been programming your mental programs? The answer lies in the complex process of **socialization**—that is, as we go through our everyday lives, we are continually influenced by all sorts of authorities (such as parents, teachers, religious leaders, political leaders, etc.) who tell us what to think about all sorts of things. One of those authorities is the mass media with their flow of messages that constantly tell us how to think about what it means to be well known, successful, happy, witty, attractive, and many other things. Through the way they present news, they tell us what is important and what is not. Through the way they tell entertainment stories, they show us how to behave in all kinds of situations. Through the way they present messages from advertisers, they shape our perception of what our personal problems are and how we can buy products to solve those problems quickly. Thus, the media are constantly tinkering with our mental programs to get us to think and behave in ways that serve their goals. Because the programs that use their codes run automatically in our subconscious minds, we are typically unaware of their subtle influence on us. Unless we periodically analyze this programming, we cannot know the extent to which the media have programmed us. When we find that particular media messages have programmed us into a habit that satisfies their needs while exploiting us, then we need to reprogram that code so that it helps us rather than harms us.

INCREASING MEDIA LITERACY

The purpose of this book is to help you increase your level of **media literacy.** In order to do this, I need to present you with information on many different topics. But information alone will not make you more media literate. You need to use the information, so each chapter has this section—Increasing Media Literacy—where I will present you with some guidelines to help you use the information from that chapter. Each chapter also presents some Applying Media Literacy exercises to help you practice using the information and generate new insights. The more you think about the things you do in these exercises, the more aware you will become of how the mass media operate and how they are influencing you subtly in your everyday lives. That increasing understanding is an essential first step toward your using the media better to achieve your own goals and to reduce the potential for media influence to program you into unhappiness.

The more you are aware of how the mass media operate and how they affect you, the more you gain control over those effects and the more you will separate yourself from typical media users who have allowed the mass media to program the way they think and behave. Let's get started on this task of increasing your awareness by examining two habits you likely take for granted: media exposure habits and product buying habits.

Media Exposure Habits

The media have programmed our media exposure habits by presenting all kinds of messages on every conceivable topic. They continually try to attract us to those messages they think we will find most interesting then do everything they can to encourage us to keep coming back to those messages for habitual exposures over and over.

What media exposure habits do you have? To begin this analysis, estimate how many hours you typically spend with the media each week. Don't worry about being super-accurate at this point; just make a wild guess. Then work through Applying Media Literacy 1.1.

Product Buying Habits

Many people criticize the media—especially their advertising messages—for making us buy things we don't need. While this criticism sounds accurate on the surface, it is faulty. The media do not force us to spend our money on things we don't need; instead, the media alter our beliefs about what we need. They move us beyond thinking of needs as things we absolutely must have to survive and lead us to believe that we have all kinds of other needs that are just as important. For example, they make us believe that we have many types of social needs—that is, we must look, act, and smell a certain way or other people will not like us. They make us believe that we need to achieve certain kinds of lifestyles in order to be successful, attractive, or happy. Once they have convinced us of the importance of these needs, we go shopping to buy those advertised

How Much Time Do You Spend With Media?

This exercise asks you to try to be as accurate as possible in recording the number of hours you spend with each kind of medium each week. Write your number of hours and minutes next to each medium in the following list. Think about an average week. Remember that you can be doing more than one of these at the same time.

_____ Reading magazines

_____ Reading newspapers

_____ Reading textbooks and other materials for classes

_____ Reading for pleasure

_____ Listening to the radio (in your car, portable players, at home, etc.)

_____ Listening to recorded music (non-radio, MP3 player, stereo system at home, etc.)

_____ Watching films at theaters

_____ Watching TV (messages of all kinds on your TV at home)

_____ Watching videos (on your computer, smartphone, and other screens)

_____ Working on a computer (word processing, doing research, etc.)

_____ Communicating on a computer (e-mailing, texting, social networking, etc.)

_____ Playing on a computer (games, visiting websites for entertainment, etc.)

_____ TOTAL (sum of all the figures down the column)

Now that you have completed this inventory, compare your inventory total to the wild guess you made before starting this exercise.

* Are those two numbers the same?

* If they are not the same, which is larger?

* Does this surprise you? Why?

Next, look for differences in the amount of time you spend with different kinds of media in your inventory.

* Do you have a zero on some lines?

- If so, why have you been avoiding those media?
- Have you had bad experiences with those media in the past?

* Which lines have the largest numbers?

- Why do you spend so much time with those media?
- Is it purely a habit, or are you continually generating wonderful experiences with those media?

Now ask yourself THE BIG QUESTION: Am I spending my time most with those media that are delivering the information and entertainment that would most strongly satisfy my own natural needs?

products that will help us satisfy that increasing list of personal needs. Advertisers have programmed many of us into a shopping habit. People in America go to shopping centers about once a week—more often than they go to houses of worship—and Americans now have more shopping centers than high schools. A decade ago, 93% of teenage girls surveyed said that shopping was their favorite activity (Schwartz, 2004), and that figure has not changed. Advertising works by programming our automatic routines so that we shop even when it would be in our best interest to do other things.

Let's analyze your product buying habits by looking at what kinds of products you have been buying. Applying Media Literacy 1.2 begins with an analysis of your food buying habits. At the most basic level, all you need to consume each day is some bread and tap water in order to survive. However, few of us think only in terms of survival when it comes to food. We also need variety. We need to experience different tastes and textures of food. We have psychological needs for food—that is, we eat some foods to excite us when we are bored and other types of foods to comfort us when we are sad. However, there are times when the media convince us we have a need but this lasts only long enough for us to buy a product. But then when we get the product home, we realize that we don't really have a need for it, and it just sits there unused. Are there any foods in your kitchen that have sat there for a week or two without you eating them? If so, think about why you had a need to buy those foods then why that need evaporated and you were stuck with the product.

As for grooming, we could get by with one bar of soap and a toothbrush. Or could we? How many different kinds of needs do you have for grooming products? Is this more or less than your friends? Have you been convinced by ads to buy certain grooming products but then never use them?

As for clothing, we could function with the clothes we are wearing and one spare outfit. But I am guessing that you have more than two outfits of clothing. Why? Group them according to your needs—that is, which are your social clothes, your business clothes, your exercise clothes, and so on? Which set of clothes contains the greatest number of outfits? Why? Do you have clothes in your closet that you rarely wear—or never wear? Why did you buy them? Work through Applying Media Literacy 1.2.

What Are Your Needs?

Now that you have undertaken an analysis of your media habits and your product buying habits, you are ready to analyze your personal needs. Take out a sheet of paper, and write down your needs. This may be difficult if you have not thought much about this before, but let's get started. Begin by simply listing all your needs as they pop into your head. At this point, simply brainstorm and list everything you can. You may want to carry this list around for a few days so you can add to it as other needs occur to you.

What Are Your Product Buying Habits?

1. First, go through your kitchen cabinets and pantry.

   - How many prepared foods (in boxes, cans, and bags) do you have compared to natural foods (milk, fresh fruit, fresh vegetables, etc.)?

   - What proportion of those products are advertised brands, and what proportion are unadvertised or generic?

2. Next, check your bathroom.

   - How many health and beauty aids do you have?

   - How many of those products are for basic health needs, and how many are image enhancers?

   - What proportion of those products are advertised brands, and what proportion are unadvertised or generic?

3. Now go through your clothes closet.

   - How many changes of clothes (outfits) do you have?

   - How many pairs of shoes do you have?

4. Finally, think about how you spend your time.

   - How much time do you take getting washed, groomed, and dressed each day?

   - How much time (how many times) do you spend eating and snacking?

   - What do you do with your leisure time? Are you active in satisfying your needs, or are you passively sitting in front of the TV or listening to music, where you are being told by others what your needs should be?

Next, organize your list into categories. Group all like needs together. For example, you might have several social needs (e.g., make more friends, become more popular), health needs (lose weight, exercise more, etc.), career needs, family needs, school needs, and so forth.

After you have your categories, rank order your groups. Which set of needs is most important to you? What set is second and so on?

The bottom line to all this analysis is to compare your needs to all the products you own and see how well there is a fit. Have you been spending the largest portion of your money on satisfying your most important needs? How about your time—that is, have you been devoting most of your time to satisfying your most important needs? How well have the products you purchased and use the most been satisfying your needs?

Think of what you have done so far on this series of Applying Media Literacy exercises as only a beginning. In the days and weeks to come, think more about your needs and keep clarifying them. Then, as your needs become clearer and clearer, keep comparing them to how you are spending your time and money. This comparison will show you where you are using your resources to satisfy your real, lasting needs and where you are wasting your resources on things that do not satisfy you. Then make the adjustments to your habits to bring them more in line with satisfying your most important needs. When you do this, you are taking more control over programming your own **mental codes.**

KEY IDEAS

- We live in an information-saturated culture where new information is being created at an accelerating rate.

- We cannot physically avoid the flood of information from the mass media, so we have developed automatic routines to filter out almost all of these messages.

- These automatic routines are governed by mental programming that has been influenced by parents, institutions, and experiences we have in our everyday lives.

- The mass media also influence our mental programming through our constant exposure to their messages every day throughout our lives.

- When our automatic routines truly satisfy our own needs, they are very valuable because they are so efficient. However, when our automatic routines instead serve to satisfy the needs of others—such as advertisers and media programmers—they can make us unhappy and harm us.

- When we periodically analyze our automatic routines, we can separate the mental programming that serves to satisfy our real needs from that which takes us in directions that can harm us.

FURTHER READING

Silver, N. (2012). *The signal and the noise: Why so many predictions fail—but some don't*. New York, NY: Penguin Press. (534 pages with index)

The author documents the dramatic increase in information over the past several decades and argues that most of this information is noise, which makes it more difficult—rather than easier—to make good predictions and forecasts.

Wright, A. (2007). *Glut: Mastering information through the ages*. Washington, DC: Joseph Henry Press. (252 pages with index)

The author, who characterizes himself as an information architect, takes an historical approach to showing how humans have evolved in the way they generate, organize, and use information. He argues that all information systems are either nondemocratic and top-down (a hierarchy) or peer-to-peer and open (a network). Tracing the development of human information, he uses perspectives from mythology, library science, biology, neurology, and culture. He uses this historical background to critique the nature of information on the Internet.

KEEPING UP TO DATE

For some chapters, the material I talk about is very fluid and quickly changes. Therefore, some of the facts and figures I present may be out of date by the time you read a particular chapter. To help you keep up to date, I have included some sources of information that you can check out to get the most recent figures available.

Infoniac.com (www.infoniac.com/hi-tech)

This site presents information about the growth of information in the world, and more generally, it provides information about new developments in technologies.

Pingdom (royal.pingdom.com)

This is a blog written by members of the Pingdom team on a wide variety of topics concerning the Internet and web tech issues. Pingdom is a company that provides Internet services to companies around the world.

***Statistical Abstract of the United States* (www.census.gov/compendia/statab)**

The U.S. Department of Commerce releases a new statistical abstract every year. For updates on this material in this chapter, go to the Information & Communications section.

WorldWideWebSize.com (www.worldwidewebsize.com)

This site constantly updates the size of the web from how many webpages are indexed by the major search engines.

$SAGE edge™

Sharpen your skills with SAGE edge at **edge.sagepub.com/potterintro**

SAGE edge for Students provides a personalized approach to help you accomplish your coursework goals in an easy-to-use learning environment.

▶ Becoming more media literate enables you to take control over your engagement with the media in order to achieve your own goals in life.

Test Your Knowledge: True or False

Before reading this chapter, think about which of the following statements you believe to be **true** and which you believe to be **false**.

1. People often criticize the media for the wrong things.
2. Media literacy is essentially critical thinking.
3. Everyone already has some degree of media literacy.
4. Some people are already so media literate that there is no more room for improvement.

Now read the chapter to see if you are right or if you have some faulty beliefs about media literacy.

Answers can be found on page 247.

2

HOW TO THINK ABOUT MEDIA LITERACY

As you learned in the first chapter, we are constantly flooded with a huge number of messages from the mass media. We must screen out all but a tiny percentage. To help us do this screening with the least amount of mental effort, we rely on automatic routines where our minds efficiently filter out media messages without thinking about the process until a particular message triggers our attention. This automatic processing is governed by mental codes that have been influenced by your history of media exposures. Becoming more media literate enables you to understand these codes better and to reprogram them so that you can use the media and their messages much better to achieve your own goals in life.

This chapter will show you what media literacy is. But first, we need to examine some of the assumptions people make about media literacy so we clear away the faulty **beliefs.**

TAKING OUT THE TRASH: CLEARING AWAY FAULTY BELIEFS ABOUT MEDIA LITERACY

Everyone holds many beliefs about the media. Some of these beliefs are accurate but many are faulty. The faulty beliefs can get us into trouble, because they trap us into thinking about the wrong things and they make us think that we are powerless to change. These traps lead people to talk in circles, and this prevents them from moving forward to a

Learning Objectives

After studying this chapter, you will be able to do the following:

1. Analyze faulty ideas about the media and media literacy so that you can avoid falling into the traps of that faulty thinking.

2. Explain the proactive definition of media literacy.

3. Define the three key components of media literacy.

4. Describe seven skills that can be used as tools for building useful knowledge structures.

5. Assess your own knowledge structures about the mass media.

point where they can use media literacy to improve their own lives. Let's examine five of these traps. Once you see what these traps are, you can avoid being caught in faulty reasoning.

Media Are Harmful

Perhaps the most prevalent trap is getting caught in the belief that the media are harmful so that the purpose of media literacy is to get us to avoid all media or at least help us avoid the risks of harm. The trap lies in believing that the media are *only* harmful. Of course there are risks with media exposures, like there are risks with many things we do in our everyday lives. But there are also many wonderful benefits that can be acquired through media exposures. Therefore, the purpose in media literacy is not to help people avoid all media or even any particular kind of message; instead, the purpose of media literacy is to help people recognize the difference in messages between potential harm and potential benefits.

This trap is frequently seen when a new medium captures the public's attention and critics complain only about the dangers of that new medium and ignore the potential for positive advantages. For example, the newest media have stimulated criticism from people like John Sutherland, an English professor at the University College of London, who argues that Facebook reinforces narcissistic drivel and that texting has reduced language into a "bleak, bald, sad shorthand" (quoted in Thompson, 2009). He says that today's technologies of communication that encourage or even require shorter messages like Twitter have shortened people's attention spans and therefore limited their ability to think in longer arcs, which is required for constructing well reasoned essays.

Fortunately there are sometimes people who take a more optimistic position with the arrival of each new mass medium and point out its positive effects. For example, Andrea Lunsford, who is a professor of writing and rhetoric at Stanford University, is convinced that the newer information technologies have actually increased literacy. She says, "I think we're in the midst of a literacy revolution the likes of which we haven't seen since Greek civilization." In addition, she argues that these new technologies of communication are not killing our ability to write well but instead pushing it in new directions of being more personal, creative, and concise. She reached this conclusion after systematically analyzing more than 14,000 student writing samples over a 5-year period. She explains that young people today are much more adept at understanding the needs of their audiences and writing messages especially crafted to appeal to them. For today's youth, writing is about discovering themselves, organizing their thoughts concisely, managing impressions, and persuading their readers.

Media literacy is not just about fearing the media and worrying about protecting one's self and others from their potentially negative effects. Media literacy is also about developing an appreciation for the many positive things the media offer us and developing our abilities to take advantage of those positive things. Thus, we need to develop a balanced perspective on the media and their influence. Media literacy is also about *adapting* to our changing world rather than *ignoring* those changes or *denying* that those changes are happening.

© Sven Hagolani/Corbis

▶ Media literacy increases a person's ability to access a wide variety of messages, no matter what technology is used to transmit them.

Media Literacy Will Destroy My Fun With the Media

Another trap in thinking about media literacy is that it requires a lot of dry analysis and that this will destroy a person's experience of fun with the media. People who fall into this trap use the analogy of analyzing a joke by arguing that when we analyze why a joke is funny, we lose the humor. Or when we overanalyze what our favorite characters do in movies, we reduce our liking of those characters. With these people, analysis is regarded as an acid that eats away at their fun, so they try to avoid analysis.

This is a trap because media literacy is not about dissolving messages with academic discourse; instead, it focuses on digging below the surface to see more things in the message. This can more often lead to greater appreciation of the messages rather than less fun.

Media Literacy Requires the Memorization of a Great Many Facts

It is a trap to think that media literacy focuses on the acquisition of a large number of facts. This is faulty for several reasons. One faulty reason is that media literacy is more focused on knowledge than on facts. Facts by themselves are not knowledge any more than a pile of lumber is a house. Knowledge requires structure to provide context and thereby exhibit meaning. Facts are ephemeral, while knowledge is enduring. Facts go out of date quickly. If your education is simply about the acquisition of a large number of facts, then your education will lose value each year as more and more facts go out of date. But if your education has shown you how to transform facts into knowledge, then you have a structure of meaning that increases in value each year. A characteristic of higher media literacy is the ability to transform information into **knowledge structures** and the willingness to exercise that ability.

Another reason that this belief is faulty is because media literacy requires more than knowledge; it requires the strengthening of a person's **skills** and the person's **personal locus.** This is because knowledge cannot be memorized; instead, it has to be constructed by you. And the construction process relies on tools (which are your skills) and a plan (which is your personal locus).

Media Literacy Is a Special Skill

People often talk about media literacy as if it is "critical thinking." This term has little usefulness in defining media literacy because it has so many different meanings. Some people think critical thinking is simply being critical of the media, while other people have many different meanings (see Box 2.1). While each of these definitional elements has value to increase understanding of media literacy, when we load them all onto one term it gets confusing.

In a larger sense, it is a trap to think that media literacy is any one particular kind of skill; instead, benefits come from the use of a cluster of skills. Furthermore, the skills that are the most useful to media literacy are skills that we already have to various degrees and already use every day.

These are the skills of analysis, evaluation, grouping, induction, deduction, synthesis, and abstraction (see Figure 2.1). We all have some ability with each of these skills, so the media literacy challenge is *not to acquire* these skills; rather, our challenge is *to get better* at using each of these skills as we encounter media messages.

Media Literacy Requires Too Much Effort

A fifth trap in thinking about media literacy is to believe that it requires too much effort because there is so much involved in becoming media literate. This is a trap if you think that media literacy is a category, rather than a continuum. It is faulty to think that you have to do 1,000 difficult things in order to enter the category of media literacy.

Media literacy is not a category—like a box—where either you are in the category or you are not. For example, either you are a high school graduate or you are not; either you have a driver's license or you do not. Instead, media literacy is best regarded as a continuum—like a thermometer—where there are degrees. We all occupy some position on the media literacy continuum. There is no point below which we could say that someone has no literacy, and there is no point at the high end of the continuum where we can say that someone is fully literate; there is always room for improvement.

There is always *opportunity* to improve. Many of these opportunities require very little effort. When you understand the media literacy perspective (to be explained in the next section), you will begin to see all sorts of opportunities to improve your level of media literacy in your everyday lives.

BOX 2.1 : CRITICAL THINKING

There are many different meanings for critical thinking:

* Criticizing the media and not accepting many of their practices

* Becoming more open-minded

* Analyzing media messages in more depth to appreciate the craft of production

* Thinking more broadly about the media and their effects on society

* Elevating one's quality of experience with the media

* Becoming more aware of the economic and political impact of the media

* Regarding the media in a more cultural context

* Becoming more skeptical of the media and their influence on individuals

* Developing a more refined aesthetic sense of quality in media messages

* Being more active in processing media messages rather than taking things for granted

INCREASING MEDIA LITERACY

Now that you have seen the traps in thinking about media literacy and how to avoid them, it's time to focus on what media literacy is. In this section, I present you with the core set of ideas that includes a definition and its three key components.

The Definition

Media literacy is a set of perspectives that we actively use to expose ourselves to the mass media to interpret the meaning of the messages we encounter. We build our perspectives from knowledge structures. To build our knowledge structures, we need tools, raw material, and willingness. The tools are our skills. The raw material is information from the media and from the real world. The willingness comes from our personal locus.

What is a perspective? I'll illustrate this with an analogy. Let's say you wanted to learn about the earth. You could build a 100-foot-tall tower, climb up to the top, and use that as your perspective to study the earth. That would give you a good perspective

Figure 2.1   The Three Components of Media Literacy

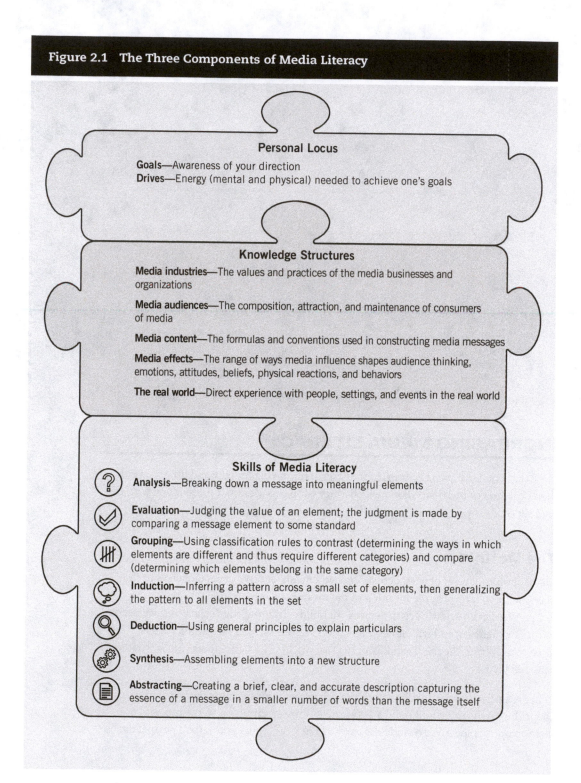

Personal Locus

Goals—Awareness of your direction
Drives—Energy (mental and physical) needed to achieve one's goals

Knowledge Structures

Media industries—The values and practices of the media businesses and organizations

Media audiences—The composition, attraction, and maintenance of consumers of media

Media content—The formulas and conventions used in constructing media messages

Media effects—The range of ways media influence shapes audience thinking, emotions, attitudes, beliefs, physical reactions, and behaviors

The real world—Direct experience with people, settings, and events in the real world

Skills of Media Literacy

Analysis—Breaking down a message into meaningful elements

Evaluation—Judging the value of an element; the judgment is made by comparing a message element to some standard

Grouping—Using classification rules to contrast (determining the ways in which elements are different and thus require different categories) and compare (determining which elements belong in the same category)

Induction—Inferring a pattern across a small set of elements, then generalizing the pattern to all elements in the set

Deduction—Using general principles to explain particulars

Synthesis—Assembling elements into a new structure

Abstracting—Creating a brief, clear, and accurate description capturing the essence of a message in a smaller number of words than the message itself that would not be blocked by trees so that you could see for perhaps several miles in any direction. If your tower were in a forest, you would conclude that the earth is covered with trees. But if your tower were in a suburban neighborhood, you would conclude that the earth is covered with houses, roads, and shopping centers. If your tower were inside the Mercedes-Benz Superdome in New Orleans, you would conclude something quite different. Each of these perspectives would give you a very different idea about the earth. We could get into all kinds of arguments about which perspective delivers the most accurate or best set of ideas about the earth, but such arguments are rather useless. None of these perspectives is better than any other. The key to understanding the earth is to build lots of these towers so you have many different perspectives to enlarge your understanding about what the earth is. And not all of these towers need to be 100 feet tall. Some should be very short so that you can better see what is happening between the blades of grass in a lawn. And others should be hundreds of miles away from the surface so that you can tell that the earth is a sphere and that there are large weather formations constantly churning around the globe. The more perspectives you have from which to experience the media, the more you will be able to see and appreciate in the media, their messages, and their effects on you.

The Big Three

The three key components of media literacy are personal locus, knowledge structures, and skills. These three are necessary to build your wider set of perspectives on the media. Your personal locus provides mental energy and direction. Your knowledge structures are the organizations of what you have learned. Your skills are the tools.

PERSONAL LOCUS Your personal locus is composed of goals and drives. The goals shape the **information processing tasks** by determining what gets filtered in and what gets ignored. The more you are aware of your goals, the more you can direct the process of information seeking. And the stronger your drives for information are, the more effort you will expend to attain your goals. However, when your locus is weak (i.e., you are not aware of particular goals and your drive energy is low), you will default to media control where you allow the media to exercise a high degree of control over exposures and information processing.

The more you know about your personal locus and the more you make conscious decisions to shape it, the more you can control the process of media influence on you. The more you engage your locus, the more you will be increasing your media literacy.

KNOWLEDGE STRUCTURES Knowledge structures are sets of organized information in your memory. Knowledge structures do not occur spontaneously; they must be

©iStockphoto.com/erikrei

▶ Exercising media literacy transforms the many discrete pieces of information you encounter through messages into an organized knowledge structure.

constructed with care and precision. They are not just a pile of facts; they are constructed by carefully crafting pieces of information into an overall design. The structure helps us see patterns. We use these patterns as maps to tell us where to get more information and also where to go to retrieve information that we have previously built into our knowledge structures.

Information is the essential ingredient in knowledge structures. But not all information is equally useful to building a knowledge structure. Some information is rather superficial. If all a person has is the recognition of surface information such as lyrics to TV show theme songs, names of characters and actors, settings for shows, and the like, he or she is operating at a low level of media literacy, because this type of information addresses only the question of *what*. The more useful information comes in the form of the answers to the questions of *how* and *why*. But remember that you first need to know something about the *what* before you can delve deeper into the questions of *how* and *why*.

With media literacy, we need strong knowledge structures in five areas: media industries, media audiences, media content, media effects, and the real world. With good knowledge in these five areas, you will be able to make better decisions about seeking out information, working with that information, and constructing meaning from it that will be more useful in serving your own goals.

In this book, I will help you get started on the first four of these knowledge structures. These four are focused on a different major facet of the media: industries, audiences, content, and effects. The fifth knowledge structure—the real world—is just as important. However, in order to build your knowledge structures about the real world, you need to seek out your own direct experiences rather than rely on what the media tell you. For example, the best way to learn about political campaigns is not to read about them in books or websites or to watch news reports. The best way to learn about political campaigns is to run for office yourself. When you run for a major office—or even when you help someone else run—you acquire a wealth of real-world information that will help you make good assessments about the credibility of media messages about political campaigning. Likewise, people who have played sports will be able to appreciate the athletic accomplishments they see on TV to a greater depth than those who have not physically tested themselves with those challenges. People who have had a wide range of relationships and family experiences will have a higher degree of understanding and more in-depth emotional reactions to those portrayals in the media.

Knowledge structures provide the context we use when trying to make sense of each new media message. The more knowledge structures we have, the more confident we can be in making sense of a wide range of messages. For example, you may have a very large, well-developed knowledge structure about a particular TV series. You may know the names of all the characters in that TV show. You may know everything that has happened to those characters in all the episodes. You may even know the names and histories of the actors who play the characters. If you have all of this information well organized so that you can recall any of it at a moment's notice, you have a well-developed knowledge structure about that TV series. Are you media literate? Within the small corner of the media world where that one TV show resides, you are. But if this were the only knowledge structure you had developed, you would have little understanding of the content produced by the other media. You would have difficulty understanding trends about who owns and controls the media, about how the media have developed over time, about why certain kinds of content are never seen while other types are continually repeated, and about what effects that content may be having on you. With many highly developed knowledge structures, you could understand the entire span of media issues and therefore be able to "see the big picture" about why the media are the way they are.

Let's see how well developed your knowledge structures are about the mass media (see Applying Media Literacy 2.1). If you are not able to answer many of these questions, don't worry too much about it. Most people struggle with these questions. However, this struggle should be taken as an indicator that your knowledge structures could be a lot better when it comes to the mass media. The following six chapters will help you acquire a great deal of the information you need to make these knowledge structures a lot stronger.

SKILLS To construct our knowledge structures, we need to use skills. What skills are most important to media literacy? Many people answer this question with this fuzzy phrase: critical thinking. This term is very popular within writings about media literacy but it creates a problem because everyone seems to have a different definition for what this is (see Box 2.1). While each of these definitional elements is important and useful, putting them all together into one term creates a lot of confusion. You can avoid this problem of fuzzy thinking by focusing on seven specific skills that can be used as the essential tools for building useful knowledge structures. These are the skills of **analysis, evaluation, grouping, induction, deduction, synthesis,** and **abstracting.** We use these tools to mine through the large piles of facts so that we can uncover the particular facts we need and brush away the rest. Once we have selected the facts we need, we shape those facts into sets of information and carefully fit those pieces of information into their proper places in a knowledge structure.

Assessing Your Knowledge Structures

Let's do a quick assessment of your knowledge structures about the mass media. For now, don't worry about whether your answers are correct or incorrect; you will find that out as you read through the book. Instead, think about how many of these 20 questions you feel confident in answering. Even if you are not able to answer more than a few—or any—of these questions with confidence, that is okay. For now! You are not expected to have any of this information in your memory banks.

Mass Media Industries

1. How many mass media are there?
2. Can you list the mass media ordered by how old each is?
3. What is the most dominant mass medium today?
4. What is the most influential force shaping the mass media today?
5. Why is advertising regarded as the engine that powers the mass media industries?
6. How do the mass media businesses maximize their profits?
7. Why is risk so high in the mass media industries?

Mass Media Audiences

8. What is long tail marketing?
9. Why do the mass media businesses no longer seek large, general audiences?
10. What are the major segmentation schemes used by mass media businesses?
11. How is audience exposure different from audience attention?
12. What is the transported exposure state?
13. How do audiences typically make filtering decisions?
14. How is meaning matching different than meaning construction?

Mass Media Content

15. What is the most important content formula used by mass media message producers?
16. Do you know what a genre is? If so, how many genres of content can you name?
17. What are the three meta-genres of mass media content?

Mass Media Effects

18. Can you tell the difference between process effects and manifested effects?
19. What is the difference between an attitudinal effect and a physiological effect?
20. How many factors of influence that lead to media effects can you name?

Analysis is the breaking down of a message into meaningful elements. As we encounter media messages, we can simply accept these messages on the surface or we can dig deeper into the message itself by breaking them down into their components and examining the composition of the elements that make up the message. For example, with a news story, we can accept what a journalist tells us or we can analyze the story for completeness—that is, we can break the story down into its who, what, when, where, why, and how to determine if the story is complete or not.

Evaluation is making a judgment about the value of an element. This judgment is made by comparing a message element to some standard. When we encounter opinions expressed by experts in media messages, we could simply memorize those opinions and make them our own. Or we could take the information elements in the message and compare them to our standards. If those elements meet or exceed our standards, we conclude that the message—and the opinion expressed there—is good, but if the elements fall short of our standard, then we judge the message to be unacceptable.

There is a lot of evidence that people simply accept the opinions they hear in media messages without making their own evaluations. One example of this is the now widespread opinion that in the United States the educational system is not very good, and a big reason for this is that children now spend too much time with the media—especially TV. To illustrate, the National Center for Education Statistics (NCES) is an agency of the U.S. federal government that uses standardized testing to assess the level of learning of America's youth in reading, science, and mathematics each year and then compares their levels of learning with youth in 65 other countries. The 2012 Student Assessment report says that adolescents in the United States are ranked 24th in reading, 28th in science, and 36th in mathematics (National Center for Education Statistics [NCES], 2012). Critiques of the U.S. educational system use information like this to argue that adolescents spend too much time with the media, and this makes their minds lazy, reduces their creativity, and turns them into lethargic entertainment junkies. If this happens, children will not value achievement and will not do well in school.

This belief is faulty because it blames the media, not the child or the parent, for poor academic performance. It also focuses only on the negative effect and gives the media no credit for potentially positive effects. However, when we look carefully at the research evidence, we can see that the typically reported finding is wrong and that when we look even more carefully, there are several effects happening simultaneously. For example, the typically reported finding is that TV viewing is negatively related to academic achievement. And there is a fair amount of research that reports this conclusion. What makes this faulty is that this relationship is explained better by something else—IQ. School achievement is overwhelmingly

▶ Evaluation is an essential media literacy skill. Weigh the evidence against popular opinions on a possible link between children's media consumption and their academic performance.

related to IQ. Also, children with lower IQs watch more TV. So it is IQ that accounts for lower achievement and higher TV viewing. Research analyses that take a child's IQ into account find that there is no overall negative relationship; instead, there is a much more interesting pattern (see Potter, 1987a). The negative relationship does not show up until the child's viewing has passed the threshold of 30 hours per week. Beyond that 30-hour point, the more TV children watch, the lower their academic achievement, and that effect gets stronger with the more hours they watch beyond that threshold. This means that academic achievement goes down only after TV viewing starts to cut into study time and sleep. But there is no negative effect for less than 30 hours of viewing per week. In fact, at the lowest levels of TV viewing, there is actually a positive effect—that is, a child who watches none or only a few hours a week is likely to do less well academically than a child who watches a moderate amount (around 12 to 15 hours per week). Thus, the pattern is as follows: Children who are deprived of the source of information that TV provides do less well in school than children who watch a moderate amount of TV; however, when a child gets to the point where the amount of TV viewing cuts into needed study time, academic performance goes down. TV—as well as the Internet and all other forms of the media—have potentially positive as well as negative effects. TV exposure can displace constructive behaviors such as studying, but TV can expand our experience, teach us valuable social lessons, and stimulate our imaginations. Preventing children from watching TV can prevent a potentially negative effect, but it also prevents positive effects as well.

When we pose the question, "What effect does viewing TV have on a child's academic performance?" we could give the simple, popular answer: There is a negative effect. But now you can see that this answer is too simple—it is simpleminded. It is also misleading because it reinforces the limited belief that media effects are negative and polarized and that the media are to blame.

The reason faulty beliefs are such a dangerous trap is because they are self-reinforcing. By this, I mean that as people are continually exposed to faulty information, they feel even more secure that their faulty beliefs are accurate. They feel less and less motivated to challenge them. When someone points out that the information on which their beliefs are based is faulty, they do not accept this criticism because they are so sure that they are correct. Thus, over time, they are not only less likely to examine their beliefs but also less tolerant of the possibility that beliefs other than their own are correct.

Grouping is the skill we use to put elements into categories. It essentially requires us to compare and contrast across elements to determine how the elements are different (contrasting) so that we can create the groups. Then we need to determine how the elements are the same (comparing) so that we can put similar elements together into the same group.

The key to using the grouping skill well is constructing one or more classification rules, which tell us which characteristics to look for in the elements when doing the comparing and contrasting. For example, if we want to group content on TV, one classification rule might be the intention of the programmer, so we look for characteristics in TV messages to tell us whether the programmer's intention was to entertain us, to inform us, or to persuade us.

The media tell us what classification rules are, so if we accept their classification rules, we will end up with the groups they want us to use. But if we make the effort to determine which classification rules are the best ways for us to organize our perceptions of the world, we will end up with groupings that have more meaning and more value for us.

Induction is inferring a pattern across a small number of elements and then generalizing the pattern to all elements in the larger set. When we examine the result of public opinion polls, we can see that many people are using elements in media stories to infer patterns about real life, and this creates faulty beliefs about real life. For example, when people are asked about health care in this country, 90% of adults say that the health care system is in crisis; this is what many news stories and pundits tell the public. But when people are asked about their own health care, almost 90% feel that their health care is of good quality. About 63% of people think other people's doctors are too interested in making money, but only 20% think their own doctor is

©iStockphoto.com/belterz

▶ Faulty reasoning can lead to false beliefs. For example, many people think that violent crime is more prevalent than crime rates indicate, following exposure to frequent media reports of sensationalized crimes.

too interested in making money. People are using elements they have learned in media messages to dominate their perception of a pattern in real life. They accept a faulty belief because they do not take their own real life experience into account when inferring a pattern—that is, they do not use induction well, instead preferring to use elements from mass media stories and not the elements from their own lives when inferring a pattern.

This faulty use of induction also shows up in other beliefs. For example, public opinion polls about crime for years have shown that typically only about one person in six thinks crime is a big problem in their own community, whereas five out of six say that crime is a big problem in society (Whitman & Loftus, 1996). People think this way because most do not experience crime in their own lives and therefore do not think it is a big problem where they live. However, they are convinced that it is a big problem in society. Where could the public get such an idea? From the media's fixation on deviance in the news. Also the news media prefer to present *sensationalized* events rather than *typical* events. So when a crime is reported, it is usually a violent crime, following the news ethic of "if it bleeds, it leads." Watching evening newscasts with their highlighting of crime and violence leads us to infer that there must be a high rate of crime and that most of it is violent assaults. But in reality, less than 20% of all crime is violent. More than 80% of all crime is property crime, with the victim not even present (U.S. Bureau of the Census, 2013). Furthermore, the rate for violent crime has been declining in this country since the mid-1980s, yet very few people are aware of this decline. Instead, most people believe that violent crime is increasing because they continually see crime stories and gory images in the media. They have fashioned their opinions on sensationalized events, and this type of information provides no useful basis to infer an accurate picture about crime. As for education, 64% give the nation's schools a grade of C or D, but at the same time, 66% give their public school a grade of A or B. As for religion, 65% say that religion is losing its influence on U.S. life, whereas 62% said religion is becoming a stronger influence in own their lives. As for responsibility, almost 90% believe that a major problem with society is that people don't live up to their commitments, but more than 75% say they meet their commitments to families, kids, and employers. Nearly half of the population believes it is impossible for most families to achieve the American Dream, whereas 63% believe they have achieved or are close to the American Dream. And 40% to 50% think the nation is moving in the wrong direction, but 88% of Americans think their own lives and families are moving in the right direction (Whitman, 1996).

Deduction is using general principles to explain particulars—typically with the use of syllogistic reasoning. A well-known syllogism is (1) All men are mortal (general principle). (2) Socrates is a man (particular observation). (3) Therefore, Socrates is mortal (conclusion reached through logical reasoning).

When we have faulty general principles, we will explain particular occurrences in a faulty manner. One general principle that most people hold to be true is that the media, especially TV, have a very strong negative effect on other people. They have an unrealistic opinion that the media cause other people to behave violently. Some people believe that if you allow PSAs (public service announcements) on TV about using condoms, children will learn that it is permissible and even a good thing to have sex. This is clearly an overestimation. At the same time, people *under*estimate the influence the media have on them. When they are asked if they think the media have any effect on them personally, 88% say no. These people argue that the media are primarily channels of entertainment and diversion, so they have no negative effect on them. The people who believe this say that they have watched thousands of hours of crime shows and have never shot anyone or robbed a bank. Although this may be true, this argument does not fully support the claim that the media have no effect on them; this argument is based on the false premise that the media only trigger high-profile, negative behavioral effects that are easy to recognize. But there are many more types of effects, such as giving people the false impression that crime is a more serious problem than it really is or that most crime is violent.

Synthesis is the assembling of elements into a new structure. This is an essential skill we use when building and updating our knowledge structures. As we take in new information, it often does not fit into an existing knowledge structure, so we must adapt that knowledge structure to accommodate the new information. Thus the process of synthesis is using our new media messages to keep reformulating, refining, and updating our existing knowledge structures.

Abstracting is creating a brief, clear, and accurate description capturing the essence of a message in a significantly smaller number of words than the message itself. Thus, when we are describing a media message to someone else or reviewing the message in our own minds, we use the skill of abstracting. The key to using this skill well is to be able to capture the "big picture," or central idea, of the media message in as few words as possible.

KEY IDEAS

- The five key traps you need to avoid when thinking about media literacy are as follows:

  o The media are always harmful.
  o Increasing my media literacy will destroy my fun with the media.
  o Increasing my media literacy will require me to memorize a great many facts.
  o Media literacy is a special skill.
  o Increasing my media literacy will require too much effort.

- Media literacy is a set of perspectives that we actively use to expose ourselves to the mass media to interpret the meaning of the messages we encounter.

- The three key components of media literacy are personal locus, knowledge structures, and skills.

FURTHER READING

Adams, D., & Hamm, M. (2001). *Literacy in a multimedia age*. Norwood, MA: Christopher-Gordon. (199 pages, including glossary and index)

Coming from an educational technology background, the authors argue that media literacy needs to include media analysis, multimedia production, collaborative inquiry, and networking technologies. They present many practical ideas to help teachers guide their students to learn how

to get the most out of messages in all forms of media.

Potter, W. J. (2013). *The skills of media literacy*. Las Vegas, NV: Knowledge Assets, Inc. (224 pages, including references and glossary)

This book presents a detailed description of the seven essential skills of media literacy along with exercises to help readers develop those skills.

$SAGE edge™

Sharpen your skills with SAGE edge at **edge.sagepub.com/potterintro**

SAGE edge for Students provides a personalized approach to help you accomplish your coursework goals in an easy-to-use learning environment.

▶ Video content has adapted from being watched on a traditional TV to being watched on laptops and other mobile devices through websites such as YouTube, founded by Chad Hurley and Steven Chen (pictured).

Test Your Knowledge: True or False

Before reading this chapter, think about which of the following statements you believe to be **true** and which you believe to be **false**.

1. Although civilization is more than 4,000 years old, the mass media have been around for less than two centuries.

2. Film is the oldest of all the mass media.

3. The mass media as a whole employ one of the largest workforces in the U.S. economy.

4. There are currently more women than men working in the mass media industries.

Answers can be found on page 247.

3

MASS MEDIA INDUSTRIES: HISTORICAL PERSPECTIVE

In this chapter, I present you with a map of the most important ideas about the how the mass media industries have developed over time to arrive at what they are today. In the first section of this chapter, I show you the key developments that led to the creation of the mass media. Then we will look at how the mass media industries have developed over time using a life cycle metaphor. This builds to a discussion of how the mass media industries look today. The final section helps you to use these historical patterns to increase your level of media literacy.

PRE-MASS MEDIA

Humans have always communicated with one another for as long as there have been humans. Initially this communication was accomplished through speech utterances and body language; then humans began creating symbols that could be preserved. The earliest known symbols are in the form of paintings on the walls of caves from about 30,000 BC. Then humans developed writing systems around 4,000 BC. Writing remained an individual activity where one person recorded his or her thoughts on a single surface (e.g., clay, parchment) that preserved those thoughts and allowed another person to read them at a later time. People who wanted to make multiple copies of the writing had to create a copy by hand one copy at a time.

Not until the 15th century was a technology invented that allowed for multiple copies of a piece of writing to be made

Learning Objectives

After studying this chapter, you will be able to do the following:

1. Apply the life cycle pattern to organize information about the mass media by describing how the media grow, mature, peak, decline, and adapt.

2. Identify the stage of development for each of the mass media.

3. Identify the factors currently strongest in each mass medium that are responsible for its current stage of development.

4. Recognize the differences in the sizes of the workforce across the mass media.

5. Apply the information you learn in this chapter toward increasing your own media literacy.

relatively quickly when Gutenberg invented a printing press using movable type. During the next several centuries, the printing press was improved, but it wasn't until the middle 19th century when additional technological inventions greatly expanded human's ability to communicate. The invention of the telegraph allowed messages to be sent over long distances very quickly, and the invention of photography allowed humans to capture, store, and share images for the first time. Then in the 20th century, the number of **technological innovations** greatly expanded human's capacity for communication first with the invention of the motion picture, wireless transmission of information with radio then TV, then the invention of computers and the Internet to give all humans the ability to interact in large numbers immediately all over the world.

The amount of technological innovation that took place in the 20th century was far greater than all the technological innovations in human history combined up until that time. This set off a period of change in human communication that happened so fast and so recently that we are still trying to make sense of it.

One way that scholars have attempted to make sense of all this change in human communication was to draw a distinction between interpersonal communication that has been around for thousands of years with mediated communication where the new technologies were used to disseminate messages to many people instantaneously even when they were spread out geographically. Scholars labeled this mediated form of communication **mass communication** because messages were being mass produced much like the way that products were being mass produced in factories. Scholars further believed that there was a **mass audience** for the media, where the term *mass* did not refer to a *large* audience as much as it referred to a certain *type* of audience, where all people were the same—that is, they had the same needs and reacted the same way to media messages. Sociologists in the early 20th century believed that society had become so industrialized with standard jobs, standard products, and standard lifestyles that society had turned people into parts of a large public machine and that individuals were becoming both isolated and alienated from other members of society. They argued that heavily industrialized countries were not just producing standard products at a high rate for the public but that they were also shaping the lives of people by turning them into a mass audience where messages reached everyone quickly and where everyone simply assimilated the same messages as they were presented. Thus, people were vulnerable to the power of the mass media.

This initial belief that the mass media were creating a mass audience was gradually rejected as sociologists began noticing that not all people were reacting to media messages the same way (Bauer & Bauer, 1960; Cantril, 1947; Friedson, 1953). However, the term *mass communication* is still used, but there is no evidence to support the belief that all people are members of the same mass audience. Instead, there are many audiences. Today, even the highest rated prime-time TV series does not attract more than about 3% of the total viewing audience. Even with events such as the Super Bowl, only about 35% of Americans watch. And more important, the people who do watch the Super Bowl do not all experience the same thing. Some viewers are elated as their team is winning, others are depressed as their team is losing, some are happy that there is a reason to party, and others have no idea which teams are playing the game. There is little common experience. Also, during the viewing, people talk to each other and help each other interpret events.

Does this mean there is no difference between communicating in person and communicating with a technological channel? The answer is that there is a difference, but that difference is not keyed to the type of audience or the type of technological channel. Instead, it is keyed to the businesses that use those channels for communication. Thus, there are mass media and non–mass media. A mass medium is a business that uses technological channels of communication strategically to attract certain kinds of audiences that will serve its economic goals then condition those audiences for repeated exposures. For example, Mark Zuckerberg uses the technologies of computers and the Internet to offer a communication platform called Facebook. His purpose is to attract as many users as possible then to condition those users for continual usage of Facebook so that he can achieve his economic goal of generating income from advertisers and others who want access to his data and are willing to pay him large sums of money for that information. In contrast, when you access your personal Facebook page, your goal is to stay in contact with your friends. Therefore Facebook, the business that provides a platform, is a mass medium; you, the person who uses the platform to contact friends, are not a mass medium. Using this definition, there are nine types of mass media—books, magazines, newspapers, recordings, motion pictures, radio, broadcast TV, cable TV, and computers/Internet. While these titles each refer to a technological way of disseminating messages to audiences, it is not the channels that are the mass media; instead, it is the businesses that use these platforms to achieve their economic goals.

DEVELOPMENT OF MASS MEDIA

If you were to start reading through the hundreds of books and thousands of websites that provide information on the mass media industries, you would encounter a great amount of detail—dates, names of inventors, names of businesses, historical occurrences, business practices, complicated charts of who owns what, and tons of financial data. It is easy to get lost in all that detail and not see the big picture of the remarkable similarities in the way each of the mass media has developed and evolved over time. In this section, I will keep the focus on that big picture by using a life cycle

▶ Launching a new mass medium successfully requires more than just technological innovations; marketing innovations are also necessary.

metaphor to show those patterns. This **life cycle pattern** is composed of five stages: **innovation** (or birth), **penetration** (or growth), **peak** (maturity), **decline,** and **adaptation.**

Innovation Stage

Each of the mass media industries began as a technological innovation that made a channel of transmission possible. For example, there would be no film industry if someone had not invented the motion picture camera and projector. However, technology by itself is not enough to create a mass medium. A mass medium is more than a technological invention; there have been many technological innovations that have failed. So the innovation stage is also characterized by **marketing innovations** in addition to technological innovations. This means that someone had to create a business that would use the technology to deliver messages and thus build audiences.

A successful marketing innovation begins with an entrepreneur recognizing a need in the population and then using a new technology to satisfy that need in a way that people begin recognizing the value of the new medium and how it can help them. To do this, the entrepreneur must have a mass-like orientation—that is, he or she must exploit the channel's potential to attract particular audiences then continue to use that channel to condition those audiences for repeat exposures. For example, in the early 1900s, after the motion picture camera and projector were invented, some entrepreneurs turned their living rooms into theaters and began charging people to watch movies. These entrepreneurs found that there was a market for this kind of entertainment, so they took steps to grow that market by renting out storefronts to accommodate larger audiences; then they rented concert theaters and then built their own theaters that were primarily for the showing of films. This growing number of large theaters increased the demand for more movies. This stimulated other entrepreneurs to create film production companies to make and distribute films to the theaters. Without all these entrepreneurs who recognized a public need and marketed their services to grow that need into a habit, the technology of the motion picture camera and projector would never have developed beyond a curious invention.

Analysis

What is your favorite mass medium? Can you identify the technological innovation that made this mass medium possible?

Penetration Stage

Once an innovation has created a new mass media channel, that channel needs to appeal to a very large, heterogeneous population if it is to be effective as a mass medium. This is called penetration. The penetration stage of a medium's development is characterized by the public's growing acceptance of that medium. The public's reaction to a new medium is based on the medium's ability to satisfy existing needs or to create new needs among many members of the public.

Sometimes, the public has a need that is already being satisfied by existing media, but a new medium comes along that can satisfy those needs better in some way. For example, in the 1940s, people were satisfying their need for entertainment with films and radio. But then broadcast TV came along. TV was perceived as being better than radio, because it offered pictures in addition to sound. TV was also perceived as being better than film, because it was more convenient—that is, brought many hours of entertainment into a person's home each and every day, so there was no need to leave the house, get a babysitter, find a parking place, or buy a ticket.

As each medium grows, it is influenced by factors that shape its growth. These factors include the public's need and desire for the medium, additional innovations that change the appeal of other competing media; political and regulatory constraints, and the economic demands of the private enterprises that own and operate the mass media businesses.

Peak Stage

The peak stage is reached when the medium commands the most attention from the public and generates the most revenue compared to other media. This usually happens when the medium has achieved maximum penetration—that is, a very high percentage of households have accepted a medium, and the medium cannot grow in penetration anymore. Of course, it can continue to absorb a greater proportion of an audience member's time and money. For example, broadcast TV reached a peak in the 1960s after taking audiences away from radio and film. Broadcast TV also had taken national advertisers away from magazines and radio.

©iStockphoto.com/djgunner

▶ When a medium reaches its peak, it has secured the maximum proportion of its audience's time and money.

Until the 1990s, broadcast TV remained at a peak as the most dominant mass medium, because people were spending more time with broadcast TV every day compared to any other medium. Also, most people regarded broadcast TV as their primary (and often only) source of entertainment and news.

Decline Stage

Eventually, a peak medium will be challenged by a newer medium and go into a decline. In the decline stage, the medium is characterized by an erosion of audience size leading to an erosion of revenues. A decline in audience size results not from a decline in need for a particular kind of message but by those message needs being satisfied better by a competing medium that is growing in penetration and moving toward its own peak.

Adaptation Stage

A medium enters the adaptation stage of development when it begins to redefine its position in the media marketplace. Repositioning is achieved by identifying a new set of needs that the medium can meet, because the old needs it used to fulfill are now met better by another medium. For example, after radio lost its audience to TV, radio adapted by doing three things. First, it stopped competing directly with TV by eliminating its general entertainment programs such as soap operas, situation comedies, and mystery dramas. Instead, radio shifted to music formats where disc jockeys would play popular songs one after another. Second, it abandoned its strategy of trying to appeal to a general audience and instead segmented the market according to musical tastes, and each station aimed its programming at the people in one of those niches. So now in each radio market, there is likely to be a top 40 station, a rhythm and blues station, a jazz station, an album-oriented rock station, a golden oldies station, a country and western station, a classical music station, and so forth—each appealing to a different group of listeners. Third, it realized that with the invention of the transistor radio in the 1950s, it could be portable whereas TV could not. So radio developed playlists that formed a kind of background mood-shaping experience as people drove in their cars, laid out on beaches, and talked on the phone.

For the past several decades, broadcast TV has been in decline as it fights off challenges by cable TV and computers. Broadcast TV is trying to adapt much like radio did in the 1950s by trying to be more mobile and by programming to niche audiences.

Deduction

Can you use the definitions of each stage of development to deduce a conclusion about which stage currently represents each of the nine mass media?

CURRENT PICTURE

Now let's look at the big picture of where we are today. We'll compare the development of the different mass media industries to get a sense of which are the newest and when each was the strongest.

Life Cycle Pattern

Take a minute to look at the life cycle patterns displayed in Figure 3.1. Notice that the print media of books, newspapers, and magazines are the oldest, with each of them moving out of their innovation stage more than a century ago. Computers are the newest mass medium, with its innovation stage finishing about the time you were born. Notice also that all of the mass media, with the exception of cable TV and computers,

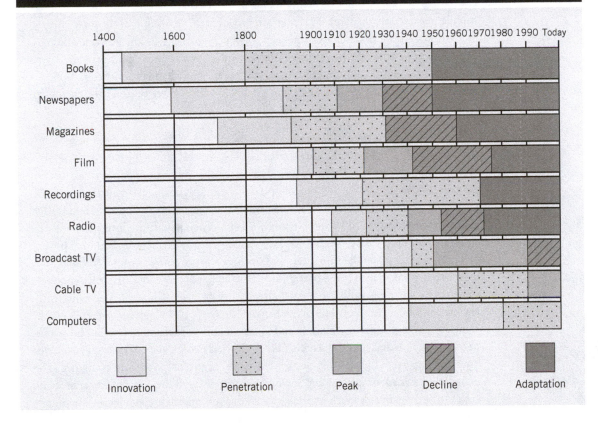

Figure 3.1   Life Cycle Patterns

are currently in the adaptation stage. This means they are all trying to figure out how to coexist with the other up-and-coming media as well as with each other.

Although the life cycle pattern is a good template for showing patterns, it is not perfect. For example, notice that several of the media (books, magazines, and recordings) never reached a peak. This does not mean that those media are not important or successful; it only means that those media never achieved dominance as the most important mass medium at a given time.

Indicators of Peak

We are at an interesting time in the development of the media industries. Broadcast TV has left the peak stage, which lasted for about 40 years, during which time it accounted for almost all of the TV audience. But cable channels have been eroding broadcast TV's hold on the audience, and now broadcast TV has slipped below 50% of the TV-viewing audience, and its revenues are now lagging behind that of cable TV. Cable has been at the peak for more than a decade but is threatened by the medium of computers (which includes receiving media messages on desktops, laptops, notebooks, mobile phones, and the like). The computer medium is showing that it can be the delivery system for books, newspapers, magazines, recordings, film, and video; it can deliver those messages anywhere through a wire or wireless; and it provides the additional feature of being interactive so that users can easily make copies of messages, transform them, and pass them along to others. For all of these reasons, the medium of computers is well on its way to a peak.

We are currently in a very dynamic and interesting time with the development of the mass media. The newer technologies that can be grouped under the title of computer are changing the way audiences access media messages by giving them much more control and variety. Take film, for example. In 2010, Americans spent almost twice the money on home viewing of movies (on-demand videos, digital downloads, and DVDs) than going to theaters ("Unkind Unwind," 2011). When people are limited to theaters to view films, they have only about a dozen choices at any given time, and they must be at the theater when the film starts and sit there for the entire running of the film unless they want to miss some of it. However, when people watch a film through their cable provider or especially from a website, they have a virtually unlimited range of choices, and they can watch the film whenever they want and interrupt whenever they want. Access to news is much faster and up to date on websites than waiting for printed newspapers or magazines to be delivered. Access to books and recordings is faster when downloading them to handheld devices than driving to a brick-and-mortar store. The newer media are growing fast and moving quickly through the penetration stage. They are putting growing pressure on the older media, forcing them to continue adapting.

Convergence

The key to understanding the nature of the
mass media industries today is to realize how the
influence of **convergence** has been so powerful over
the past decade and will continue to be well into
the future. In the most general sense, convergence
simply means the moving together over time of
things that were previously separated. With the
media, convergence means the blending together
of previously separate channels of communication
such that the characteristics that have divided those
channels into distinctly different media have
been eroding. In this section, we'll examine how
three types of convergence—technological, marketing, and psychological—have
been changing the nature of the mass media.

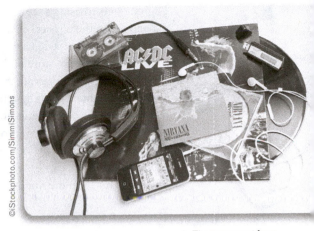

▶ The movement from analog to digital— from vinyl LPs and audiocassettes to CDs and MP3s, for instance—has been key to technological convergence.

TECHNOLOGICAL CONVERGENCE **Technological convergence** refers to how
innovations about storing and transmitting information have brought about changes
to the mass media industries. The key technological innovation that has been driving
convergence is not the computer per se but the software code that runs computers.
This software code is digital—that is, it is written, stored, and read as discrete,
individual numbers that are arranged in sequences to communicate patterns. While
computers and digital code have been around for more than a half century, it was not
until about two decades ago that the media began moving away from **analog coding**
and began using **digital coding** instead. Analog coding is the recording, storage,
and retrieval of information that relies on the physical properties of a medium. For
example, from the early days of sound recording engineers used an analog method of
storing the information of sound recordings. The primary medium of transmitting
recordings was the vinyl disc. The recording was pressed into the disc in the form
of a groove that was composed of tiny fluctuations in the depth and width of the
groove. A needle moved through the groove as the vinyl disc revolved on a turntable.
The needle picked up the tiny fluctuations in the groove and translated them into
electrical impulses that were sent to an amplifier then to a speaker where those
impulses were translated into movements in the speaker, which sent out waves of
compressed air to human ears. In the 1970s, recording companies began shifting
from vinyl discs to magnetic tapes, but the analog system of coding was still used.
Both the vinyl discs and tapes were subject to wear and tear; the messages degraded
with use. Then, in the 1990s, recording companies began translating music into
digital code and storing that code on compact discs (CDs), which could be read with
a laser, and this greatly reduced the wear and tear on the recording.

Digital refers to using a sequence of symbols or bytes (usually numbers) that are not dependent on the physical characteristics of any one medium. With analog, sounds are stored and retrieved in a very different manner than are photographic images, so it is not possible to store both on the same device or to copy one into the other. However, when messages are translated into the digital format, they all share the same fundamental coding system so they can be moved seamlessly across all kinds of media. Thus, the computer is not simply a channel that allows you to access messages on the Internet. It also allows you to access messages previously available only on paper (newspapers, magazines, books, and photographs) as well as recordings, video, and films. Thus the barriers that have traditionally separated the different media into distinct channels of distribution have broken down.

Translating analog messages to digital offers several major advantages. Perhaps the biggest advantage is that digital code is standard and can be read by any medium while the analog code is different for each medium. This standard code allows for ease of making copies of a message and accessing those copies on many different kinds of platforms—your MP3 player, computer, smartphone, car radio, home TV, etc. Another big advantage is that the digital code can be compressed so that all the music on an album could be put on a CD, which is much smaller than the old vinyl discs. Advances in compression technologies have now made it possible to store thousands of albums on a device the size of your thumb. Because of these advantages, all of the mass media have been switching over from analog to digital means of recording, storing, transmitting, and retrieving their messages.

While digitization of messages has been the major technological development leading to convergence, there have also been several other important technological developments that have helped this trend. One of these is the switching from copper wire to fiber optics in the sending of signals to TVs and computers. With the combination of compression of digitized information and fiber optics, both the amount of information and its speed have been increased thousands of times over the past few decades. This has led to the availability of two-way communication. Now computer users can both upload and download enormous files—like huge software programs and videos—in a matter of seconds.

The newest technological innovation has been smartphones. The typical smartphone now has more computing power than Apollo 11 had when it landed a man on the moon (Gibbs, 2012). It allows users to make phone calls, send texts, play music, read books, take pictures, and record video. With the use of apps, you can use smartphones to access the Internet, play games, present coupons, and pay for purchases at brick-and-mortar stores, track people on GPS, trade stocks, and follow traffic patterns in real time. In the United States, 9 out of 10 adults carry a mobile device, and by the eighth grade, 80% of kids have their own cell phone (Cloud, 2012). And in many parts of the world, more people have access to a mobile device than have a toilet or running water. Of all smartphone users, 20% check their phones every 5 to 10 minutes. Three quarters of 20-year-olds sleep with their phones (Gibbs, 2012).

MARKETING CONVERGENCE **Marketing convergence** is a powerful influence that has changed the way media programmers regard audiences and how they develop their messages. In the past, media companies used to define themselves by channels— that is, newspapers saw themselves as a print medium only. However, technological changes have forced media businesses to move away from distinctions by channel of distribution and focused much more on the messages and the audiences. So newspapers now are focused more on the idea of news and are looking for ways to market their messages through all kinds of channels, not just print.

In the past, movie studios produced only films for theaters; magazine companies produced only print magazines; and recording companies produced only records. The channel limited their distribution and kept them in a box where they competed only with other like companies in the same box. But now media companies think outside the box of their channels; they have broadened their marketing by thinking about all the ways they can distribute their messages across as many channels as possible.

With technological convergence, channels are much less important than they used to be. Now the message is more important than the channel of transmission, so mass media companies now focus on identifying the message needs of different kinds of people then develop messages specifically to meet those needs. They translate that message into as many forms as possible to attract and hold that audience—film, TV, websites, etc. This procedure has two major advantages. One advantage is that a single message can generate many streams of revenue, so once the media company pays to have the message produced, it can collect revenues several times. The second advantage is that when the message appears in one channel, it stimulates audience members to expose themselves to the message in other channels. For example, people who read the Harry Potter books are stimulated to see those characters, settings, and events depicted in a movie. They want to read about the actors in those movies in magazines, newspapers, and fan websites.

AP Photo/Pottermore

▶ Harry Potter author J. K. Rowling and Sony partnered to create Pottermore, an interactive website that allows users to engage with the series through another channel in addition to the movies and books.

This trend toward convergence also has changed the way media companies view audiences. In the past, the big media companies would try to attract the largest audiences possible. In order to do this, they would make sure their messages could appeal to everyone without offending anyone with language or with certain themes that a part of the general audience might find distasteful. Thus, they adopted the programming principle of **lowest common denominator (LCD)**. Programming has now shifted to what is called **long tail marketing.** To understand what a long tail is, think of the bell curve, which is referred to as a normal distribution by statisticians and college professors who "grade on the curve." On any characteristic—height, weight, IQ, scores on tests, etc.—people are arranged in a distribution that ranges from lowest to highest and most people cluster in the middle of the distribution. Let's take height, for instance. Adult males can range from under four feet tall to over seven feet tall, which is a range of about 40 inches. Within this overall range, about two thirds of adult males are clustered in the middle five inches (between five foot seven inches and six feet), which forms the fat part of the curve. On either side of this fat part are fewer people who are either shorter or taller than the majority; these small areas on either side of the fat part are the tails. The tails are rather short on both sides of the fat part of the height distribution—there are almost no adult males who are taller than seven feet or shorter than four feet. However, when it comes to personal interests like preferences for music or entertainment, the fat part of the distribution is not so fat; there are fewer people who share the same needs than there are people who share the same height. For example, the highest rated TV series draws less than 3% of the U.S. population with everyone else spread out along a very long tail of preferences for entertainment. Thus long tail marketing refers to finding out what the special needs are for each of the many small niche audiences that form the long tail.

In the past, media companies would focus on the fat part of the distribution, because that is where most people are. But now, savvy media companies know that the "fat" part of the curve is not very large; instead, most people are arrayed out across a very long tail—that is, people are spread out over lots of different interests. Therefore, to make a lot of money, media companies need to develop messages for a lot of different niche audiences.

Long tail marketing is now a viable marketing strategy given the trends that were previously discussed. Huge media conglomerates have deep pockets and can afford to pay for the research necessary to discover these new niche interests then accept the risk of developing new messages. The Internet allows for more experimentation and creativity. To illustrate, old-time brick-and-mortar bookstores had limited shelf space, so they had to be selective in choosing which books to stock. But Amazon is web-based, so it can market all books; thus, it has something to offer to every niche market—no matter how tiny—throughout the entire long tail of interests. This means that Amazon does not need to focus only on best-selling books (books ranked in the top 10 of sales). Instead, Amazon has built its business by long tail marketing—that is, over half of Amazon's sales come from low-ranked books (books ranked lower than 130,000) (Bollier, 2008). Because Amazon offers hundreds of thousands of books for sale on every conceivable topic, it is easier for Amazon to generate sales of 1 million copies of books by selling 10 copies each of 100,000 different books than to try selling 1 million copies of a single book.

PSYCHOLOGICAL CONVERGENCE Convergence is not just a technological or marketing force; it also has profoundly changed the psychology of the audience (Jenkins, 2006). **Psychological convergence** refers to changes in people's perceptions about barriers that previously existed that are now breaking down or totally eliminated due to recent changes in the media. These changes have served to help people see things in a different way and have provided them with tools to act on those changes in perception. One of these changes in perception concerns geography; geographical barriers are no longer important. With e-mail, instant messaging, **social networking sites (SNSs),** and mobile phones, people can stay in close contact psychologically with friends and colleagues even when those people are not physically present. There has also been the breaking down of sociological barriers, such as social class or ethnicity. With newer media platforms, a person can cross all those barriers to make contact with anyone—often not even aware of people's social class or ethnicity. With the removal of these geographical and sociological barriers, people have been redefined their social spheres.

Convergence has changed the way people think about the media and use them. Digitization has allowed people to access messages from various platforms and merge those into their own messages. The interactive features of many platforms have allowed users to bring together all kinds of previously unacquainted people into a single network of friends or professional colleagues. Thus, there is a convergence of people's individual needs with the available of ways to satisfy those needs. People are more active now and do not have to wait for media companies to recognize their needs; instead, they can assemble their own messages as their needs arise. People do not think of themselves only as consumers of the media but also as essential contributors.

▶ New media technology has led to changes in how, when, and where we choose to use media.

Profile of Mass Media Workforce

The media employ a wide variety of people in many different business and occupations. However, you may be surprised to learn that the media employ only a very small percentage of the total workforce—fewer than 2 million people, which is less than 1% of the adult population in the United States. While the general rate of growth in employment is expected to be about

Abstracting

Can you define convergence in the media industries in 25 words or less?

8% across all industries in this country in this decade (2008 to 2018), the media are expected to grow about 10% (U.S. Bureau of Labor Statistics, 2011).

Let's take a look at where these people work. There are two ways to examine this. One way is to examine the relative size of the workforce and businesses across the different media (see Table 3.1). Another way is to examine how people identify with occupations.

The largest employer within the media industries has been newspapers along with film and video production. Software publishing has recently grown rather large in terms of employees and especially in terms of establishments (unique businesses). On the other end of the range is cable TV and sound recording.

Table 3.1	Number of Employees and Number of Establishments Across Media Industries		
Mass Medium	Number of Employees	Number of Establishments	Average Emp. Per Est.
Software Publishing	397,145	8,302	47.8
Newspapers	231,384	7,624	30.3
Film/Video Production	133,365	13,484	9.8
TV Broadcasting	124,875	2,113	59.1
Radio	101,652	6,756	15
Book Publishing	64,969	2,622	24.8
Internet Publishing and Broadcasting, and Web Search	159,673	6,887	23.2
Cable TV and other Subscription Programming	47,699	747	63.8
Record Production	1,037	357	2.9

Source: U.S. Bureau of the Census. (2012). Country business patterns. http://censtats.census.gov/cgi-bin/cbpnaic/cbpdetl.pl

It is also important to look at employment from an additional perspective to get a more accurate picture because a lot of people who work in the media occupations do so only part time, like with actors or musicians. Also, there are people who contribute a great deal to various media industries without being employees of any of those businesses. For example, 70% of authors and writers are self-employed, which means that they get paid when they sell their work to a book publisher or producer of a movie or video project without ever being considered an employee of a media company. Figure 3.2 displays salary data for many of the occupations in the media industries. Notice that

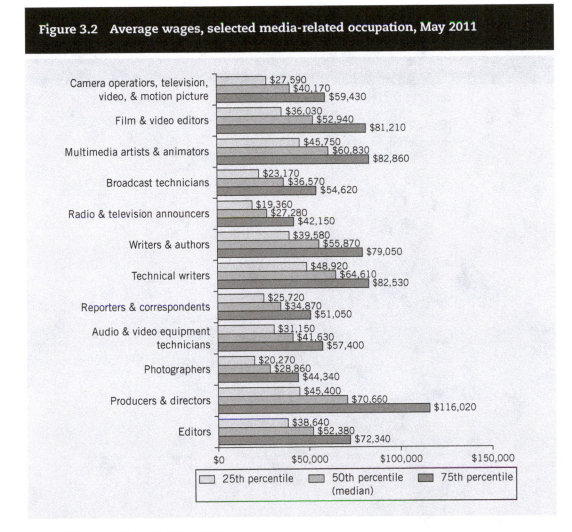

Figure 3.2   Average wages, selected media-related occupation, May 2011

Source: U.S. Bureau of Labor Statistics (2013a).

there is a considerable range of pay within each occupation with people in the 75th percentile being paid two to three times as much as those people in the 25th percentile. This range can be explained by experience (with people new to the industries being paid less than more experienced workers) and size of market (with people in small markets being paid less than workers in larger, more attractive markets). Notice also that the salaries for some occupations (such as producers and directors) are much higher than salaries of other workers (such as camera operators). These differences can be explained by talent—that is, it takes a considerably higher degree of talent to produce or direct a TV show or movie than it does to operate a camera. To look at how employment for media-related industries is growing, see Figure 3.3.

Figure 3.3 Numeric and percent changes in projected employment, selected media-related occupation, 2010–2020

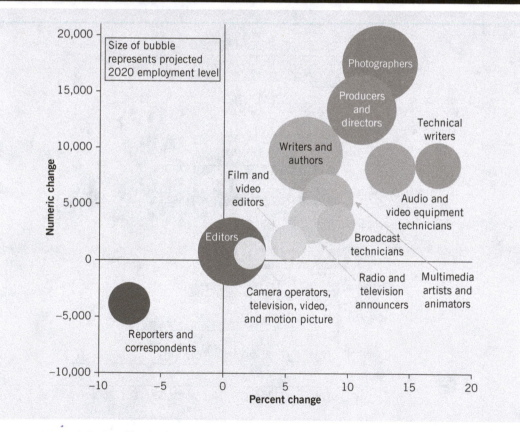

Source: U.S. Bureau of Labor Statistics (2013b).

DEMOGRAPHIC PATTERNS When looking at the total labor force in this country, we can see a trend toward more and more women becoming employed outside the home. Now, about 45% of the labor force is female. With the mass media industries, there has been a growth in the number of women employed, but there are still many more men working in the mass media than there are women.

The media industries that have the highest percentage of women employed are magazines and books, where women make up more than 50% of the labor force. The most growth in terms of the percentage of women has been in the newspaper industry. In 1960, only 20% of all people working on newspapers were women, but this percentage has been growing slightly each year. A major reason for this increase has been because newspapers have been moving away from the traditionally male-oriented press jobs and into more clerical and technologically oriented jobs. In broadcasting, 23% of all employees were women in 1960. This remained fairly static until the early 1970s, when the federal government began monitoring hiring practices in businesses. Since that time, there has been a gradual increase to the current figure of about 30%.

In motion pictures, about 40% of all employees are women, but this varies depending on the sector of the industry. In the large exhibition sector (ticket takers, concession clerks, projectionists, etc.), about 45% of all employees are women. But with the production sector (actors, directors, producers, and writers), 95% are men.

JOURNALISM A popular profession within the media industries is journalism. In this journalistic community, there are about 67,000 reporters and correspondents, 23,000 writers and editors, and 67,000 radio and TV announcers and newscasters. Most are male, White, and young. About one third of working journalists are women, which is an unusually low percentage given that about two thirds of students in journalism schools over the past decade have been women. Only 7.5% are minorities (3.7% are African American, 2.2% Hispanic, 1% Asian American, and 0.6% Native American). More than half of U.S. journalists are younger than 35, and only 10% are 55 or older. Almost all have a college degree, either with a major in the skill of journalism or another content-based area, such as English, American studies, and political science.

©Digital Vision/Digital Vision/Thinkstock

▶ The job market for journalists is expected to decline, while growth is expected for media jobs in public relations and advertising.

Grouping

Can you use what you now know about the mass media industries to categorize them into two groups (highly attractive and not attractive) in terms of a career for you?

In the United States, there are more than 300 universities with journalism/mass communication programs, and each year, about 20,000 bachelor degrees are granted by those journalism programs.

ADVERTISING According to the American Association of Advertising Agencies, there are about 160,000 people currently employed in advertising agencies in the United States: about 24% in creative, 15% in account management, 10% in media, 10% in financial, 8% in special support services, and the rest in secretarial and clerical areas (i.e., about 33%). Women account for 55% (U.S. Bureau of Labor Statistics, 2011).

STATUS Women who are employed in the media industries usually hold positions of lower status, earn less money, and have less education. For example, in newspapers, women hold about 120 managing editorships at 1,700 newspapers in the United States. As far as policymaking positions on newspapers, women hold about 361 (11%), whereas men hold 3,057 (89%). With book publishing, about 64% of editors, vice presidents, and professionals are men; however, there is better representation in the smaller publishing houses.

INCREASING MEDIA LITERACY

Now that you have been presented with some information about how the mass media industries have developed over time and how the forces of convergence are shaping its development today, it is time to try using some of that information to increase your own media literacy. Let's begin by thinking about the idea of convergence. See how well you can work through Applying Media Literacy 3.1.

Next, think about the workforce in the mass media industries (go back and see Table 3.1 and Figures 3.2 and 3.3). Does the relative sizes of the industries surprise you? If you were thinking about a career in the mass media, were you thinking of working in one of the industries that employs a lot of people or only a few people? Why do you think there are such large differences across the sizes of the workforce across industries?

Finally, let's see how creative you are about predicting the future of the mass media industries. As you saw from the life cycle structure in this chapter, a newer medium comes along every few decades, and as it grows, it takes over the functions of some

Thinking About Convergence in the Mass Media Industries

Technological Convergence

1. What device do you typically use that allows you to access messages from two or more different media industries at the same time?

2. How easy is it to use this device?

3. What are the limits of this device? What other types of media messages would you like to get on the device that it currently will not allow you to get?

Marketing Convergence

1. Can you think of examples of when you were accessing messages from one particular media industry (such as a film) and you were stimulated by that message to access a message from another media industry (such as recordings)? List as many examples as you can recall.

2. For each example that you listed, can you identify the media companies who were marketing those messages? Can you see patterns where a media company has attracted your attention to a particular media message (such as a film) then stimulated you to access another media message that was also marketed by that same company?

Psychological Convergence

1. Think about when your parents were your age. What are you able to do with the media that they were not able to do? What are the key differences?

2. How important are these key differences? Do you think your parents would be different today if they had grown up with the media you use the most?

of the existing media. It looks like we are getting ready for a new mass media to come along; what do you think that new medium will be? What functions will that new medium be able to do better than any of the existing media? If you struggle with these questions, don't worry. These are tough questions. It's always easier to look backward and explain what already happened than to predict the future with confidence. However, if you are creative enough and perceptive enough to predict what will come next, then you have a bright future in shaping the mass media industries throughout your career!

Synthesis

Given what you now know about the mass media industries, can you make a good guess about what the next mass medium might be?

- Historically, the mass media industries have followed a life cycle pattern of development (innovation, penetration, peak, decline, and adaptation stages), but now the most powerful force shaping its current nature is convergence.

- Currently the computer and Internet industry is on the rise and competing with the cable TV industry to take over the peak. The remaining mass media industries are working to adapt to the rise of the computer and Internet industry.

- The strongest force shaping the development of the mass media industries today is convergence—technological, marketing, and psychological convergence.

- Historically, the mass media industries have been defined by their channels of distributing messages—book, newspaper, magazine, film, recording, radio, broadcast TV, cable TV, and computer—but over the past few decades the forces of convergence have broken down the old channel distinctions and have shifted the focus away from the characteristics of distribution and onto the needs for media messages in distinct niches of audiences.

- The mass media industries are rather small in terms of the size of their workforces.

> ## FURTHER READING

Neuman, W. R. (Ed.). (2010). *Media, technology, and society: Theories of media evolution*. Ann Arbor: University of Michigan Press. (231 pages with index)

This edited volume consists of 10 chapters written by various scholars. Seven chapters trace the development of a different mass medium—newspapers, telephone, film, radio, TV, cable, and the Internet. The remaining three chapters focus on theories of media evolution, privacy ad security policy, and the future of ownership.

Seguin, J., & Culver, S. H. (2012). *Media career guide: Preparing for jobs in the 21st century* (6th ed.). Boston, MA: Bedford/St. Martin's. (122 pages with index)

This is a practical guide to help college students prepare for a career in any facet of the mass media industries. Its seven chapters offer a lot of practical advice about how to develop a job search strategy; how to get an internship and maximize that experience; and how to write cover letters, resumes, and thank you notes.

> ## KEEPING UP TO DATE

U.S. Bureau of Labor Statistics (www.bls.gov/ces/home.htm)

This is a website run by an agency of the federal government that reports information on all kinds of occupations in the United States, including salaries, duties, and required educational training.

Vault.com (http://www.vault.com/wps/portal/usa)

This is a website that provides lots of useful information about various industries, particularly relevant to media literacy are the industries of publishing, newspapers, Internet and new media, music, broadcast and cable, advertising, and public relations.

Zap 2 It (http://www.zap2it.com)

This website provides ratings of TV shows and figures about popularity of various Hollywood movies.

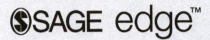

Sharpen your skills with SAGE edge at **edge.sagepub.com/potterintro**

SAGE edge for Students provides a personalized approach to help you accomplish your coursework goals in an easy-to-use learning environment.

©iStockphoto.com/RiverNorthPhotography

▸ Comcast Spotlight, the local advertising division of Comcast, provides opportunities for advertisers to reach fragmented audiences.

Test Your Knowledge: True or False

Before reading this chapter, think about which of the following statements you believe to be **true** and which you believe to be **false**.

1. The primary goal of media businesses is to maximize profits.
2. Profit is defined as the total income that a business is able to generate.
3. The most important player in the economic game is the advertiser.
4. People with the most talent are paid the most money by the media.

Answers can be found on page 247.

4

MASS MEDIA INDUSTRIES: THE ECONOMIC GAME

Economics is essentially about resources. As a consumer of mass media messages, your key resources are money and time. Every day, you give up your time and money to various media businesses in exchange for entertainment and information. Our expenditures of resources for media exposures increases each year and now has reached an average of almost $1,078 per person and over 3,500 hours per household per year (U.S. Bureau of the Census, 2013).

Are you average or above average in terms of how much of your personal resources you exchange for media exposures each year? To answer this question, take a few minutes to complete the inventory in Applying Media Literacy 4.1 to estimate how much money you give to the media each year, both directly and indirectly.

THE MEDIA GAME

Economics is best viewed as a game where the players bring their resources to a market and negotiate with other players in resource exchanges. The goal of the game is to leave the market at the end of each day with resources of greater value than the resources you brought to market at the beginning of the day. If your end-of-day resources are of greater value, you are a net winner for that day.

Learning Objectives

After reading this chapter, you will be able to do the following:

1. Apply the game metaphor to organize your knowledge about media economics.

2. Identify the role of advertising in the mass media economic game.

3. Describe the three major strategies mass media businesses use to be successful.

4. Develop a plan to help you increase your ability to play the economic game more successfully.

Estimating How Much Money You Spend on the Media

1. Before you go any further, stop and make a general estimate about how much money you spent on all forms of the media over the past year. Write your estimate here:

   $ _____

2. Now, let's itemize those expenditures. Think back a year from today and try to remember how much money you spent on each of the following over the past 12 months. If you want to do this accurately, get out your checkbook register and credit card receipts.

   $ _____ Cable subscription (take monthly bill and multiply by 12)

   $ _____ Magazine subscriptions

   $ _____ Individual issues of magazines

   $ _____ Newspaper subscriptions

   $ _____ Individual newspapers

   $ _____ Textbooks

   $ _____ Other books (pleasure reading, gifts, reference books, etc.)

   $ _____ Movie theater admissions

   $ _____ Rental and downloading costs of movies

   $ _____ Radios, TVs, DVD players, MP3 players, etc.

   $ _____ Repairs on media equipment

   $ _____ Computer hardware and peripherals (printer, game controllers, etc.)

   $ _____ Computer software and/or manuals

   $ _____ Computer services subscription (Internet service provider [ISP], website access, etc.)

   $ _____ Musical recordings

   $ _____ Video or computer games

   $ _____ Video games at arcades

   $ _____ TOTAL (sum of all the figures down the column)

3. How close are your figures in #1 and #2?

4. Does the amount of money you spent surprise you? Why?

The Players

In the mass media economic game, there are four types of players: (a) you, the consumer; (b) the advertisers; (c) the media companies; and (d) the employees of media companies. Each type of player brings a different set of resources to the game.

We are the consumers, and our resources include not only our money but, even more importantly, our time. We seek to exchange our money and time for entertainment and information. We, as consumers, are the largest group with over 330 million people in this country and over 7 billion people worldwide. We have the greatest amount of resources. If we pulled out of the game entirely, the game would collapse. However, our resources are dispersed over so many people that no one individual feels he or she has that much power in playing the game. This feeling is a mistake. While no one individual has a significant amount of power to change the overall game, each of us has the power to alter the game significantly for ourselves. If we play the game well, we continually increase the value of the entertainment and information we get in return for our time and money. But playing the game well requires that we keep track of our resources as well as our changing needs and that we negotiate better exchanges of resources. If we don't play the game well, we will make poor economic exchanges and continually get shortchanged on our expenditures of time and money.

©iStockphoto.com/STILLFX

▶ How much time and money do you spend on media each year? Turn to the Applying Media Literacy exercises in this chapter to find out.

The advertisers are a second group of players. Advertisers bring money to the game. They negotiate an exchange of their money for time and space in the media to present their ads to their target audiences. Advertisers want to get access to their target audiences for the lowest cost possible. So they look for media **vehicles** that have constructed the largest assemblages of the audience members they want without also including other kinds of audience members they do not want. For example, sellers of tennis rackets want to get their ad messages in front of as many people who play tennis as possible, but they do not want to pay a lot of money to get access to a large audience that might also include toddlers, invalids, and people who hate tennis. So they look for media vehicles (such as particular sports TV shows, Internet sites, and magazines) that have constructed an audience of only tennis players and negotiate a good ad price to get access to that smaller, **niche audience.**

The media companies are the third group of players. These businesses bring money, messages, and audiences to the game to compete in three different markets simultaneously. First, each media business competes in the talent market for the services of the best writers, journalists, actors, directors, musicians, website designers, and so on. Second, media businesses compete in the audience market—that is, they present the messages produced by their talented employees in such a way to attract the greatest number of people within certain types of audiences. In the media industries of magazines, newspapers, cable, and Internet, those companies sell subscriptions, so they want to maximize their revenue by attracting as many subscribers as possible. Media companies also sell messages in the form of books, musical recordings, and DVDs. Third, media companies compete in the advertising market. When media companies have constructed quality niche audiences, they have something valuable to offer advertisers who want to get their messages in front of certain types of consumers.

The media employees comprise the fourth group of players. Employees bring their time, skills, and **talent** to the game. Talent has less to do with artistic ability than with the ability to attract large audiences. Sometimes, the two conceptualizations of talent are the same, but more often the two are very different. For example, Miley Cyrus and Justin Bieber have shown a demonstrated ability to attract huge audiences although their singing ability is no better than millions of other people. Also, there are many TV stars who are not particularly good actors yet they are in high demand by TV producers because these actors can attract large audiences. The celebrities who can attract the most attention are paid the most (see Table 4.1).

Another elite set of employees are the media company managers, who are often also partial owners of the companies. The talent of these managers is to oversee the construction of messages and their distribution so that those messages are experienced by the greatest number of targeted consumers. In essence, the talent of managers is to construct these audiences by attracting consumers and maintaining those audiences over time by making the exposures continually rewarding to the audience members. These media managers also have a talent that is in short supply so they are also paid very well (see Table 4.2). While you may recognize a few names on this list, most people who have created and who run the large media companies are not known to the general public. Only a few are famous, but notice that their economic value is often far greater than their very famous employees (compare the money columns in Tables 4.1 and 4.2).

The Goal

For all four types of players, the general goal is to maximize the value of the exchange for themselves. However, value is computed in very different ways for different players. For the media businesses, employees, and advertisers, value can be computed quantitatively—numbers of dollars. But for consumers, value is regarded as satisfaction, and that's difficult to quantify, so they do not carefully analyze the economic game in order to determine whether they are a **net winner** or **net loser** in their

Press Association via AP Images

▶ Taylor Swift has challenged the current music industry model by withholding her album *1989* and then removing all her music from Spotify, a digital music-streaming service.

Table 4.1 Annual Income of Highly Paid Media Celebrities

Millions	Person	Profession
$620	Dr. Dre	Music Producer
115	Beyonce Knowles	Singer
105	Floyd Mayweather	Boxer
100	The Eagles	Musicians
100	Steven Spielberg	Director/Producer
95	Howard Stern	Radio Personality
95	Simon Cowell	TV Personality
90	Glen Beck	TV Personality
90	James Patterson	Author
86	Mark Burnett	Director/Producer
82	Bon Jovi	Musicians
82	Oprah Winfrey	TV Personality
81	Bruce Springsteen	Musician
80	Justin Bieber	Singer
80	Cristiano Ronaldo	Soccer Player
77	Dr. Phil McGraw	TV Personality
75	One Direction	Singers
75	Robert Downey Jr	Actor
72	LeBron James	Basketball Player
71	Paul McCartney	Musician
70	Tyler Perry	Director/Producer
70	Ellen DeGeneres	TV Personality
66	Rush Limbaugh	Radio Personality
66	Michael Bay	Director/Producer
66	Calvin Harris	Musician

Figures in left column represent 2014 income in millions of dollars

Source: The Highest Paid Celebrities (2012).

Table 4.2   Salaries of Media Managers

Name	2013 Pay	Company, Job
Sumner Redstone	93.4	Viacom, Chairman
Leslie Moonves	66.9	CBS, Chairman & CEO
Philippe P. Dauman	37.2	Viacom, CEO
Robert A. Iger	34.4	Walt Disney, Chairman & CEO
Brian L. Roberts	31.4	Comcast, Chairman & CEO
Rupert Murdoch	28.9	21st Century Fox, Chairman & CEO
Marissa Mayer	24.9	Yahoo, CEO
Jon Feltheimer	12.6	Lions Gate, CEO
Reed Hastings	4	Netflix, CEO

Note: Pay figures are in millions of dollars and include total compensation including base salary and bonuses paid in 2013.

Source: Shaw & Maglio (2014).

Evaluation

Can you assess the talents of your friends and make a judgment about which friend has the most talent to attract a particular kind of audience?

economic exchanges. As long as consumers feel some satisfaction, they will continue accessing the same types of messages. In contrast, the other three types of players continually focus their attention on how well they are playing the economic game. Businesses can compute the value of their exchanges by performing the simple calculation of adding up all their revenue and then subtracting out their expenses, thereby determining their **profit**. If they are able to make a profit, they are a net winner because their revenues (what resources take in) exceed their expenses (resources they give up). And if the size of the profit continues to grow each year, those businesses become more powerful because they amass more resources.

As consumers of media messages, we play this economic game every day. So we need to ask ourselves this: If most media businesses are net winners, who are the net losers? Am I a net loser—that is, am I giving up more valuable resources than I am receiving back? The more you understand the game, the better you will be able to position yourself to be a net winner in these economic exchanges.

Advertising Is the Engine

Advertising is the engine that drives the growth of the media industries. The cost of doing business in the United States has greatly increased as advertising continually becomes a stronger economic force. In 1900, about $500 million was spent on all forms of advertising. By 1940, it was $2 billion, so it took 40 years to multiply four times. In 1980, it was $60 billion, or a growth of 30 times in those 40 years. By 2012, it had increased to more than $245 billion with 27.4% going to online advertising, which was a bigger share than all advertising money spent on TV (broadcast and cable) and radio combined (Screenwerk, 2014).

▶ Facebook provides an opportunity for advertisers to reach targeted audiences based on location, age and gender, interests, or connections and also to track the effectiveness of advertisements.

Why is advertising so important to our economy? There have been some dramatic changes of the economy of this and other Western countries over the past 100 years and especially over the past 50 years that have worked in combination with advertising to increase both the sale of goods and services as well as the importance of advertising. First, there has been a decline in the proportion of farmers and blue-collar workers and an increase in the proportion of white-collar workers. This means that people are not as self-sufficient and must buy their food and clothing. Second, there has been a high level of employment, which gives people the resources to buy goods and services. We have more discretionary income, which makes it possible for us to purchase things at a point well beyond the mere subsistence level. Over time, the standard of living has steadily increased as people's earning power increases and their expenditures for food, clothing, automobiles, housing, media, and luxuries have all increased.

Advertising has been the engine for this growth. Advertising makes it possible for new goods to enter markets and let us know immediately that they are available. With more product successes, more and more companies are willing to introduce an even wider range of new products. These companies fuel advertising agencies with money, which is passed through to the media. As the media grow, they offer more information and entertainment to us. More of us spend more time with the media,

Abstracting

Can you explain why advertising is so important to the economy in 25 words or less?

thus generating many more audiences, which the media rent out to advertisers. The money cycles from us to products, to the manufacturers of those products, to those companies' advertising agencies, to the media. Advertising drives this cycle faster and faster each year. If we stopped buying advertised products, the cycle would slow down and eventually stop.

MEDIA INDUSTRIES' STRATEGIES

The media industries have developed some general economic strategies over the years that make them successful at playing the economic game and achieving their goals. Three major strategies are illuminated in this section: maximizing profits, constructing audiences, and reducing risk.

Maximizing Profits

Almost all mass media are profit-oriented enterprises. As businesses, they are run to make as large a profit as possible. Profit, which is the difference between a company's revenue (total income) and expenses (total costs), is the payoff or reward for doing business. There are two ways of increasing profit: increasing **revenue streams** and decreasing expenses.

INCREASING REVENUE STREAMS A major strategy employed by media businesses to maximize their overall revenue is to increase the number of revenue streams. Given the way audiences have been fragmenting into smaller and smaller slivers, the level of revenue that can be generated by any one audience has been decreasing. So to work around this problem of fragmenting audiences, media businesses have had to develop multiple revenue streams. One way to do this is to try to develop several ways to generate money from the same audience. For example, a film studio will develop an action adventure movie to attract a certain kind of audience to buy tickets at a theater when the movie is first released. Although movie studios typically spend $50 million advertising a film, they know that many films will not earn this much at the box office. So the studios sell the movie on DVDs and through downloads from Internet sites. They also lease the movie to foreign distributors, and this adds another revenue stream. They lease the film to the airlines for showing during flights. They also sell downloads of the music from the film. Often, they try to produce toys, clothing, or other artifacts from the film and sell those to the public. They sometimes hire writers to turn the movie into a book. Or they could hire someone to translate the movie into a comic book format. And they also sell product placements in the films. All these revenue streams increase the total revenue and thus give the film more of a chance to be profitable. This strategy is not limited to film but applies to all the media industries.

This strategy of increasing revenue streams can also be seen in all the merger and acquisition activity across the media industries. When a media company becomes a conglomerate, controlling the distribution of messages in many media channels can easily market a single message across many channels and thus quickly create multiple revenue streams for that one message.

MINIMIZING EXPENSES One of the largest expenses across all the media industries is personnel—especially for what is called **above-the-line employees.** These are the people who have the talent to attract audiences. In contrast, other employees (such as receptionists, secretaries, ticket takers, etc.) are called **below-the line employees.** Because the talent of above-the-line employees is at a premium, media companies must pay huge sums to hire this talent. To compensate for this increasing cost of talent, companies are pressured to keep the below-the-line costs down. Most of the positions in the media industries are fairly low-level jobs that entail routine assignments that can be done by many different people with little training. These are the secretaries, receptionists, ticket takers, and low-level craftspeople. A bit higher than this are the assistant producers, camera operators, disc jockeys, and the like. Some of these people have special talent and quickly move up to the top of their industry, but most of them do not.

The media pay the people with a lot of talent a lot of money because these people are required for a company to generate large revenues. To counterbalance the large payments to talent, companies reduce expenses by paying clerical people as little as possible. Because the supply of potential workers for entry-level positions is so much larger than the demand, media companies can pay near minimum wage and get good workers.

The media reduce expenses through **economies of scale** and **economies of scope.** Economies of scale exist when marginal costs are lower than average costs—that is, when producing an extra unit of a product decreases as the scale of output expands. Large production runs are good because they spread out the start-up expenses over many units; thus, with each additional unit manufactured, the per-unit cost continues to go down (Doyle, 2002). To illustrate, let's say you are a magazine publisher and your cost of operation (cost of paying all your reporters, editors, salespeople, office staff, rent on building, depreciation of all your equipment, supplies, phones, other utilities, etc.) is $60,000 per week. This is your fixed cost. If you print only one copy of the magazine each week, you will have to sell it for $60,000 just to cover your fixed costs.

If you print two copies, you would have to sell each for $30,000 to cover all your costs; your average fixed cost per copy is cut in half. If you print 60,000 copies, your average fixed cost per copy is only one dollar. Thus, your average fixed costs keep going down as these costs are spread over more and more copies.

However, when you print more copies, the cost of paper, ink, and distribution increases; these are your variable costs because they vary according to how many copies you print. The more copies you print, the more paper and ink you will need, and the price you pay for a roll of paper or a gallon of ink will go down because you can buy these materials in bulk and get big discounts. Although your total cost for ink and paper will go up when printing more copies, your *average* variable cost for these will go down. This is known as economies of scale. The bigger the scale of your business, the more likely your costs will go down either through the ability to demand greater discounts or because you are able to operate more efficiently beyond a certain point.

The media companies, like any business, want to keep their expenses down, so they will find the point at which the combination of both their average fixed costs and their average variable costs are lowest. Beyond this point, distributing more copies only serves to increase unit costs and thus reduce profit. So newspapers, magazines, books, and recordings each seek the point where their average total costs (the sum of average fixed costs and average variable costs) are lowest.

With economies of scale, broadcast television, radio, and websites are different from the other media. They have no variable costs, only fixed costs. For example, with radio, there is no cost to the station of adding an additional listener to the audience. Listeners pay for their own radio receivers, and they pay for the electricity to run them. The station has no distribution costs other than the electricity of the broadcast signal, and the power used to broadcast a station's signal is the same whether 100 or 100,000 sets are tuned in. It is fixed. With no variable costs and with a very high first-copy fixed cost, radio stations keep dropping their average total costs with each additional audience member added. For this reason, the broadcast media (both radio and TV) are strongly motivated, more than any other medium, to increase the size of their audiences. The same pattern holds with websites.

Economies of scope also serve to reduce a firm's expenses per unit. Economies of scope are achieved through multiproduct production—that is, there are variations on the product produced. Recall the previously given example about a movie company generating many revenue streams for a single movie. As the revenues increase for each new revenue stream, the expenses remain relatively low—that is, once you have produced the movie, it is relatively inexpensive to record it on videocassettes and DVDs. By increasing the scope of distributing the same product, very little additional costs are incurred, and yet the potential for revenues increasing is great.

Digitization has made economies of scope even more attractive, because it creates little cost to retransmit a message in many different channels. Also, digitization allows for compression of greater amounts of data or more layers of content to be packed into a product. Now you can buy a DVD with an entire movie. It also can have interviews with the writer, director, and stars; outtakes; director's cut; alternative endings; and so on.

Grouping

Can you compare and contrast the techniques that achieve economies of scale with techniques that achieve economies of scope?

Constructing Audiences

Because advertising is the principal source of revenue for most of the commercial media throughout the world, media companies are in the business of constructing desirable audiences and renting them out to advertisers. Because the cost of building an audience is high, mass media businesses need to condition their audiences for repeated exposures so the businesses can recover those costs over time.

ATTRACTING PEOPLE TO NICHE AUDIENCES The radio and magazine industries have been very successful for years in attracting people to a niche audience. Recall from the previous chapter that radio was displaced by TV as the dominant medium in the middle of the last century. In order to pull itself out of a decline and adapt, radio switched from a quantitative to a qualitative audience strategy, and each radio station developed a certain sound to appeal to one kind of listener. For example, one station will use rap music to attract urban youth, whereas another station will use golden oldies to attract the aging baby boomers. The audience for each of these stations is relatively small compared to the audience for radio during its peak years, but if a company owns several radio stations, then each of those small audiences can add up to a large total.

Relatively small, highly targeted audiences have great value to many advertisers, because special groups of people have special needs. Businesses that are marketing products for a special audience will pay a premium to the media vehicles that attract that special audience. For example, joggers as a group have a special need for information on running practices, equipment, and training techniques. They support several magazines that publish nothing but this type of information. Manufacturers of jogging equipment pay a premium to place ads in these magazines, knowing that the buying of advertising space in these magazines is a very efficient purchase, because the ads placed there will be reaching their most likely customers.

This niche orientation is called long tail marketing, which was introduced in the previous chapter. The market for products of all kinds as well as media messages is

Induction

Can you see a pattern in the way
your favorite websites attract
your attention?

now much less concentrated on a few hits and is much more spread out across thousands of alternatives, each of which generates a small amount of sales. Our economy has shifted away from a focus on relatively few hits (mainstream products) and is moving toward servicing the needs of thousands of tiny markets forming a long tail. To illustrate, the recording industry used to focus on signing only those musical groups that could produce gold records (at least 500,000 sales) and platinum records (at least 1 million sales). But then with the introduction of MP3 players in 2001 and the widespread use of music-sharing platforms on the Internet, the recording industry moved much more into long tail marketing; by 2006, there were 8 million unique song tracks being sold and shared.

Long tail marketing relies on aggregators, which are platforms that bring together buyers and sellers of all kinds of products and services. Anderson (2006) says there are five kinds of aggregators: physical goods (Amazon, eBay), digital goods (iTunes), advertising services (Google, Craigslist), information (Google, Wikipedia), and communities/user-created content (Facebook, Bloglines). These aggregators rely on recommendations to direct users to the products and services they are most likely to buy. These aggregators make filtering decisions so that users can have a more efficient buying experience and not have to slog through all the hundreds of thousands of choices.

What makes long tail marketing so successful is the widespread use of technologies that many people can use to create products and messages, the removal of limitations in bottlenecks of distribution, and limits on product lines in stores. The cost of reaching those small niche audiences has fallen dramatically. Now everything is available. Now it is easier than ever to create media messages in many forms (print, musical recordings, video) and make them widely available (blogs, Amazon, iTunes, YouTube, Facebook, etc.)

We are now in the middle of a major retailing shift away from brick and mortar stores to web-based stores. Brick-and-mortar stores have limited shelf space and can only offer a small percentage of products, but virtual sites on the Internet can offer a much more extensive selection of products. For example, of the more than 200,000 films, TV shows, documentaries, and other video that have been released commercially, the average video brick-and-mortar store carries only about 3,000. Thus, web-based movie rental services are better than even the largest brick-and-mortar stores. For example, 138 million Americans shop at Walmart each week, making Walmart the biggest single seller of music in the country, accounting for 20% of all records sales, but 99% of music albums available today are not in Walmart. Web-based retailers, such as Apple iTunes, offer 40 times as much selection as Walmart; and eBay offers thousands of times as many products as even a large department store (Anderson, 2006).

CONDITIONING AUDIENCES Once a mass media business has constructed an audience, it needs to keep that audience so it can continue to rent it out to advertisers. The mass media businesses are not especially interested in providing a message for a single exposure, like a rock concert promoter might. The mass media want to stay in business over the long term and this requires that once they have been able to attract an audience that they hold on to it for repeated exposures. Therefore, they must condition their audience members so that they develop a habit of exposure.

Induction

Can you see a pattern in the way your favorite websites condition you to want to keep coming back for repeated exposures?

Reducing Risk

All businesses face risk. About 90% of new businesses fail shortly after being founded, and venture capitalist firms that finance new businesses for a living are happy when 20% of their investments are successful. Risk is especially high with new media businesses, like with Internet start-up companies and even with established companies that must continually develop new messages, like Hollywood films. Very few Hollywood films earn enough at the box office to cover their initial production costs, and less than 2% of films released each year in the United States account for 80% of box office returns (Schumpeter, 2011).

How do media companies reduce the risk that their messages will fail to attract a large enough audience to recover their initial costs of production? Media businesses have shifted their thinking toward something called the **marketing concept.** Instead of beginning with messages then trying to find audiences for those messages, media businesses begin with audience needs then construct messages to meet those needs. With the marketing concept, managers conduct research to identify particular niche audiences and then find out what the unmet needs are for those audiences. Then the media develop messages to meet those previously unmet needs. Beginning with research first and product development second reduces risk of message failure once the messages are released into the market.

This procedure is used frequently by the media industries. Researchers analyze what works, and then they develop shows that are sequels or spinoffs of successful shows. Hollywood is fond of sequels because they reduce risk. This is why the number of sequels increased each year until 2011: They reached an all-time high when a sequel of a major Hollywood movie was released every other week (Lussier, 2011). For example, *Spider-Man 2* cost $200 million to produce, which is a huge investment risk. However, it earned back all that investment in the first several weeks at the box office and then went on to earn a total of over $370 million from all its revenue streams over the next few years. Based on this success, the producers made *Spider-Man 3* with a budget of $258 million and that movie earned even more money (Sammy, 2012).

INCREASING MEDIA LITERACY

Now it is time to ask yourself this: Am I a net winner or net loser in the economic game I play with the mass media every day? To arrive at a good answer to this question, you need to consider the value of your resources—that is, how do the costs of the resources you give up compare to the benefits from the resources you receive? Your main resources are your time and money. Earlier in this chapter, you estimated your expenditure of resources of money and time. These are your costs.

Now let's analyze your benefits. The benefits received from exposure to media messages are typically the resources of information and entertainment. So you need to think about the degree of satisfaction from the information and entertainment you have been receiving from the mass media. The task of clarifying these benefits is more difficult than the task of inventorying your costs because they are difficult to quantify. With costs, it is relatively easy to list hours of exposure and dollars spent. But with benefits, the "yardstick" you must use to measure them is much more personal and subjective. Of course, there may be some areas where quantification is possible. For example, perhaps you spend a lot of time on Facebook with the goal of increasing your number of friends; so if your number of friends constantly increases, then you are constantly increasing the benefits of your exposure. Another example is the playing of computer games where your scores constantly improve as you spend more hours and money playing. However, with most media exposures, there is no quantifiable yardstick; instead, we all need to use our subjective judgment and answer two questions. The first question is this: Am I generally satisfied by what I get from all my media message exposures? To answer this question, you need to think about your general standards for media messages and compare your pattern of exposure to those standards. If you conclude that your general patterns of media exposure deliver the right amount of information and entertainment than you typically expect, then you believe that the exchange of resources is fair—that is, you are getting what you wanted from your media exposures. If you conclude that you are getting more than you expected, then you regard yourself as a net winner. But if you feel you are constantly getting less than you expected, then you are regarding yourself as a next loser—that is, you keep giving up your valuable time and money when you continually feel that you are not getting back sufficient value in return. Of course in our everyday lives, we all feel shortchanged from time to time. We cannot win every exchange, so we cannot worry about that. However, if you feel that there is a long-term pattern of being shortchanged, then you need to consider doing something different.

Our economic analysis is not yet complete. We need to ask a second question, which is this: How good are my standards? If your standards are too low, then everything you encounter will meet those standards and typically exceed them. In this case, you may be regarding yourself as a net winner, but this perception would be faulty because you are selling yourself short.

The key to being a net winner starts with valuing your resources well in this economic game. For example, let's say you find something in your parents' attic that you think may be valuable. You take it to an antique dealer to sell it. The dealer offers you $60 for it. Should you accept the $60 and sell it to the dealer? If you have no knowledge of antiques and no idea about how rare the piece is, you are operating in the dark. You might think you are savvy negotiator and ask for $100, then settle for $80, feeling good that you "got the dealer to raise her offer" by $20. But maybe the piece is worth $1,000. If you don't have a good operating knowledge about what your resources are worth, you will continually fall into one of two traps. One trap is to *overvalue* your resources, and no one will want to enter into exchanges with you. The other trap is to undervalue your resources, in which case you make lots of exchanges, but you continually are shortchanged. When you have little self-awareness of the value of your resources, you can only play the game to lose.

Now let's return to the cost–benefit analysis. As for costs, think beyond financial resources and also consider what your time is worth. If your time is worth nothing, then anything you receive in return for giving up that time is a bonus! But if your time is valuable, then think about how you could spend your time to match—or exceed—that value. As for benefits, think in terms of how valuable the information is that you get from the mass media. Is it credible? Is it simple to understand? Is it useful for your personal needs? Then think about how valuable the entertainment is that you get from the mass media. Is it exciting and involving, or is it boring? Do you look forward to these exposures, or do you engage in them simply to pass the time? Think about the range of your media exposures. Have they grown narrower each year? Or are you expanding your exposure to a wider range of media platforms; a wider range of music; a wider range of types of movies; and a wider range of magazines, newspapers, and websites as you search for a wider range of information?

The more you think about those expenditures and the value of what you are receiving in return, the more you are thinking from a media literacy perspective. If you are happy

Synthesis

Now that you have learned more about the economic perspective, can you construct a personal plan to increase the value of your exchanges and become more of a net winner with the media?

with your answers and come to realize that you are a net winner in these exchanges with the media, then this media literacy perspective has helped you appreciate the media—and yourself—more. If, instead, your answers have led you to realize that you are a net loser in these exchanges and that the media have conditioned you to fulfill their goals rather than your own, then this media literacy perspective has helped you see a problem that you have been overlooking—a problem that has likely been making you unhappy.

In your overall cost–benefit analysis, however, it is not likely that your answers have been all positive or all negative; instead, you are likely to have reasoned that with some of your exchanges you have been a net winner and with others you have been a net loser. In this case, the media literacy perspective has helped you see a difference; therefore, you need a strategy to protect your exposures that result in you being a net winner and grow your winnings while developing another strategy to negotiate more from those exposures where you have been a net loser. In developing new strategies to overcome past problems, think about how you can increase your benefit streams while reducing your costs. Think about how you can find those messages that satisfy your personal needs better. And think about how you break the media's hold on your habits that have been conditioned to satisfy their needs rather than your own needs.

KEY IDEAS

- Media economics can be viewed as a game where the major players (you, the consumer; advertisers; the media businesses; and employees of the media businesses) negotiate exchanges of their existing resources for other resources that they value more.

- The businesses in the media industries engage in tough competition with each other to acquire limited resources, play the high-risk game of appealing to audiences, and achieve a maximum profit.

- The media businesses are very successful at playing the economic game because they follow three strategies:

  1. They maximize profits by increasing revenues and decreasing expenses.

  2. They construct niche audiences and then condition audience members into habits of continual exposures.

  3. They reduce their risks by using the marketing concept.

- Advertising is the engine that keeps the game going and increases the exchange of resources.

- As consumers, we exchange our resources of time and money in order to receive information and entertainment.

- In order to become more media literate, we need to evaluate our resource exchanges periodically to make sure that we are getting full value for the resources we give up.

FURTHER READING

Albarran, A. B. (2010). *The media economy*. New York, NY: Taylor & Francis. (202 pages with index)

The author covers a lot of ground in this relatively short book. He includes chapters on theories, technologies, regulatory issues, globalization, and labor issues.

Anderson, C. (2006). *The long tail: Why the future of business is selling less of more*. **New York, NY: Hyperion. (238 pages including index)**

Anderson convincingly shows that marketers of media messages—as well as all products—have moved away from depending on hits for generating all their sales and instead are now mining sales

from thousands of non-hits, each of which has low sales but added together generate huge revenue.

Vogel, H. L. (2011). *Entertainment industry economics: A guide for financial analysis* (8th edition). **New York, NY: Cambridge University Press. (655 pages including appendices, glossary, and index)**

This textbook presents a wealth of details about the economics of each of the media industries in 15 chapters. It presents a lot of facts and figures (rather than anecdotes and insider stories) about the economic history and current nature of the entertainment industries primarily in the United States.

KEEPING UP TO DATE

Advertising Age (http://adage.com/datacenter/article?article_id=106352)

This website provides lots of information about the leading media companies.

Forbes (www.forbes.com/forbes-400)

This website provides stories on economics and rank ordered lists of wealthy people.

$SAGE edge™

Sharpen your skills with SAGE edge at **edge.sagepub.com/potterintro**

SAGE edge for Students provides a personalized approach to help you accomplish your coursework goals in an easy-to-use learning environment.

▶ Newspapers such as *The New York Times* have not only adapted technologically but have also adapted to appeal to niche audiences.

Test Your Knowledge: True or False

Before reading this chapter, think about which of the following statements you believe to be **true** and which you believe to be **false**.

1. Success in media businesses requires them to attract the greatest number of people possible from the total population.

2. Long tail marketing refers to selling things to people over the long term instead of immediately.

3. The media are successful in reinforcing our exposure patterns so that we develop habits.

4. The media are much better at satisfying our existing needs than in creating new needs.

Answers can be found on page 247.

5

MASS MEDIA AUDIENCE: INDUSTRY PERSPECTIVE

The central challenge for each mass medium is to create and maintain audiences. In order to meet this challenge, they have developed a three-stage strategy of first identifying opportunities in the total population, then attracting those audiences, and finally conditioning those audiences for repeated exposures. This chapter is structured to explain each of these three stages. Then it shifts the focus to get you thinking about how to increase your media literacy.

IDENTIFYING OPPORTUNITIES

The mass media's perspective on the audience used to be that the audience was a "mass"—that is, a collection of everyone where all people exhibited the same needs for information and entertainment. Their goal was to attract the largest audience possible, so they developed messages to appeal to every type of person. The larger the audience they could assemble, the more they could charge advertisers for access to those audiences. So media programmers were motivated by a simple quantitative goal—that is, they had a drive to increase the number of people in their audiences.

Over time, however, mass media programmers realized that not everyone shared the same needs for information and entertainment. The more they examined audience needs, the more they realized that those needs were fragmented. Those who wanted entertainment split into people who wanted fantasy and some wanted reality. And within the reality preference group, there were people who wanted

Learning Objectives

After reading this chapter, you will be able to do the following:

1. Describe what is meant by a "niche audience" in the media business.

2. Describe the three-step strategy that media businesses use to construct and maintain audiences.

3. Identify three families of segmentation schemes that media businesses use to identify audience niches.

4. Explain how media businesses attract niche audiences for media exposures.

5. Be wary about how media businesses condition audience members for repeat exposures.

6. Develop a personal strategy to use the information in this chapter to increase your media literacy.

Analysis

Can you identify three of your personal needs that are satisfied by media exposures?

competitions (e.g., game shows, sports) and others who wanted more of an everyday narrative of celebrities (*Keeping Up With the Kardashians*), exotic people (*Amish Mafia*), or of people like them. Media programmers changed their goal from a simple quantitative one to a more complex qualitative one where they attempted to identify different kinds of audiences as distinguished by their individual needs. This shift in goal required a shift in strategy. Now media programmers start with identifying audience needs and then developing media messages to attract those niche audiences, and once they have attracted them, the media work hard to condition those audiences for repeated exposures.

Thus, media programmers are in the business of constructing niche audiences. For example, if a website designer wants to attract an upscale, highly educated, professional audience, the designer must identify an interest these people would have—for example, an interest in golf. The web designer then works to assemble content that will satisfy the needs of that niche audience better than does the content provided by other websites that are also trying to attract members of the same niche audience. The web designers must then find out where this potential audience is spending its time and put ads in those places in order to attract those people to the newly designed website on golf. Once the website starts attracting these people, a sales staff will sell access to this audience to interested advertisers, such as stores that sell golf equipment, travel agencies, luxury car dealers, and jewelers.

Each person is a member of many different niche audiences. You are a member of a local community that the local newspaper and cable TV franchise targets. You are a member of virtual communities when you get on the Internet—communities that quickly form and may last for only one evening. You are a member of certain hobby groups that are targeted by certain websites and magazines, although other members of your audience are spread out all over the world and will never meet you in person.

Grouping

Think about the needs that your friends and family members have for media entertainment. Can you arrange those people into niche groups according to their needs?

Mass media businesses are constantly looking for message needs in the general population. Key to meeting this challenge is dividing the total population into marketing segments then identifying the segment that has the greatest potential to be attracted by a particular kind of media message. This is accomplished by thinking about audience needs by segmenting the total audience into niches as defined by certain characteristics. This audience segmentation task usually follows one of several segmentation schemes.

"Time & Life Pictures/Getty Images"

John Shearer/Invision for AMC/AP Images

▶ While the term *mass communication* is still used, media programmers have shifted attention away from the large and anonymous mass audience (left) toward more targeted and individualized niche audiences (right).

Geographic Segmentation

The oldest form of market segmentation is by geography. A company would begin a business in a certain locale and produce products that the people in that locale wanted. Because of limits on distribution, that company would only do business in that one area. If that company wanted to expand, it would move out from its home locale to other places in the region where the product met a need. If there was a nationwide need, then the company could expand into national distribution, which many companies did; thus, **geographic segmentation** has become less useful. This type of segmentation scheme is most important to newspapers, radio, and local TV where there are geographical boundaries to their coverage areas. But it has also been useful to other media in thinking about getting their messages out to certain regions of the country.

Demographic Segmentation

Another popular form of market segmentation has been with the use of demographics: **demographic segmentation.** Demographics focus on the relatively enduring characteristics about each person—such as gender, ethnic background, age, income, and education. These are fairly stable characteristics that have been

Analysis

Within your total set of needs, can you identify the particular needs that are triggered by where you live?

quite useful in classifying us into meaningful audience segments. Although people can change their status on some of these (such as education and income), such change requires a great deal of effort and takes some time to evolve.

Like with geographic segmentation, the usefulness of demographics as an audience segmentation device has been diminishing. Decades ago, when adult women typically stayed home and raised children, it made sense to focus the marketing of household and child care products on women only. But now that there are so many single-parent households and that the number of women in the workforce is about the same as men, gender has lost its value as a way of identifying a target market for most marketing campaigns.

Ethnicity also used to be a stronger demographic segmenter than it is today as the range of income, education, political views, and cultural needs is much greater within any ethnic group than it is across ethnic groups. With the tremendous growth of credit, household income has not been as useful a segmenter. Educational level is also less useful. Sixty years ago, having a college degree put you in an elite group—the top 5% of the population. But now, over 20% of American adults have at least one college degree, and another 20% have earned some college credit. While demographics are still valuable as a segmenter for some products and some media messages, other segmentation schemes are required for most products and media messages.

These are the relatively enduring characteristics of people. The reasoning here is that women are likely to have different needs than men; teenagers will have different needs than the elderly; higher educated people will have different needs than high school dropouts; and rich people have different needs than poor people. While this is a still a useful segmentation method, it is rather crude. For example, not all women have the same needs, and the needs of women are not always so different than the needs of men.

Psychographic Segmentation

Over time, marketers have developed more sophisticated ways of segmenting the general population into marketing niches according to people's needs. An umbrella term for these more sophisticated segmentation methods is *psychographics*, which is an approach to segmentation that is based on people's values and lifestyles. There are many examples of **psychographic segmentation.** Two stand out as being very influential.

Analysis

Within your total set of needs, can you identify those particular needs that can be traced to your age or gender?

TWELVE AMERICAN LIFESTYLES William Wells, director of advertising research at Needham, Harper & Steers in Chicago, developed the 12 American lifestyles that include Joe the factory worker and his wife Judy, Phyllis the career woman and her liberated husband Dale, Thelma the contented homemaker, and Harry the cigar-chomping middle-aged salesman. Each of these creations represents a different lifestyle. For example, Joe is a lower-middle-class male in his 30s who makes an hourly wage doing semiskilled work. He watches a lot of TV, especially sports and action/adventure programs; he rarely reads. He drives a pickup truck and knows a lot about automotive parts and accessories. In contrast, Phyllis is a career woman in her 30s with a graduate degree. She reads a lot, and when she watches TV, it is usually news or a good movie. She likes fine food, dining out, and travel.

VALS TYPOLOGY VALS was developed at the Stanford Research Institute (SRI; now known as SRI International) by Arnold Mitchell. After monitoring social, economic, and political trends during the 1960s and 1970s, Mitchell constructed an 85-page measurement instrument that asked questions ranging from people's sexual habits to what brands of margarine they ate. He had 1,635 people fill out the questionnaire, and the answers became the database for his book *Nine American Lifestyles*, published in 1980. In the book, Mitchell argued that people's values strongly influence their spending patterns and media behaviors. So if we know which value group a person identifies with, we can predict a great deal about the products and services he or she will want. For example, one of the groups is called experientials. The people in this value grouping like to try new and different things to see what they are like. They like to travel. They are early users of new types of products. And they are constantly looking for something different.

The VALS typology has made SRI very successful, with revenue of more than $500 million per year. By the mid-1980s, SRI had 130 VALS clients, including the major TV networks, major ad agencies, major publishers such as *Time*, and major corporations such as AT&T, Avon, Coke, General Motors, P&G, R.J. Reynolds, and Tupperware. For example, Timex, a giant corporation best known for its watches, wanted to move into the home health care market with a selection of new products, including digital

▶ At the cutting edge of audience segmentation, psychographics segment consumers by lifestyle.

thermometers and blood pressure monitors. It decided to focus on two VALS segments: societally conscious and the achievers. Everything about the packaging and the advertisements was chosen with these two groups in mind. Models were upscale, mature in comfortable surroundings with plants and books. The tagline was "Technology where it does the most good." Within months, all of Timex products were the leaders in this new and fast-growing industry.

Over the years, as the American culture has changed, VALS has changed its segments to keep up. Today, the VALS typology of segments looks very different than it did in the early 1980s. By keeping up with changes in people's lifestyles over the years, VALS has remained a valuable tool to mass media programmers and marketers.

Psychographic segmentation schemes are less crude ways of focusing on people's needs, and this makes these methods better than geographic or demographic methods. However, psychographics is still an indirect method. But with the rise in popularity of social networking sites (SNSs) on the Internet, media programmers now have a way to segment the population directly on needs. By mining the data of what people talk about—what they like and what they complain about—marketers can develop a much more clear ideas of which needs are not being met and a much more precise estimate of how many people would make up their niche audiences.

ATTRACTING AUDIENCES

Attracting audience attention is critical for the thousands of advertisers who spend hundreds of billions of dollars each year to get their messages out to their target audiences. But as more and more advertisers as well as media outlets compete for the attention of the public, attention has become the scarce resource of the information economy. In their fascinating book *The Attention Economy: Understanding the New Currency of Business*, Davenport and Beck (2001) argue, "In postindustrialized societies, attention has become a more valuable currency than the kind you store in bank accounts. Understanding and managing attention is now the single most important determinant of business success" (p. 3).

After a media organization has selected a niche audience to target, it must develop content to attract people into that audience. The mass media employ two tactics to do this. First, they try to appeal to your existing needs and interests. Second, they use **cross-media promotion** and **cross-vehicle promotion** to attract your attention.

Appeal to Existing Needs and Interests

The mass media do not develop vehicles and messages and then go looking for an audience. Instead, they conduct research to try to identify the message needs of potential audiences; then, they develop that content. Not everyone has the same needs and interests, so the media can identify a range of different types of people as defined by those different needs. For example, some people are very interested in sports, but other people are more interested in news and public affairs. These are two important niches for the media. Each of these has subniches. Some sports fanatics might like baseball, whereas others cannot stand baseball but love football.

How do media companies know what the existing needs are? The easiest way to answer this question is to look at what messages are already being consumed. The messages that already are attracting the most attention within a niche audience demonstrate that there is a particular existing need. The new competitors then try to create their own messages to attract that same audience by appealing to that same need. This is why many new films, TV shows, and popular songs typically look and sound like last year's most popular films, TV shows, and songs.

Programmers know that we have a relatively narrow exposure repertoire—that is, a set of message types we attend to—so if the new competitors can make their messages very similar to what we are already attending to, we will likely pay attention to those new messages also. Messages that are too different than what we are already exposing ourselves to will not break through the automaticity. We typically stay in this state of automaticity until something triggers our attention, and then we pay attention to it. Therefore, media programmers look for what has triggered our attention in the past, and they construct their messages in a similar manner so their messages will also trigger our attention.

Although we have a wide variety of media and messages available to us, we usually select a small subset of them that tend to serve our needs best. This fact about a small set of message preferences—or media repertoire—was clearly established several decades ago when there were far fewer media choices than we have today. Several decades ago, Ferguson (1992) found that even in cable TV households with more than 100 channels, TV viewers typically watched only 5 to 8 channels and ignored the rest. Also, having a remote control to change TV channels or a device to record shows was not found to increase the size of a person's channel repertoire. Thus, when the media expand the number of messages offered, individuals do not increase the range of their exposures; instead, the expanded number of messages increases the number of niche audiences. With a larger range of messages available, individuals can find particular messages that better serve their needs. Today, as the newer **interactive media** make it possible to have even greater choice in how we use the media, each of us still has a relatively narrow focus on the types of media and messages we like best.

Analysis

(?)

When looking at your favorite website, can you identify the elements that were designed specifically to appeal to people with your same needs?

Cross-Media and Cross-Vehicle Promotion

Media programmers must find potential members of their audience in other audiences so the programmers can promote their new messages and thus attract people to the audience they are trying to construct. Programmers therefore will engage in a great deal of cross-media promotion and cross-vehicle promotion.

Several decades ago, media programmers were most concerned about branding their particular vehicles and trying to build loyalty to those vehicles. For example, local TV stations wanted you to watch only them. A newspaper wanted you to be loyal to that newspaper and get your news only there—not from magazines, TV, or the radio. But with the rise of media consolidation, media programmers have shifted their focus to the message and away from the vehicle. So, for example, a political commentator on the radio might also be asked to post a column on a website and appear on a TV show where the company that owns the radio station also owns the website and the TV station. That company might also own a magazine and book publishing firm, in which case the commentator would be encouraged to write a column for the magazine and publish a book. When this media conglomerate company brands its message—the commentator—the company then tries to market that message through as many media and vehicles that it owns so as to increase the number of revenue streams without adding much to the already existing expenses. Therefore, media companies think of audiences more in terms of messages that would attract them rather than as groups of people limited to one medium or one vehicle.

Differences across media are also blurring over time. Newspapers have become more like magazines in their editorial outlook, featuring more soft news and human interest pieces that are not time sensitive and that appeal more as entertainment than as information. Trade books are becoming shorter and less literary. And computers with their games, encyclopedias, and webpages are becoming more like films, books, magazines, and newspapers. Given the focus on messages and the convergence of channels, the content is becoming much more of a focus than is the delivery system.

Several decades ago, some futurists argued that we are moving toward convergence where all the media will be one—"a single, high capacity, digital network of networks that will bridge what we now know as the separate domains of computing, telephony,

▶ Oprah Winfrey, referred to as the "Queen of All Media," uses cross-vehicle promotion techniques to promote her books, magazines, movies, and TV network.

© Pictorial Press Ltd / Alamy

broadcasting, motion pictures, and publishing" (Neuman, 1991, p. x). This convergence has been happening and continues to happen, as you saw in Chapter 3. The differences between channels of disseminating information have become much less important; in contrast, the differences in consumer needs across niche audiences has become much more important.

Evaluation

Think about all the devices that are now labeled with the term TV. Can you make a judgment about how useful this term is in today's media environment?

CONDITIONING AUDIENCES

Once a mass media organization has attracted you to a message, it immediately tries to condition you for repeated exposures. This drive toward **audience conditioning** is an essential strategy for all mass media. The costs of attracting members of an audience to their first exposure to a message are so high that media organizations must rely on repeated exposures in order to recoup their initial investment and eventually make a profit.

The mass media have conditioned us to certain behavioral patterns of exposure. These are continually reinforced until they become habits; then they are reinforced some more so that we do not change our habits. Think back to the Applying Media Literacy 1.1 exercise you completed in Chapter 1 on the time you spend with various media. When you made those estimates, you were relying on your recall of long established habits of media exposure.

Media exposures are inertial. This means that when we are paying attention to a particular message, we tend to keep paying attention to that message, and when we are in an automatic state, we tend to stay in that state and filter out all the messages around us. For example, let's say you go to YouTube and watch one of your favorite videos. YouTube will suggest additional videos you might want to view next. These suggestions are formulated based on your history of watching other videos. YouTube wants to hold on to you as a continuing audience member so it keeps suggesting content you might like. Then, as you watch each suggested video and are entertained, you are being conditioned to want to return to YouTube tomorrow and the day after and the day after that. Successful websites—whether they deal with information, entertainment, music, video, or the printed word—all try to do the same thing. They offer you apps that you can download and use for free on your mobile devices. They want to condition you to continually use their services so it becomes a habit that you cannot live without.

INCREASING MEDIA LITERACY

Let's analyze how well the media industry has identified your needs and attracted you into certain niche audiences. Begin Applying Media Literacy 5.1 by thinking about

What Audience Segments Are You In?

1. Pick three of your favorite media messages and write the name of each on the column heading line.

Show 1: _____   Show 2: _____   Show 3: _____

_____   _____   _____

_____   _____   _____

_____   _____   _____

_____   _____   _____

_____   _____   _____

_____   _____   _____

_____   _____   _____

_____   _____   _____

_____   _____   _____

_____   _____   _____

_____   _____   _____

_____   _____   _____

_____   _____   _____

_____   _____   _____

_____   _____   _____

_____   _____   _____

_____   _____   _____

2. Now look at the lists of products and try to imagine who the advertisers had in mind as a target audience when they decided to advertise in these shows.

   * Are those products oriented more toward males or females, or doesn't it matter?

   * What age group are the products aimed at?

   * What economic level are the products aimed at?

   * What educational level are the products aimed at?

   * What geographical location are the products aimed at, or doesn't it matter?

   * What values do the advertisers think you have?

3. Did you notice any ads for other media messages? If so, what other kinds of messages were those ads trying to get you to see? Do you watch those other shows? Why or why not?

4. Think about how the messages were constructed in those TV shows. Can you notice anything that the message designers have done to condition your for repeated exposures?

your three favorite TV shows—the TV series you watch as often as you can. Once you have identified three of your favorite shows, list the advertisements that come with those messages and work through the rest of the exercise. Among all those ads for products and services, were there also ads for other media messages (such as other TV shows, films, recordings, websites, etc.)? These are examples of cross-promotions. Are you currently a member of the audience for any of those cross-promoted media messages? If not, why not? Have you tried exposing yourself to those messages and found them not to your liking? Or have you not been exposed to them at all? If not, why not?

Now try doing Applying Media Literacy 5.1 again but this time with your favorite magazines. Are you in the same kinds of niche audiences? Is there more or less cross-promotion with these magazines compared to the TV shows?

Finally, try doing the exercise with your favorite websites or social networking platforms. Are you in the same kinds of niche audiences as with the more traditional media of TV and magazines? Is there more or less cross-promotion with these interactive media compared to the more traditional media? Do you notice any difference in the way these interactive media are conditioning you for repeated exposures?

KEY IDEAS

- The mass media segment the general population into marketing niches according to their needs.

- The mass media attempt to attract certain people into niche audiences by creating the types of content they want.

- Because the cost of attracting audiences is so high, the mass media condition people in those audiences for repeat exposures.

- Increasing one's media literacy about the industry's perspective on audiences entails analyzing which audiences you find yourself in and then evaluating whether being in those particular audiences is the best way to satisfy your needs.

- When we are well aware of our needs, we can use the mass media as an essential resource to satisfy a wide variety of needs.

- When we are *not* aware of our real needs, the most aggressive of the mass media will herd us into audiences for their most profitable messages. Increasing media literacy gives you more control so you can use the mass media as a tool in achieving your needs rather than allowing the mass media to us you as a tool to achieve their needs.

FURTHER READING

Davenport, T. H., & Beck, J. C. (2001). *The attention economy: Understanding the new currency of business*. Boston, MA: Harvard Business School Press. (253 pages with index)

This is a very readable book written by two business school professors who explain why attention deficit is such a serious problem in our economy. But they are not social critics who are interested in pointing out a problem then exploring recommendations for ameliorating the problem. Instead, they write more as marketing consultants who provide suggestions to businesses about how to attract the public's attention.

Napoli, P. M. (2011). *Audience evolution: New technologies and the transformation of media audiences*. New York, NY: Columbia University Press. (248 pages)

Written by a professor at Fordham University, this book shows how the conceptualization of audiences have changed over time, particularly with the development of the newer media technologies that serve to fragment society. The scholarly analysis of this phenomenon focuses on political, economic, and social perspectives.

Neuman, W. R. (1991). *The future of the mass audience*. New York, NY: Cambridge University Press. (218 pages)

Neuman begins with a good, balanced discussion of the difficult idea of post-industrialism and with the conflict between fragmentation and homogenization. He argues that education contributes to fragmentation, with people able to peruse their specialized interests. Family has changed as women entered the workforce in a large percentage. He also shows that media use has fragmented. He argues that this is not a new issue but is a continuing and central problem of political communications. The key issue is that of balance: between the center and the periphery, between different interest factions, between competing elites, and between an efficient and effective central authority and the conflicting demands of the broader electorate (p. 167). This is the conflict between community and pluralism.

ⓈSAGE edge™

Sharpen your skills with SAGE edge at **edge.sagepub.com/potterintro**

SAGE edge for Students provides a personalized approach to help you accomplish your coursework goals in an easy-to-use learning environment.

© Comstock/Stockbyte/Thinkstock

▶ Though we are inevitably exposed to numerous messages, we must choose which stimuli to pay attention to in order to make sense of them.

Test Your Knowledge: True or False

Before reading this chapter, think about which of the following statements you believe to be **true** and which you believe to be **false**.

1. A high level of exposure is called attention.

2. The media exert an influence on people with subliminal messages.

3. There are important differences in exposure states that have more to do with different experiences than with different degrees of attention.

4. It is easier for people to increase their media literacy when they are field dependent.

Answers can be found on page 247.

6

MASS MEDIA AUDIENCE: INDIVIDUAL PERSPECTIVE

There has been a huge increase in the amount of information generated and its aggressive competition for our **attention.** New technologies have made it possible to generate more information and to transmit it at the speed of light through fiber optics and Wi-Fi. But the human brain has not been able to evolve as fast as the new technologies have, and this disparity raises important questions such as the following: What does it mean to be exposed to media messages? How do humans handle all this information without drowning in the flood? How do we as humans process the meaning from those messages?

EXPOSURE IS NOT THE SAME AS ATTENTION

Given the huge number of media messages flooding our culture, can we conclude that we are exposed to them all or must we pay attention to them in order to be exposed? In everyday language, **exposure** is a term that is often used synonymously with the term *attention*, but with media literacy, it is important to make a clear distinction between the two terms.

Exposure

In order to clarify what we mean when we say that a person was "exposed" to a media message, we need to consider three criteria: the physical criterion, the perceptual criterion, and

Learning Objectives

After reading this chapter, you will be able to do the following:

1. Distinguish between exposure and attention.

2. Recognize the three criteria for exposure.

3. Explain how media experiences vary across the four exposure states.

4. Distinguish among filtering, meaning matching, and meaning construction decisions during media exposure.

5. Recognize how your level of media literacy is influenced by four natural abilities.

the psychological criterion. Only when all three criteria are met can we conclude that a person was indeed exposed to a media message.

THE PHYSICAL CRITERION The most foundational criterion for exposure is physical presence. A person must experience some proximity to a message in order for exposure to take place. The physical requirement for exposure means that the message and the person occupy the same physical space for some period of time. Thus, space and time are regarded as barriers to exposure. If a magazine is lying faceup on a table in a room and Harry walks through that room, Harry is physically exposed to the message on the cover of the magazine but not to any of the messages inside the magazine unless Harry picks it up and flips through the pages. Also, if Harry does not walk through that room when the magazine is on the table, there is no **physical exposure** to the message on the cover of the magazine. Likewise, if a TV is turned on in the lunchroom during the noon hour then is turned off at 1:00 p.m., anyone who walks through that room after 1:00 p.m. is not physically exposed to TV messages.

Physical proximity is a necessary condition for media exposure, but it is not a sufficient condition. A second necessary condition is **perceptual exposure.**

THE PERCEPTUAL CRITERION The perceptual requirement refers to a human's ability to receive appropriate sensory input through the visual and auditory senses. There are limits to a human's sense organs. For example, human sensitivity to sound frequency extends from around 16 Hz and 20,000 Hz but sounds are heard best when they are between 1,000 Hz and 4,000 Hz (Metallinos, 1996; Plack, 2005). A dog whistle is pitched at a frequency higher than 20,000 Hz, so humans cannot perceive that sound—that is, it is outside their range of human sensitivity to sounds. With the human eye, people can see light, which travels at a certain frequency, but not sound, which travels at another frequency. Any auditory or visual signal that occurs outside of a person's sense organs' ability to perceive it is non-exposure.

The perceptual criterion, however, has a feature beyond simple sensory reception; we must also consider the sensory-input/brain connection. There are instances when the sensory input gets to the brain, but when the brain transforms the raw stimuli—such that we cannot perceive the raw stimuli and therefore cannot be thought of as being exposed to the raw stimuli—instead, we are exposed to the transformed stimuli. For example, when we watch a movie in a theater, we are exposed to individual static images projected at about 24 images per second. But humans cannot perceive 24 individual images in a given second, so our brains miss seeing the 24 individual static pictures and instead "see" motion. Also with film projection, there is a brief time between each of those 24 individual images every second when the screen is blank, but the eye–brain connection is not quick enough to process the blanks so we do not "see" those blanks as blanks; instead, we only "see" smooth motion. If the projection rate of images were to slow down to under 10 images per second, we would begin to see a flutter—that is, our brains would begin to see the blanks, because the replacement of still images is slow enough for the eye–brain connection to begin processing them.

Stimuli that are outside the boundaries of human perception are called subliminal. Subliminal messages cannot be perceived—that is, humans lack the sensory organs to take in stimuli and/or the hard wiring in the brain to be sensitive to them.

There is a widespread misconception that the mass media put people at risk for "subliminal communication." This belief indicates a confusion between subliminal and subconscious. There is an important distinction that needs to be made between subliminal and subconscious, because they are two very different things and they have two very different implications for exposure. Subliminal refers to being outside a human's ability to sense or perceive; thus, it is always regarded as non-exposure. However, once media stimuli cross over the subliminal line and are able to be perceived by humans, it can be regarded as exposure. However, this does not mean that all exposure is conscious, and this brings us to the third criterion in our definition: psychological.

©iStockphoto.com/AleksandarNakic

▶ Three types of exposure—physical, perceptual, and psychological—are required before we pay attention to a media message.

THE PSYCHOLOGICAL CRITERION In order for the psychological criterion to be met, there must be some trace element created in a person's mind. This trace element can be an image, a sound, an emotion, a pattern, etc. It can last for a brief time (several seconds in short-term memory then cleared out) or a lifetime (when cataloged into long-term memory). It can enter the mind consciously (often called the central route) where people are fully aware of the elements in the exposure, or it can enter the mind unconsciously (often called the peripheral route) where people are unaware that those elements are entering their minds (see Petty & Cacioppo, 1985). Thus, there is a great variety of elements that potentially can meet this psychological criterion. The challenge then becomes organizing all these elements into meaningful

Abstracting

Can you explain the difference between subliminal and subconscious in 25 words or fewer?

sets and explaining how different kinds of elements are experienced by the individual and how they are processed as information.

Attention

In order for attention to a media message to occur, people must first be exposed to that message—that is, they must meet all three criteria for exposure. However, something else must also occur. That something else is conscious awareness of the media message. Thus, exposure to media messages can be split into two categories: conscious exposure and unconscious exposure. The idea of attention refers to conscious exposure, not unconscious exposure.

As you can now see, there are a lot of things that have to happen in order for us to pay attention to a media message. And when we do pay attention to a media message, that attention can vary. By *vary*, I do not simply mean that there are differences in degree of attention from a little attention to a great deal of attention. What I mean by *vary* is that there are different kinds of attention. This brings us to the next topic of **exposure states** where I will explain the different kinds of attention that we experience when we are exposed to media messages in our everyday lives.

Exposure States

Thus far, I have made a distinction between unconscious exposure and conscious exposure to media messages. Unconscious exposure means that people meet the physical criterion, the perceptual criterion, and the psychological criterion but that they are not aware of the messages during that exposure. During this type of exposure, information enters a person's unconscious mind through a peripheral route (kind of like a back door) and leaves traces in their memory. This type of exposure happens automatically—that is, we do not have to think about it. It is governed by the automatic code constantly running in the back of our minds. Let's call this type of exposure the state of automaticity.

Now let's examine conscious exposure. From a media literacy perspective, it is too simple to call everything else attention because there are different kinds of conscious attention. With media literacy, it is important that we consider four exposure states: **automatic state, attentional state, transported state,** and **self-reflexive state.** Each of these states is a qualitatively different—rather than a quantitatively different—experience for the audience member. By this, I mean that these four are not distinguished by degree of attention; instead, they are categories that are different in the kind of experience

Abstracting

Can you describe the key difference between exposure and attention in 25 words or fewer?

people have in each of the four states. Switching between states is not caused by increasing or decreasing attention; instead, the crossing the line from one state to another results in a qualitatively different experience with the message. Let's examine each of these four exposure states in some detail.

AUTOMATIC STATE In the automatic state of exposure, people are in environments where they are exposed to media messages but are not aware of those messages—that is, their mind is on automatic pilot while they screen out all the messages from conscious exposure. There is no conscious goal or strategy for seeking out messages; however, screening out of messages still takes place. This screening out continues automatically with no effort until some element in a message breaks through people's default screen and captures their attention.

In the automatic state, people can look active to outside observers, but they are not thinking about what they are doing. People in the automatic state can be clicking through a series of websites without paying attention to the messages on those sites. While it may look to an observer that the person is actively searching the web, the person may be just randomly clicking through webpages while thinking about something totally different. Even when there is evidence of exposure behavior, this does not necessarily mean that people's minds are engaged and that they are "making" decisions. Rather, the decisions are happening to them automatically because they are being governed by the mental code running in the back of their minds.

We are in the automatic state often in our everyday lives. Think about driving to school today. Although you performed many complicated tasks (starting the car, backing out of your parking spot, navigating through traffic, avoiding threats from other drivers and road hazards, finding a parking place, etc.), you are likely to have a memory of very few of those details. For example, how many cars did you pass? What colors were those cars? Who was driving those cars? What were their license plates? Although you were exposed to all this information to answer these questions, you cannot provide more than very sketchy answers.

Exposure to much of the media is in the automatic state. People have no conscious awareness of the exposure when it is taking place, nor do they have a recollection of many of the details in the experience if they are asked about it later. This is especially the case when people are multitasking. Someone might be listening to music, surfing the web, and talking to a friend on the phone; while the person may be paying attention to the phone conversation, he is in an automatic exposure state with regard to the music and the webpages. If his attention suddenly shifts to an image on a webpage, then he slips into the automatic state with the phone conversation and no longer pays attention to what his friend is saying. Multitasking severely reduces a person's cognitive advantages (i.e., ability to concentrate on a particular message) but enhances his or her emotional gratifications (i.e., receiving pleasure from more than one thing at a time) (Wang & Tchernev, 2012).

ATTENTIONAL STATE The attentional exposure state refers to people being aware of the messages and actively interacting with the elements in the messages. This does not mean they must have a high level of concentration, although that is possible. The key is conscious awareness of the messages during exposures.

Within the attentional state, there is a range of attention depending on how much of a person's mental resources one devotes to the exposure. At minimum, the person must be aware of the message and consciously track it, but there is a fair degree of elasticity in the degree of concentration, which can range from partial to quite extensive processing depending on the number of elements handled and the depth of analysis employed.

TRANSPORTED STATE When people are in the attentional state but then are pulled into the message so strongly that they lose awareness of being apart from the message, they cross over into the transported state. In the transported state, audience members lose their sense of separateness from the message—that is, they are swept away with the message, enter the world of the message, and lose track of their own social world surroundings. For example, watching a movie in a theater, we often get so caught up in the action that we feel we are involved with that action. We experience the same intense emotions as the characters do. We lose the sense that we are in a theater. Our concentration level is so high that we lose touch with our real-world environment. We lose track of real time; instead, we experience narrative time—that is, we feel time pass like the characters feel time pass. If someone behind us in the movie theater starts talking, it really disturbs us because that person's talking interrupts the enjoyment we feel in the transported state by reminding us that we are in a movie theater rather than being swept away into the movie itself.

▶ In the transported state of attention, we are pulled into a media message so strongly that we lose track of our surroundings.

©Stockphoto.com/annedde

This transported state typically occurs when people are playing video and computer games. Players lose track of real-world time and place as they submerge themselves deeply into the game world.

The transported state is not simply the high end of the attentional state. Instead, the transported state is qualitatively different than the attentional state. While attention is very high in the transported state, the attention is also very narrow—that is, people have tunnel vision and focus on the media message in a way that eliminates the barrier between them and the message. People are swept away and "enter" the message. In this sense, it is the opposite of the automatic state where people stay grounded in their social world and are unaware of the media messages in their perceptual environment; in the transported exposure state, people enter the media message and lose track of their social world.

SELF-REFLEXIVE STATE In the self-reflexive state, people are hyperaware of the message *and of their processing of the message.* It is as if they are sitting on their shoulder and monitoring their own reactions as they experience the message. This represents the fullest degree of awareness—that is, people are aware of the media message, their own real world, and their position in the real world while they process the media message. In the self-reflexive exposure state, the viewer exercises the greatest control over perceptions by reflecting on questions such as the following: Why am I exposing myself to this message? What am I getting out of this exposure and why? Why am I making these interpretations of meaning? Not only is there analysis but there is meta-analysis. This means that people are not only analyzing the media message but they are also analyzing their analysis of the media message.

While the self-reflexive and transported states might appear similar in that they are characterized by high involvement by audience members, the two exposure states are very different. In the transported state, people are highly involved emotionally, and they lose themselves in the action. In contrast, the self-reflexive state is characterized by people being highly involved cognitively and are very much aware of themselves as they analytically process the messages.

> **Grouping**
>
> Can you compare and contrast the four exposure states by identifying the ways in which they are the same and the ways in which they are different?

DECISIONS DURING EXPOSURES

As we are exposed to media messages, we are constantly confronted with decisions. The types of decisions can be organized in a three-step procedure of **filtering decisions, meaning matching decisions,** and **meaning construction decisions** (see Table 6.1). First, we encounter a message and are faced with the task of deciding whether to filter the message out (ignore it) or filter it in (process it). If we decide to filter it in, then we must make sense of it—that is, recognize the symbols and match our learned definitions to the symbols. Next, we need to construct the meaning of the message.

Table 6.1 Three Tasks of Information Processing

	Filtering Message	Meaning Matching	Meaning Construction
TASK	To make decisions about which messages to filter out (ignore) and which to filter in (pay attention to)	To use basic competencies to recognize referents and locate previously learned definitions for each	To use skills in order to move beyond meaning matching and to construct meaning for one's self in order to personalize and get more out of a message
GOAL	To attend to only those messages that have some kind of usefulness for the person and ignore all other messages	To access previously learned meanings efficiently	To interpret messages from more than one perspective as a means of identifying the range of meaning options, then choose one or synthesize across several
FOCUS	Messages in the environment	Referents in messages	One's own knowledge structures

Credits from left: ©iStockphoto.com/denis_pc; © iStockphoto.com/ t_kimura ; ©iStockphoto.com/bulentgultek

Sometimes we engage in this sequence of tasks in a very conscious manner, such that we are aware and control our decisions. However, most of the time, we engage in this sequence of tasks unconsciously—that is, our minds are on automatic pilot where our mental code automatically makes filtering and meaning matching decisions while avoiding the meaning construction process altogether. Let's examine each of these three information processing tasks in more detail.

Filtering Decisions

As we go through each day, we are constantly flooded with information. In order to protect ourselves from being overwhelmed, we continually block out most of that flood of information by automatically ignoring most of it and paying attention to only a very small percentage of it. For example, think about when your cell phone, iPad, or computer signals that you have received a text. Sometimes you read it and answer it, but other times you ignore it, especially when you're receiving hundreds of texts a day. When you see the signal for a text and decide whether to respond or not, you are filtering consciously. But let's say you have a spam filter on your device where certain kinds of texts and e-mails are blocked and only a certain kind are allowed through. In this case, your spam filter may be blocking thousands of messages each day automatically so you don't have to be bothered by them.

Spam filters provide a great service—that is, until you think about who has programmed your spam filter. Maybe there are some messages that you do not want filtered out, but your spam filter has been programmed to block them. When someone important to you sends valuable messages that are blocked by your spam filter, this is a frustrating problem. To solve this problem, you need to get into your spam filter and reprogram its selection process to unblock those messages you want to get through. We all have a kind of spam filter running in the back of our minds every day to filter out almost all of the media messages available to use. We can see evidence of this spam filter working when we look at our media exposure habits—that is, there are some media and certain types of messages that we completely avoid.

©iStockphoto.com/mrPliskin

▶ Ignoring the flood of information does not protect us from being influenced by it.

The media create much of our filtering code for us. They do this primarily by conditioning us for repeat exposures of the messages we like. This conditioning creates and reinforces exposure habits. When we follow our exposure habits, we leave no time to explore other media or other types of messages.

There is also evidence that the media are trying to be even more proactive in determining our filtering codes. For example, Amazon focuses your attention on a handful of books based on what it knows about your history of book buying. Also, Netflix offers 140,000 movies and TV shows, but you can't see a listing of them all. Instead, it personalizes what it shows you, thus focusing your choices on what you say you like most. Now, about 60% of all Netflix rentals come from personalized guesses of what Netflix thinks you would like.

Internet companies employ sophisticated algorithms to churn through all the information they have about you to infer conclusions about what you like, then use those inferred conclusions to direct you to particular products and wall you off from other products in the name of efficient filtering. These algorithms are very sophisticated and very powerful in sorting through massive data files. The danger is that they have built-in assumptions that consumers are not aware of, and often, these algorithms can be harmful. Imagine the following scenario. Let's say a company assembles a huge database about college students by pulling together information from Facebook pages, credit history, health history, parents' income level, etc. Then someone in that company develops an algorithm that churns through all that data and rank orders all the college students on potential for success and economic wealth. And let's say that the company's algorithm ranks you at the bottom as a probable loser but ranks your roommates at the top as probable winners. The company sells its rankings to other companies who then send your roommates all kinds of great offers for low interest credit cards, coupons for exciting trips, opportunities to network with successful professionals, and so on. Meanwhile, you are ignored by these marketers because you are regarded as an undesirable target audience. But your roommates go on to live very successful and happy lives because of all the opportunities offered by marketers who bought data that told them that your roommates were highly desirable targets. Your roommates get higher paying jobs at graduation than you because employers looked at the rankings. Your roommates go on to get bigger raises and promotions, have better health care plans, travel more, meet more interesting people, etc. Marketers can set people off in different life paths by the opportunities they offer certain people and not others. These marketers are not trying to be evil or trying to unfairly discriminate. Instead, marketers are simply trying to be efficient and get the most for their advertising dollars by targeting their advertising to those people who have the greatest potential of becoming valued customers. So marketers depend on research companies to help them identify the right people to be the best targets for their expensive marketing campaigns.

Meaning Matching Decisions

Meaning matching is the process of recognizing elements in the message and accessing our memory to find the meanings we have memorized for those elements. This is a relatively automatic task. It may require a good deal of effort to learn to recognize symbols in media messages and to memorize their standard meanings, but once learned, this process becomes routine. To illustrate, think back to when you first learned to read. You had to learn how to recognize words printed on a page. Then you had to memorize the meaning of each word. The first time you saw the sentence "Dick threw the ball to Jane," it required a good deal of work to divide the sentence into words, to recall the meaning of each word, and to put it all together. With practice, you were able to perform this process more quickly and more easily. Learning to read in elementary school is essentially the process of being able to recognize a longer list of symbols and to memorize their **denoted meanings.** Some symbols in media messages were words, some were numbers, some were pictures, and some were sounds.

This type of learning develops **competencies.** By competency, I mean that either you are able to do something correctly or you are not. For example, when you see 2 + 3, you either recognize that the 2 and the 3 are symbols representing particular quantities or you do not. You either recognize the + symbol as indicating addition or you do not. You can either perform this mathematical operation and arrive at 5 or you cannot. Working with these symbols does not require—or allow for—individual interpretation and creative meaning construction. Competencies are our abilities to recognize standard symbols and recall the memorized denoted meanings for those symbols. If we did not have a common set of symbols and shared meanings for each of these symbols, communication would not be possible. Education at the elementary level is the training of the next generation to develop the basic competencies of recognizing these symbols and memorizing the designated meaning for each one.

▶ The process of meaning matching allows you to connect symbols to meaning—for instance, recognizing that a particular sound your cell phone makes is signaling you've received a text message.

When your cell phone makes a certain sound, you know that means you have received a text. You look at the screen and see a name and know which friend has sent you that text. You tap the screen at a certain icon, and your text message is revealed. That message has words and emoticons that convey meaning to you. In this example, the sound, name, icon, words, and emoticons are each symbols that have a specific meaning that you have learned in the past and are now able to match with its learned meaning with almost no effort. This task is accomplished automatically because you have acquired those competencies.

Meaning Construction Decisions

In contrast to meaning matching, meaning construction is a much more challenging task. It is not an automatic process, but instead, it requires us to think about moving beyond the standard denoted meaning and to create meaning for ourselves by using the skills of induction, deduction, grouping, and synthesis. We engage in a meaning construction process either when we have no denoted meaning for a particular

© Richard Levine / Alamy

▶ Research shows that how a media message such as a news story is framed, or presented, will influence how an audience interprets the message.

message in our memory banks or when the denoted meaning does not satisfy us and we want to arrive at a different meaning.

Let's say you get a text from your friend Christopher who has just broken up with his girlfriend Christine. The text message says, "Chris is not happy with your help. Thanks a bunch." This message is too ambiguous for meaning matching. For example, does the Chris in the message refer to the sender or his ex-girlfriend? Is the sender being sarcastic when he says, "Thanks a bunch" because he resents your interference? Or is he sincere because you helped him break up when he couldn't do it himself? To answer these questions, you need context about your friendship with Christopher, about his relationship with Christine, his intention to break up with her or not, etc. So you need skills rather than competencies to analyze the situation, evaluate his intention, see how this message fits into the pattern of your relationship, and then synthesize an appropriate response.

Many meanings can be constructed from any media message; furthermore, there are many ways to go about constructing that meaning. Thus, we cannot learn a complete set of rules to accomplish this task; instead, we need to be guided by our own information goals, and we need to use skills (rather than competencies) to creatively construct a path to reach our goals. For these reasons, meaning construction rarely takes place in an automatic fashion. Instead, we need to make conscious decisions when we are constructing meaning for ourselves. Also, every meaning construction task is different, so we cannot program our minds to follow the same one procedure automatically when we are confronted with a range of meaning construction tasks.

Much of our processing of media messages utilizes meaning construction. There is a large body of research that clearly shows that each of us brings a considerable number of factors with us to any media message exposure and that these factors constitute a **frame** that we use to interpret the message. Researchers typically find that the meaning that people get from news stories is not determined solely by the information provided in the story itself; meaning is also determined in part by how the audiences interpret that information (e.g., see Kepplinger, Geiss, & Siebert, 2012). Those interpretations are influenced by our own expectations, motivations, past history with the topic of a media message, and our biases.

While meaning matching relies on competencies, meaning construction relies on skills. This is one of the fundamental differences between the two tasks of meaning matching and meaning construction. Competencies are categorical—that is, either you have a competency or you do not. However, skill ability is not categorical; on any given skill, there is a wide range of ability. That is, some people have little ability, whereas other people have enormous ability. Also, skills are like muscles. Without practice, skills become weaker. With practice and exercise, they grow stronger. When the personal locus has strong drive states for using skills, those skills have a much greater chance of developing to higher levels.

The two processes of meaning matching and meaning construction do not take place independently from one another; they are intertwined. To construct meaning, we first have to recognize symbols and understand the sense in which those symbols are being used in the message. Thus, the meaning matching process is more fundamental because the product of the meaning matching process then is imported into the meaning construction process.

It's important to avoid getting the two mixed up. Consider the example of a physics exam where the professor asks students how they could use a barometer to measure the height of a building. If the professor is treating this as a meaning matching task, then there is one sanctioned answer—take a reading of barometric pressure at the foot of the building and again at the roof then using a particular formula, translate the difference in readings into feet thus computing the height of the building. But what if a student is creative and can think of other ways to use the barometer to measure the height of the building? When Niels Bohr was asked this question on a physics exam at the University of Copenhagen in 1905, he answered the question by saying that he would go up onto the roof of the building, tie a string to the barometer, lower the barometer to the group, then measure how long the string was. The professor gave him an F. Niels went to talk to the professor and argued that his answer would produce the correct solution. He also argued that there were several other answers: (1) throw the barometer off the roof then count the number of seconds it took to hit the ground then calculate the distance and (2) measure the length of the shadow of the barometer and the building then calculate the ratio. While all of these alternative methods could yield an accurate measure of the height of the building, the professor did not care, because he was looking for one particular answer that required matching the problem to the one solution he taught in his physics class. Niels Bohr took the F that day but continued to use his creative mind to become a very successful physicist, winning the Nobel Prize in Physics in 1922 for his contributions into atomic structure and quantum mechanics. The lesson from this story is that we all need to understand the nature of the tasks we are asked to perform. If the task is one of meaning matching, then we need to focus on competencies and find the matching answer to the question. But if the task is one of meaning construction, then we need to be more creative in using all kinds of skills and think divergently.

INCREASING MEDIA LITERACY

In this chapter, I have illuminated some of the practices you take for granted in your everyday life. The more you recognize the different exposure states and the different information processing tasks, the more you can use them to your advantage. How well have you been performing the information processing tasks? We will analyze your decisions in this section, but first, let's examine the natural abilities that form the foundation for performing these tasks well.

Natural Abilities

Some of us naturally do better in navigating through all the filtering choices, meaning matching tasks, and meaning construction opportunities. The reason for this is that we vary in our natural abilities. With media literacy, there are cognitive abilities and emotional abilities that are more highly developed in some of us compared to other people. While some of us are blessed with a higher level of these abilities, they are not static. That is, we can grow our abilities through exercise. We can also lose our inborn abilities through neglect.

©Comstock/Stockbyte/Thinkstock

▶ Regardless of your age, the more eager you are to embrace new experiences and new perspectives, the more media literate you will become.

People who have a high degree of these natural abilities will be more media literate and, hence, need less protection from the media. In contrast, people who have a low degree of these natural abilities will be much less able to protect themselves from potential harm from media exposures. Because these natural abilities are not related to age, we cannot rely on a person's age alone to decide whether that person is at risk for harmful effects.

In this section, I will focus on two cognitive abilities (**field independency** and **conceptual differentiation)** and two emotional abilities (**emotional intelligence and tolerance for ambiguity**). While there are other natural abilities that contribute to a person's media literacy, these four are likely the most important ones.

FIELD INDEPENDENCY Perhaps the most important ability related to media literacy is field independency. Think of field independency as your natural ability to distinguish between the signal and the noise in any message. The noise is the chaos of symbols and images. The signal is the information that emerges from the chaos. People who are highly field independent are able to sort quickly through the field to identify the elements of importance and ignore the distracting elements. In contrast, people who are more field dependent get stuck in the field of chaos—seeing all the details but missing the patterns and the "big picture," which is the signal (Witkin & Goodenough, 1977). For example, when reading a news story on a website, field-independent people will be able to identify the key information of the who, what, when, where, and why of the story. They will quickly sort through what is said, the graphics, and the visuals to focus on the essence of the event being covered. People who are field dependent will perceive the same key elements in the story but will also pay an equal amount of attention to the background elements of pop-up pictures, ads, borders, and so on. To the field-dependent person, all of these elements are of fairly equal importance, so they are as likely to remember the trivial as they are to remember the main points of the story. This is not to say that field-dependent people retain more information because they pay attention to more; on the contrary, field-dependent people retain less information because the information is not organized well and is likely to contain as much noise (peripheral and tangential elements) as signal (elements about the main idea).

Let's try one more example of this concept. Have you ever had to read a long novel and gotten so lost about 100 pages into it that you had to quit in frustration? You may have felt that just when the author was getting the story going with one set of characters, he or she would switch to a different setting at a different time with a totally new set of characters. This may have been happening every few pages! There were too many characters talking about too many different things. You were overwhelmed by all the detail and could not make sense of the overall story. This indicates that the novelist was making demands on you to be much more field independent than you could be as you read his or her novel. If you had been more field independent, you would have been able to see through all the details and recognize a thematic pattern of some sort, then use that thematic pattern as a tool to sort through all the details about characters, settings, time, dialog, and action to direct your attention efficiently to those elements that were most important.

We live in a culture that is highly saturated with media messages. Much of this is noise—that is, it does not provide us with the information or emotional reactions we want. The sheer bulk of all the information makes it more difficult to differentiate the important from the trivial, so many of us do not bother to differentiate. Instead, we default to a passive state as we float along in this stream of messages. The advantage of this automatic processing is that it screens out the noise, but the disadvantage is that it screens out much of the signal too. When we are more field independent, we can better program our attention triggers to maximize the filtering *in* of signal and at the same time maximize the filtering *out* of noise.

CONCEPTUAL DIFFERENTIATION This refers to how people group and classify things. People who classify objects into a large number of mutually exclusive categories exhibit a high degree of conceptual differentiation (Gardner, 1968). In contrast, people who use a small number of categories have a low degree of conceptual differentiation.

Related to the number of categories is category width (Bruner, Goodnow, & Austin, 1956). People who have few categories to classify something usually have broad categories so as to contain all types of messages. For example, if a person has only three categories for all media messages (news, ads, and entertainment), then each of these categories must contain a wide variety of things. In contrast, someone who has a great many categories would be dividing media messages into thinner slices (breaking news, feature news, documentary, commercial ads, public service announcements [PSAs], action/adventure shows, sitcoms, game shows, talk shows, cartoons, and reality shows).

When we encounter a new message, we must categorize it by using either a leveling or a sharpening strategy. With the leveling strategy, we look for similarities between the new message and previous messages we have stored away as examples in our categories. We look for the best fit between the new message and one of remembered messages. We will never find a perfect fit—that is, the new message always has slightly different characteristics than our category calls for, but we tend to ignore those differences. In contrast, the sharpening strategy focuses on differences and tries to maintain a high degree of separation between the new message and older messages (Pritchard, 1975). To illustrate this, let's say two people are comparing this year's Super Bowl with last year's Super Bowl. A leveler would argue that the two games were similar and point out all the things the two had in common. The sharpener would disagree and point out all the differences between the two Super Bowls. Levelers tend to have fewer categories so that many things can fit into the same category, whereas sharpeners have many, many categories. In our example, the first person would likely have only one category for Super Bowls, feeling that all the Super Bowls are pretty much the same. A sharpener might have a different category for every Super Bowl, treating each one as unique. Increasing one's level of media literacy requires one to do more sharpening of categories for media messages, media companies, and media effects.

EMOTIONAL INTELLIGENCE Our ability to understand and control our emotions is called emotional intelligence. Emotional intelligence is thought to be composed of several related abilities, such as the ability to read the emotions of other people (empathy), the ability to be aware of one's own emotions, the ability to harness and manage one's own emotions productively, and the ability to handle the emotional demands of relationships.

Those of us with stronger emotional intelligence have a well-developed sense of empathy; we are able to see the world from another person's perspective. The more perspectives we can access, the more emotional intelligence we have. When we are highly developed emotionally, we are more aware of our own emotions. We also better understand the factors that cause those emotions, so we are able to seek the kinds of messages to get us the emotional reactions we want. In addition, we are less impulsive and are able to exercise more self-control. We can concentrate on the task at hand rather than become distracted by peripheral emotions.

TOLERANCE FOR AMBIGUITY Every day, we encounter people and situations that are unfamiliar to us. To prepare ourselves for such situations, we have developed sets of expectations. What do we do when our expectations are not met and we are surprised? That depends on our tolerance level for ambiguity. If we have a very low tolerance for ambiguity, we will likely choose to ignore those messages that do not meet our expectations; we feel too confused or frustrated to work out the discrepancies. If we have a very high tolerance for ambiguity, we will likely not be bothered at all by discrepancies and let them ride. Thus we encounter problems at both the low and high ends of tolerance for ambiguity. We are most successful in developing our media literacy when we have a middle tolerance for ambiguity. This middle-level tolerance allows us to confront areas of ambiguity and not ignore them. Initial confusion does not stop us from thinking through the ambiguities. We do not feel an emotional barrier that prevents us from examining messages more closely. However, our tolerance is not so high that we allow those ambiguities to continue—that is, we feel a strong motivation to resolve the ambiguities. We are willing to break any message down into components and make comparisons and evaluations in a quest to understand the nature of the message and to examine why our initial expectations were wrong.

During media exposures, people with a low tolerance encounter messages on the surface. If the surface meaning fits their preconceptions, then it is filed away and becomes a confirmation (or reinforcement) of those

Evaluation

Can you make a judgment about which of the four natural abilities is the most helpful to you in increasing your media literacy?

preconceptions. If the surface meaning does not meet a person's preconceptions, the message is ignored. In short, there is no analysis.

Analyzing Decisions

The ideas presented in this chapter can be used to increase one's media literacy—that is, to increase one's power over making decisions. Let's first examine the filtering decision, which is usually made in the automatic exposure state, which is governed by your mental code running automatically in the back of your mind. Recall from Chapter 2 that when our mental codes are running automatically, they deliver enormous efficiency. But it is important to examine what those codes are so we can understand how the thousands of filtering decisions that are made for us every day are actually made. To illustrate what goes into these codes, let's return to the Google example. Recall the example of Google from Chapter 1 where the key word *information overload* generated a search through Google's 13.4 billion indexed webpages and found 7.3 million that mentioned that key word. Thus, Google was able to filter out 99.95% of all webpages in less than one second. While that is very efficient, Google wants to become even more efficient in helping you with filtering. Google CEO Eric Schmidt said that Google's goal was to guess what you are interested in. In December 2009, Google changed its algorithm to personalize searches. This means that your Google searches are not guided exclusively by the key words you use; those searches are also guided by information Google has gathered about your personal preferences. So what you see as a result of a Google search is determined by your key words entered, the popularity of sites, paid placement by advertisers, and Google's perception of your interests. Because of this last criterion, different results will be displayed when different people search on Google and enter the same key words. To test this, do Applying Media Literacy 6.1.

Let's think about this. If Google is really good at guessing your personal interests (from your past searches on Google), then its service increases in value to you because the results of your searches have a higher degree of refinement. But what if Google misinterprets your interests? In this case, Google searches decrease in value. If you do not periodically examine how Google structures its searches, then you are simply trusting its criteria, and that could be causing problems for you of narrowing your world down over time.

Evaluation

Do you judge Google's ability to guess your personal interests to have a good or a bad impact on your own Internet searches?

You have a Google-like algorithm constantly running in the back of your mind as it governs all your filtering decisions. As you encounter the thousands of messages every day, this algorithm is filtering out almost all this information and triggering your attention only with certain messages. What are those triggers? They are

Personalized Search Results

Step one: Get together.

You will need to compare your own search results with those of other people, so get together with a friend or small group of friends.

Step two: Brainstorm searches.

Make a list of Internet searches based on the specific interests and hobbies of the people in your group.

Step three: List key words.

Make a list of key words that you will use for each search. Try to use words that have more than one meaning. For example, the word *fish* could refer to the action of trying to catch food from a boat, searching for information, the victim in a con game, etc.

Step four: Conduct your searches simultaneously using Google.

Each person in the group conducts the same search, using the same key words, at the same time.

Step five: Analyze.

Compare and analyze your search results with your friends' search results. Are there differences in the time of the search, the number of hits, the highest ranking sites? Can you explain the differences in results according to the personal characteristics and interests of the different people who conducted the searches?

Step Six: Test for general terms

Repeat the process with relatively general terms, such as news, clothing, advertising, reality, etc. Analyze the results of each search on a general term. Are there as many differences across people when you use a general term compared to a specific term?

different for each person, so to find out what the triggers are in your filtering algorithm, you need to examine your media exposure habits and ask yourself why you are spending time with particular media and particular messages while ignoring others. If you have good reasons for your exposure habits, then it is likely the triggers in your algorithm have been programmed by you to meet your specific needs. But if you are puzzled by some of your habits, it is time to think about changing those habits to see if your needs can be met better through exposure to different media and different kinds of messages.

Your mind is filled with a good deal of mental coding that has been built up over the course of all your experiences with the media and in the real world. Are there faulty parts in that code? To continue our examination, let's move on to the decisions about meaning matching. Periodically check some of the meanings you have memorized. The simplest way to do this is to examine your vocabulary. Perhaps there are words that are used in everyday language where you have not memorized the meaning or you have acquired a wrong meaning. These can be easily identified and corrected. More difficult to spot are faulty meanings you have memorized about important facts. Perhaps you have acquired some faulty meanings by simply memorizing the incorrect fact presented by so-called experts, such as newscasters, pundits, cultural critics, etc. Perhaps the experts were later found to be wrong yet you still hold on to a memorized fact that is now faulty. Or perhaps you should not have memorized an expert's opinion but instead constructed your own opinion that fits better with your own personal beliefs and experiences. It is likely that your large set of memorized meanings contains elements that are out of date, are causing friction with what you now believe, or are faulty in some way. If you don't identify them and clear them out of your "mental dictionary," you will automatically continue to use those meanings and these dysfunctional meanings can take you farther away from your goals.

As for meaning construction, you should identify areas where decisions are most important in your life. As you use the media messages to gather more information, ask yourself if you are simply accepting that information as is or if you are transforming it to fit into your needs and goals. The more you work on transforming the raw material of information into knowledge that helps you achieve your own goals, the more your meaning construction process will operate under your control.

The meaning of media messages is not always the way it might seem on the surface. There are often many layers of meanings. The more you are aware of the layers of meaning in messages, the more you can control the selection of which meanings you want. The constant exposure to media messages influences the way we think about the world and ourselves. It influences our beliefs about crime, education, religion, families, and the world in general.

When you examine your mental codes for defective criteria and faulty facts, you need a strong personal locus to provide the mental energy needed as well as good skills. The skill of analysis is important to search out the lines of code. The skill of evaluation is important to make judgments about how useful, credible, and accurate those lines of code are. The skills of grouping, induction, and deduction are essential in looking for inconsistencies across lines of codes. And the skill of synthesis is important as a way of fixing faulty lines of code and replacing them with new codes that will work within your system of thinking and have a greater chance of delivering more valuable decisions.

People who have weak skills will not be able to do much with the information they encounter. They are likely to fall into traps of ignoring good information and fixating on inaccurate or bad information because they are unable to tell the difference and therefore make good selections among all the available information. They will organize information poorly and create weak and faulty knowledge structures. In the worst case, people with weak skills will try to avoid thinking about information altogether and become passive; the active information providers—such as advertisers and entertainers—will become the constructors of people's knowledge structures and will take control over of how those people see the world by altering their beliefs and by giving them faulty standards that they then use to create their attitudes.

KEY IDEAS

- Exposure and attention are not the same thing.

- Exposure requires that three criteria (physical, perceptual, and psychological) be met.

- Attention occurs in one of four exposure states—automatic, attentional, transported, and self-reflexive.

- As we are constantly exposed to the flood of media messages, we are continually making decisions—either consciously but more typically unconsciously—about filtering, meaning matching, and meaning construction.

- We have natural abilities that help us become more media literate. Two of the most important natural abilities are cognitive (field independency and conceptual differentiation) and two are emotional (emotional intelligence and tolerance for ambiguity).

- Increasing one's media literacy involves the active examination of mental codes periodically to identify and fix the faulty programming. Once fixed, those codes can run automatically to make thousands of decisions while on automatic pilot, with increased confidence that those decisions will make them more productive, smarter, and happier.

FURTHER READING

Brooks, David. (2011). *The social animal: The hidden sources of love, character, and achievement.* New York, NY: Random House. **(424 pages including index and endnotes)**

This is an easy-to-read book about the human brain. It presents a lot of interesting information about what is known—and what scientists think they now know—about this complex organ.

Pariser, E. (2011). *The filter bubble: How the new personalized web is changing what we read and how we think.* New York, NY: Penguin Books. **(294 pages with index and endnotes)**

In this fascinating book, Pariser provides many examples about how the mass media are making filtering decisions for you.

Potter, W. J. (2005). *Becoming a strategic thinker: Developing skills for success.* **Upper Saddle River, NJ: Prentice Hall. (183 pages with index)**

In this book, I show that success in higher education is based on how well students have mastered eight skills. Seven of these skills are also key to developing higher levels of media literacy. This book presents lots of examples and exercises for each skill.

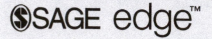

Sharpen your skills with SAGE edge at **edge.sagepub.com/potterintro**

SAGE edge for Students provides a personalized approach to help you accomplish your coursework goals in an easy-to-use learning environment.

▶ How are message formulas used on social media websites, such as those pictured?

Test Your Knowledge: True or False

Before reading this chapter, think about which of the following statements you believe to be **true** and which you believe to be **false**.

1. At a general level, all mass media messages share a common formula.

2. The most successful message producers are those people who understand the content formulas the best.

3. Audience members use the same formulas to make sense of media messages that producers use to create their media messages.

4. Increasing your media literacy requires you to stay away from negative content.

Answers can be found on page 247.

7

MASS MEDIA CONTENT

Mass media content is a huge topic area that encompasses an incredibly wide range of messages. In order to organize all this information efficiently, this chapter focuses on the ideas of message formulas and **genres**.

MESSAGE FORMULAS AND GENRES

Formulas are conventions that message producers use as guidelines when creating their messages. Audiences also use these same formulas as guides when they extract meaning from those messages. Thus these formulas are essential to both message producers as well as message receivers.

The most successful producers of mass media messages are those people who best understand and apply these formulas in order to attract audience members, hold their attention throughout the entire message, and make those audience members want to seek out additional messages from those producers. We, the audience members, have developed a relatively high degree of sophistication in using message formulas in order to follow stories and make sense of our media exposures. We know how to recognize suspenseful cues in stories and understand what they mean. We know how to infer character motivations for actions and look for the consequences of those actions as they unfold later in the stories. We know how to start playing **electronic games** and learn what the rules are through trial and error. We know how to read the material on our friends' social networking

Learning Objectives

After reading this chapter, you will be able to do the following:

1. Explain the relationship between message formulas and genres.

2. Define the next-step reality formula.

3. Describe the three meta-genres of mass media content.

4. Develop a personal strategy for dealing with mass media content in a more media literate fashion.

sites (SNSs), figure out what they are telling us, and respond in a meaningful manner. All media messages follow conventions that can be expressed as message formulas. The more we understand these formulas, the better we can construct messages as producers and the more we can get out of those messages as receivers.

Messages that share the same set of content formulas are said to be in the same genre.

This chapter is organized to present a genre structure that highlights the differences and similarities of formulas used by producers across the wide range of mass media messages. First, we will examine the most general of all mass media formulas—the one formula used by producers of all mass media messages regardless of type. Then the chapter branches into three sections in order to examine each of the three major kinds—or meta-genres—of mass media messages: narratives, electronic games, and interactive message platforms. Within each of these three sets of mass media messages, there are different genres and subgenres. When you look at Table 7.1, you can begin to see a big picture about how the wide variety of mass media messages can be organized according to the sets of message formulas they use.

Table 7.1 Mass Media Content Genres and Subgenres		
Narratives	Information	News Documentaries
	Persuasion	Commercial advertisements Public service announcements (PSAs)
	Entertainment	Drama Comedy Romance Reality
Games	Small scale (few players; constrained environment) Large scale (many players; wide open environment)	
Interactive Message Platforms	Social networking (meeting other people for personal or business reasons) Sharing (downloading music, video, and other messages; purchasing products)	

Credits from top: ©iStockphoto.com/Bibigon; ©iStockphoto.com/ihorzigor; ©iStockphoto.com/neyro2008

MOST GENERAL FORMULA: NEXT-STEP REALITY

The most general formula that is used by all mass media messages is what I call the **next-step reality** formula. This formula calls for a combination of reality elements and fantasy elements. This combination is necessary to attract the attention of all kinds of audiences and hold their attention in a satisfying way while programming them for repeated exposures.

The reality elements in media messages are necessary to send a signal to potential audience members that the message will resonate with their own real-world experiences and give them some context to help them understand the meaning of the upcoming message. Messages that contain people or characters that look and sound familiar to audiences give them the context to recognize quickly who these people are and set up expectations that make it easy to follow the action. The messages also present familiar settings and use familiar language patterns. The use of all these familiar elements helps audience members to get into the message easily and to process its meaning efficiently. Also, when the message elements are similar to the elements in their own everyday lives, audience members are led to expect that they can learn something useful from the media message that they might be able to use in their own lives.

The fantasy elements in media messages are necessary to send a signal to potential audience members that the message offers something novel that is likely to surprise them or at least add something new to their existing base of knowledge. Potential audience members do not want media messages to be exact replications of what they see every day in their lives, because they already have an everyday life where they are feeling constrained by its limits and want to see their lives expanded with new information, new feelings, and new experiences. These new things can be relatively minor as subtle tweaks on their own existence, or they can be relatively major where the message producers take audiences to exotic settings (in outer space or back in history), show them bigger than life characters, and evoke emotions (fear, lust, excitement) far more intense than people are getting in their everyday lives.

Sometimes we want much more reality than fantasy in a media message. For example, with news, we want a heavy dose of reality to see what actually happened, but we also want some novelty—that's what makes the message news. In contrast, sometimes we want much more fantasy than reality in a media message. For example, with Hollywood type movies, we want to see exotic locations as well as fabulously attractive and interesting characters in highly dramatic plots where the action is resolved in super intense climaxes. However, we also need some reality cues so we can recognize settings

Abstracting

Can you explain the next-step reality formula of media messages in 25 words or fewer?

and find characters with which we share some qualities so we can identify with those characters and experience the action through them. The most skillful producers of mass media messages are the talented people who are able to blend together reality and fantasy in a way that makes us believe that the real world is (or can be) more exciting and dramatic than we previously thought.

Audience's Perspective

Why do we expose ourselves to media messages? At the most fundamental level, we expose ourselves to the media to find information and experiences that we cannot get in real life. Most of us feel that the real world is too limited—that is, we cannot get all the experiences and information we want in the real world. To get those experiences and information, we journey into the media world and therefore expect to find something more exciting there. Our journeys into the media world are valuable to the extent that they resonate with our real world but also expand on it by showing us something new, taking our perceptions to places we have yet to visit in real life, and by stimulating our imaginations to consider new ideas. Thus, media messages must present something novel, but they must also resonate with our real-world experiences.

There are two reasons why people are motivated to go to the media rather than get experiences in real life. One reason is that it is impossible for them to get those experiences in real life. For example, for most people, it is impossible to know what the earth looks like from outer space or what the surface of other planets look like. It is impossible to know what it was like to live on a farm during the American Civil War, to be a Knight of the Round Table in medieval England, or to watch an ancient religious leader walk the earth. To get access to these images, sounds, and emotions, people must access messages from the media.

A second reason that motivates people to seek experiences from the media instead of real life is because the costs of getting those experiences in the media are far lower than the costs required in real life. For example, it is far easier to watch a presidential news conference on TV than it is to go to journalism school, get a job on a major newspaper or TV service, get credentialed as a White House reporter, and attend the press conference in person. And it is less costly emotionally to watch characters in a movie try to meet each other, establish relationships, break up, and learn from their mistakes than it is to go through all of that in real life to learn the same thing.

Therefore, people want media messages that are not so real that they are the same as their everyday lives. But neither do they want media messages that are so far removed from their experiences and needs that the messages have no immediate relevance. So people want messages that are one step removed from real life; they want messages that show what is easily possible and make it seem probable and even actual.

Programmers' Perspective

Programmers intuitively know that to attract audiences, they must take their audience's sense of reality and tweak it a bit to make it seem more interesting. Thus, the producers of media messages typically keep the elements of their messages anchored in the real world as much as possible so that they can accurately resonate with the audience's experiences in real life. But producers of media messages also know they cannot simply reproduce literal reality; there would be no point to this because it would be easier for people to stay with their own real-world experiences.

Producers of fiction know that their art is in telling stories that are "bigger" than life in some way. Producers can take an ordinary setting and a typical plot (boy meets girl) but change the characters so that they are a little more attractive or a little more interesting than people in real life. Or producers can take ordinary characters and put them in a plot that is a bit more dramatic in events and consequences than what happens to most people in real life. Skilled producers can take the audience on a journey by removing the audience one step at a time until they have taken them willingly all the way into pure fantasy. This is the formula with farce. The story begins with what looks like an ordinary everyday situation; then, step-by-step, the producer takes the audience far away from that reality but does it in a way that the audience is not lost but willingly accepts each new step into silliness. Thus, producers depend on viewers' willing suspension of disbelief. To make people willing, producers must take it one step at a time.

The next-step reality also underlies persuasive messages. For example, the typical problem–solution advertising message shows ordinary people with an ordinary problem, such as bad breath, a headache, dirty laundry, hunger for a good lunch, and so on. The advertiser invites the audience to take the step of faith into a solution—that is, to buy and use the advertised product on the promise that it will solve the problem better than any other solution—more quickly, more completely, more inexpensively, or more satisfying emotionally.

The next-step reality is a bit more difficult to understand with information-type messages. For example, if the purpose of news organizations is to report the events of the day, how can the next-step reality apply to journalists? The answer is that when journalists select what gets reported, they typically are more interested in reporting the deviant events than they are in reporting the typical events that happen every day. Recall the old saying that if a dog bites a man, it is not news, but if a man bites a dog, that is news. The twist in the event makes it news. Crimes are news because they are aberrant behaviors. Violent crimes are more newsworthy than are property crimes because they are more aberrant and more rare—in the real world.

Now let's turn our attention to the three major genres of mass media content: narratives, electronic games, and interactive message platforms. While each of these uses the next-step reality formula, they each add additional formulas that make them unique from one another.

NARRATIVES

The narrative meta-genre is characterized by a clear separation between message producers and audiences. The producers design messages, and the audience members are purely the receivers of those messages. Of course, different audience members may receive a given message in different ways (i.e., interpret different meanings and have different degrees of emotional reactions), but audience members do not change the message itself, nor are they involved in designing or distributing those messages.

Designers of mass media narratives have a particular kind of audience in mind then use those message formulas as guides to create a story that will attract as many members of that target audience as possible. They know they must have a strong beginning to the story to hook audience attention by showing them the kinds of characters and settings that resonate with them most and by promising a flow of events that will stimulate particular kinds of emotions. Then once the story is underway, producers rely on formulas that help them heighten the action in a way that keeps audience members on the edge of their seats and anxious to find out what happens next. In designing the end of the message, producers follow formulas that will provide audiences with a satisfying resolution to the problems and reinforce the message experience in a way that makes audiences want another message from the same producers.

There are three kinds of narratives distinguished by their primary intention of informing, persuading, or entertaining audiences. While it is important to understand that most media messages are a mix of these three, it is also important to understand that messages differ in terms of their primary intention. Let's examine each of these three.

Informing

Information narratives are designed primarily to give audiences something of a factual nature that they can use in their real lives. People who like to travel will expose themselves to travel narratives to experience the geography and culture of different places. Hobbyists will expose themselves to informational narratives to learn how to engage in their hobby in a better way. Many people expose themselves to news stories every day to keep up with current events about traffic, weather, performance of sports teams, actions of legislatures that can pass laws to change their lives, etc.

The most well-known **story formula** for journalists is to structure their stories to answer six questions: Who? What? Where? Where? Why? How? Journalists confronted with a new story begin by asking these questions; then they structure their story to answer each of these questions. When journalists ignore one or more of these questions in their stories, audiences find the messages unsatisfying and are likely to feel frustrated.

Another popular news-writing formula is the inverted pyramid. This formula tells the journalist to put the most important information at the beginning of the story and then add the next most important set of information. Journalists move down their list of information, ranked according to importance until all the information is in the story. This formula was developed in the early days of the telegraph, when journalists in the field would send their stories to their newspapers over telegraph lines. They needed to send the most important information first in case the telegraph line went dead before they were done transmitting the entire story. We are way past the days of dependence on telegraph lines, but the formula still has value because editors will cut stories if they run too long. For example, a newspaper editor might want to use a reporter's 20-inch story but only has room for 16 inches, so the editor will typically cut off the last 4 inches.

Although people do not expose themselves to information narratives primarily for entertainment, producers of these messages know that they need to use some entertainment conventions in order to attract and hold the attention of these audience members. So another popular formula that journalists use is what I call **simplified extended conflict (SEC).** When covering a story, journalists look for some angle of conflict that appears very simple. They believe that a story that has no conflict will not grab the audience's attention, but if the conflict is complex, the story will not hold the audience's attention. Furthermore, if the story can be played out over several days—or longer—so much the better. Political elections offer lots of good examples of the SEC. Campaigns always involve conflict between the candidates, and the media narratives usually simplify this by focusing on only two candidates and pushing other candidates into the background. Also, the campaign, which goes on for weeks or months, is typically portrayed as a race, with one candidate ahead and the other candidate running hard to catch up. Political coverage is much more about who is winning and whether the challenger can come from behind and close the gap than it is about issues. If the conflict is focused on the finer points of complex issues, the story will not appeal to as large audience. Therefore, journalists look for a simple form of conflict, and that is best seen in the "horse race" metaphor.

Other examples of SEC are the good guys against the bad guys, such as the police force against a criminal; the outsider against the insiders, such as a whistle blower exposing corruption in a large corporation; and the little guy against the big guys, such as an individual taking on city hall or big business. Journalists can present the conflict in these situations in a very simple manner and keep the conflict going over a long period of time so that audiences seek out messages every day to find out who is winning.

Journalists do this by polarizing the people or issues in the conflict, inviting the audience to identify with one side, then playing out the fight with lots of drama.

Persuading

Persuasive narratives are designed primarily to influence audience attitudes and behaviors. The typical story formula for persuasive narratives is problem–solution, which is a very simple formula. It has to be very simple because audiences rarely pay attention to any one persuasive narrative. Persuasive narratives on TV are typically 15 seconds and appear in clusters of a dozen or more ads in a commercial pod interrupting an entertainment program. Persuasive narratives in magazines, newspapers, and on websites typically are displayed on a small portion of a page or a screen.

©Stockbyte/Stockbyte/Thinkstock

▶ Part of a complete breakfast? Advertising puffery can make foods like cereals sound more nutritious than they really are.

Using this very simple problem–solution formula of storytelling, advertisers typically exaggerate our problems (in order to increase our anxiety and fear) then exaggerate their product's effectiveness as the solution (in order to motivate product purchasing). Thus, they are using the next-step reality formula by presenting real problems that we experience but then making those problems seem more critical while portraying their solutions as more dramatic. When they exaggerate their solutions, they must be careful not to present a factual falsehood that could be tested for its truth value. Therefore, their product claims are less about presenting **factual information** and more likely to be **puffery,** which is the practice of making claims for their product that sound super good on the surface but when examined closely reveal that they are not making any substantive claim that could be actually tested for its truth value. For example, have you ever seen an ad where any of the following claims were made: "the best in its class," "the most beautiful," or "the finest"? These slogans at first seem to be telling us something good about the advertised product, but upon closer examination, they are empty claims because they cannot actually be tested for various reasons. Puffery comes in many forms:

- Irrelevant comparisons: "X is the best-selling product of its kind." What kind? Maybe *kind* is defined so narrowly that there is only one brand of its kind. Also, maybe it is the best seller because it is the cheapest or because it wears out so fast.

- Comparison with an unidentified other: "X has better cleaning action." Better than what? Better than another brand? Better than not cleaning? There is an implied comparison that makes the product sound superior, but it really is a meaningless claim.

- Comparison of the product to its earlier form: "X is new and improved!" Again, on the surface, this seems like a good thing—until we start thinking about it. What was wrong with the old version? And what is wrong with this current version that will end up being new and improved again next year?

- Pseudo-claims: An example of this is "X fights cavities," but we are not told how. Is it a chemical in the toothpaste, the movement of the brush on the teeth, or the habit of brushing?

- Pseudo-survey: "Four out of five dentists surveyed said they recommend X." Who are these five? Maybe they were paid to recommend it.

The puffery formula works well for producers because it makes their persuasive narratives sound good to audiences. But it does not work well for audiences because those claims are misleading.

Entertaining

Entertainment narratives are designed primarily to elicit emotional reactions from audiences. Some of these narratives are very short, like a single joke designed to elicit laughter. And some can be fairly long where producers attempt to take audiences on a long involved journey that elicits many different emotions and at the end leaves audiences satisfied that the journey was worth it.

On the surface, it appears that the media present a wide variety of entertainment messages. But when we analyze those messages, we can see that they follow standard patterns. For example, with popular music there has been a wide variety of styles over the years, but at base, all popular music follows a set of formulas. All of these songs are built from a limited number of

Analysis

Can you identify examples of puffery when examining ads?

tones arranged in a small set of cords (notes played together) in standard sequences. Every popular song is a variation from the standard formula. The same can be said for any media message.

GENERAL STORY FORMULA There are formulas for telling stories. Screenwriter Sue Clayton analyzed successful and unsuccessful Hollywood films to try to figure out which elements are most associated with success. From this analysis, she discovered a formula, which she calls the genetic blueprint for a successful movie. This blueprint calls for 30% action, 17% comedy, 13% good vs. evil, 12% love/sex/romance, 10% special effects, 10% plot, and 8% music. This formula shows that *Titanic* and *Toy Story 2* were perfect movies (Baker, 2003). While it is doubtful that we could ever reduce the formula for a successful movie or story to a precise mathematical formula, there are certain characteristics all stories must have in order to appeal to audiences. Thus, we can identify a **general entertainment story formula.** All stories begin with a conflict or a problem. The conflict is heightened throughout the story, and the main characters try to solve the problem. Finally, during the climactic scene, the problem is solved, and the conflict is eliminated—or at least significantly reduced.

This general formula is used not only by the creators of media messages; the formula is also used by us—the audience—to help us easily recognize the good and bad characters and to quickly find where we are in the story. Stories that follow the formulas the closest usually have the largest audiences because they are the easiest to follow. The more experience we have with entertainment messages, the more we learn the story formula. We are conditioned to expect certain plot points, certain kind of pacing, certain types of characters, and certain themes. However, if a producer slavishly follows the formulas with no variations at all, the story will be so standard that it will be boring. Creativity lies in knowing when to deviate from the formula.

TRADITIONAL GENRES The overall entertainment story formula is elaborated in different ways across different genres of entertainment. Let's examine how the basic story formula is elaborated across the traditional genres of tragedy, mystery, action/horror, comedy, romance, and reality programming.

Tragedy must have characters that are perceived by the audience as noble and good. However, bad things happen to these characters either because they have a fatal flaw they cannot get around (as is the case in Shakespearean tragedies) or because fate has conspired to do them in, such as what happens in the movie, *Titanic*). What audiences enjoy about tragedies is the opportunity to compare themselves with the tragic characters and feel better off than those unfortunate characters.

With the mystery formula, an important element of the plot is withheld until the end when the mystery is solved. For example, in a "whodunit" mystery, the *who* is withheld. A serious crime usually triggers the story, and someone must use the information available to figure out who committed the crime. The suspense is in solving the puzzle. Audiences are drawn into the story as they try to solve the mystery for themselves.

The action/horror formula is primarily plot driven as good and evil fight it out in ever-deepening conflict. Characters are stereotypes or comic book types. Within several seconds after being introduced to a character, we know whether that character is a hero or a villain. Characters are static and don't change. The plot relies on fast-paced action that maximizes arousal in the audience by presented life-and-death situations. The primary emotions evoked are fear, suspense, and vengeance. Violence is a staple in almost all of these stories. The formula of violence tells us that it is okay for criminals to behave violently throughout a program as long as they are caught at the end of the show. This restores a sense of peace—at least until the commercials are over and the next show begins. Also, we feel that it is permissible for police officers, private eyes, and good guy vigilantes to break the law and use violence as long as it is used successfully against the bad guys.

With the comedy formula, minor conflict situations flare up and set the action in motion. The conflict is heightened verbally, usually through deceit or insults. Characters are developed through their unusual foibles and quick wit. The action is neatly resolved at the end of the show, and all the main characters end up happy, because their problems have been eliminated.

One subgenre of comedy is the character comedy—or the comedy of manners. Here, the humor arises out of character quirks that illuminate the craziness of everyday situations. Characters find themselves in difficult situations that we all encounter every day. As characters try to work their way through these situations, the absurdity of certain social conventions is illustrated, and this makes us laugh. Examples include *Seinfeld* and *The Big Bang Theory*. Another subgenre of comedy is the put-down comedy, where certain characters have power over other characters and exercise that power in humorous ways. Examples include *Two and a Half Men* and *The Office*. The situation comedy formula is so well known by viewers that

Jason La Veris/FilmMagic/Getty Images

▶ The sitcom *New Girl* finds humor in its quirky characters struggling to adapt to adulthood.

Nickelodeon has created some 60-second sitcoms. Because viewers have no trouble recognizing typical plots and stereotypical characters, we have no trouble following the action.

A romance story begins with a person experiencing either loneliness from a lack of a relationship or a relationship that is bad due to betrayal, jealousy, or fear. As audience members, we are led to identify with the main character and feel her pain. But she is full of hope for what seems like an unattainable goal. Through hard work and virtue, she gets closer and closer to her goal—even though she experiences frequent heart-rendering setbacks—until the story climaxes with the fulfillment of the goal, which transmits intensely positive emotions to the audience.

After years of watching stories on TV and in the movies, we have become adept at following the formulas about characters, plots, and themes. We know these formulas so well that many of us think we can write and produce our own shows. Perhaps some of us can, but producing a successful show is a very difficult undertaking. While the formulas are deceptively simple, making them work well is very difficult.

NEWEST GENRE Currently the hottest genre on TV is what is known as "reality programming." While TV has had examples of reality programming throughout its history (with game shows, *Candid Camera*, etc.), it did not become a recognizable genre until about 2000 when three of the most popular shows (*Survivor*, *American Idol*, and *Big Brother*) were unscripted series using real people instead of professional performers. Within a decade, the number of reality shows on TV had grown from 4 in 2000 to 320 in 2010 (Ocasio, 2013). This genre has grown so large that it has developed many subgenres (see Table 7.2).

The most popular of the reality series has been *Survivor*. Even before airing the first episode, CBS received 6,000 applicants who wanted to be marooned on a small island in the South China Sea and compete for $1 million (Bauder, 2000). The popularity of *Survivor* quickly generated a slew of other entries into this genre of reality programming. What these shows have in common is that each takes a handful of real people and puts them in a competitive situation. As the participants compete and reveal their personalities, audience members begin to identify with (or at least root for) certain players.

Now that you have read this section on media entertainment narratives, let's see how you are able to incorporate this information into your own ways of thinking about these stories. Try analyzing some entertainment narratives in Applying Media Literacy 7.1.

Table 7.2 The Subgenres of the Reality TV Genre

Documentary-style subgenre: Cameras record what happens in everyday life.

- Real people (*Big Brother*, *The Real World*, *The Real Housewives* franchise)
- Workers (*Ice Road Truckers*, *Ax Men*)
- Celebrities (*Keeping Up With the Kardashians*)
- Fringe groups (*Sister Wives*, *Amish Mafia*)

Reality–legal subgenre: People's behavior is recorded as they deal with legal problems.

- Court shows (*The People's Court*, *Divorce Court*)
- Law enforcement documentaries (*Cops*)

Reality competition/game show subgenre: People compete for some prize as one or more contestants are eliminated each episode.

- Performance (*American Idol*, *America's Got Talent*, *Dancing With the Stars*)
- Dating competitions (*The Bachelor*, *The Millionaire Matchmaker*)
- Job search competitions (*Top Chef*, *America's Next Top Model*, *Last Comic Standing*)

Self-improvement/makeover subgenre: Viewers are amazed as a real-world person or object is drastically improved.

- Personal makeovers (*The Biggest Loser*, *Extreme Weight Loss*)
- House makeovers (*Fixer Upper*, *Property Brothers*)

Social experiment subgenre: People are put in unusual situations, and a camera records their reactions (*Wife Swap*, *Undercover Boss*).

Hidden camera subgenre: People's actions are recorded without their awareness (*Cheaters*, *What Would You Do?*).

Supernatural/paranormal subgenre: People are put in frightening situations that purportedly involve paranormal forces (*Ghost Adventures*, *Ghost Hunters*).

Hoax subgenre: People are fooled to believe something false, and their reactions are recorded (*Undercover Boss*).

Analyzing Narratives

1. Think about one of your favorite entertainment messages, such as a TV series.

   A. What do the producers do to attract your attention to each episode?

   B. What do the producers do to tell their stories in an interesting way?

      Think about characters, plot, settings, etc.

      Which of these elements are most realistic?

      Which of these elements are mostly fantasy?

   C. What have the producers been doing that has conditioned you for repeated exposures?

2. Think about a place you typically go to get information on a regular basis on a topic.

   A. What has attracted you to this source of information?

   B. Why do you keep coming back to this source as new needs for information arise?

3. Can you think of a TV ad that uses a problem–solution formula?

   A. What is the problem depicted?

      Is this a problem you have?

      How realistic is the portrayal of this problem?

   B. What is the solution to the problem?

      How realistic is the portrayed solution?

      Do you believe this solution would work as promised in your life?

ELECTRONIC GAMES

The electronic games meta-genre is characterized by story structures that are more open than narratives. This means that electronic games invite audiences to enter a competitive experience, where there is a predefined goal and rules for playing. This is the structure. Players then perform within this structure by creating their own actions that become their story as they progress toward the goal of winning the game. Thus, the audiences create the narratives, which are the stories, by how they play the game.

Some electronic games are fairly simple with few rules and a quick resolution where an individual plays against a computer or one person (e.g., checkers, tic-tac-toe, blackjack). Other electronic games are very elaborate where an individual can join teams to play against many other players in a journey that takes players through many layers of challenges over a period of months or even years and where a complicated set of rules is gradually revealed to players as they progress through the game (e.g., World of Warcraft, Dungeons and Dragons).

Electronic games are different than other types of media messages in the sense that they do not take players through a story in the conventional narrative sense (Friedman, 1995). Instead, games offer the potential for players to construct their own stories as they move through the game. These games force the player to pay a heightened level of attention to the message stimuli, not to absorb its meaning passively but to make active decisions about that stimuli so as to enter into interactions with the game rules, characters, and environments. These decisions by the game player tend to change the arc and nature of the game. These changes give players a sense of power and a sense of wonder as they explore how far they can progress into a novel unfolding story.

What all of these electronic games have in common are digital game codes that govern game appearance and play; visual and audio features that attract users into the game; and input devices that the player uses to communicate with the digital code in playing the game (Kerr, 2006). Also, electronic games are like all of the other forms of mass media, because the games are commercial products that have been created in a manner to be highly attractive to particular niche audiences and the games themselves are constructed so as to condition habitual use of them (Giddings & Kennedy, 2006).

Many interactive media platforms have been designed to attract users who want to compete against themselves, to compete against a computer, or to compete against one or many players. With electronic games, we can begin playing any time we want and pause the game for as long as we want, we can take as much time as we want to decide our next move without our opponent complaining, and we can receive immediate feedback on our performance. With the rise of the Internet, we can now play against opponents anywhere in the world, so geography is no longer a limitation. Also, we can compete with very large numbers of players, such as with **massively multiplayer online role-playing games (MMORPGs).** And with the proliferation of mobile devices, we can take our game playing experiences everywhere we go.

Designing Electronic Games

Producers of electronic games follow formulas to make the three most important decisions in the design of their games. These are category of play, formality of play, and the affective tone (Sykes, 2006).

▶ Felix Kjellberg, known by his username PewDiePie, has over 34 million subscribers to his YouTube channel, where he posts videos of himself playing video games.

As for category of play, designers have six options when considering what the objective of their game should be. First, the objective can be competition, so audiences play the game for the pleasure of testing their skills against other players. Second, the objective can be winning against the odds; these are the games of chance, like roulette and lotteries. Third, the objective can be mimicry where players are given the opportunity to take on a new identity then engage in make believe. Fourth, the objective can be vertigo, which is the temporary destabilization of the perceptual system, such as fairground rides. Fifth, the objective can be exploration, where the game provides audiences with the opportunity to explore new worlds and discover new things. And sixth, the objective can be social play where the game provides players with the opportunity to make contact with other players and join special clans with secret languages, nicknames, initiation rights, etc. Sykes says that while there is a different niche audience for each of these six, the popular games usually combine two or more of these features in a single game to appeal to a broader base of players.

As for formality of play, game designers have a wide range in the number of rules that a game can have. At one end of this range, the game can be designed with a minimum number of rules so that players experience the spontaneous expression of the animalistic impulse to play. At the upper end of this range, the game is designed with many rules that structure highly developed rituals; players must develop a high degree of discipline to learn all the rules well and to achieve success in the game.

As for affective tone, designers must think about what they want their players to feel as they interact with the game. One feeling is aggression as players fight a series of stronger and stronger opponents; as they conquer these opponents, players themselves feel stronger and more confident in their abilities. Another popular feeling is mystery or suspense where players must figure out what is happening before something bad happens to them or others.

In addition to the design decisions outlined in the previous paragraphs, designers also follow some generic type rules to ensure that their games are able to attract players then condition them for repeat playing. There are six design rules that apply to all successful digital games. Game developers carefully follow these rules in order to reduce the risk that players will reject their games. First, there must be some reward to the player, and the rewards must only go to the good players. Bad players should be punished, but the punishment should never be for something that happened outside a player's control. Second, the game should be relatively easy to learn. Of course, some games are very complex, but the complexity is not revealed to a player in the beginning. Instead, the complexity is gradually revealed step by step as the player moves through the game. Third, the game should be predicable. The game should follow logical rules so that players can predict the outcome of their actions. Fourth, the game should be consistent. The outcome of a particular action must always be the same. Fourth, there should be a fair degree of familiarity. This means that designers should consider what players bring to the game and use it. And sixth, the game should be challenging. If it is too simple, players will quickly lose interest. Instead, designers must build in layers where players advance to greater and greater challenges to keep them playing.

Induction

As you think back on your electronic game playing experiences, can you see a pattern in the type of challenges, use of graphics, sounds, etc., that attracted and held your attention?

Experience of Playing Electronic Games

When an electronic game has been designed well, it delivers an experience to players that has been characterized as **flow** and **telescoping.** Flow is a term coined by social psychologist with the almost unpronounceable name of Csikszentmihalyi (1988). He observed people getting lost in tasks and called this experience flow. In order to achieve this state of flow, people must deeply immerse themselves in a task so that they lose all track of time and place. With digital games, players often get so involved in the playing of the game that it is as if they enter the world presented by the screen and lose the sense that they are in the real world. Players become so focused on the pleasure of the game that other needs (such as thirst, sleep, hunger, etc.) become secondary—that is, satisfying those secondary needs gets put off in the interest of satisfying the primary need of achieving the next objective in the game. The expectation of completing the next game objective is so pleasurable that everything else is forgotten while in the flow state.

Telescoping is a term used by another social psychologist with a much more pronounceable name of Johnson (2006). He used this term to refer to the way electronic game players focus on the steps within the process of moving through a game. At any given point in an electronic game, the player must focus on an immediate objective that follows from previous objectives that were successfully achieved and lead to upcoming objectives that take the player to the end of the game. This focusing on the immediate objective is viewed as the foreground, and all the other objectives are pushed into the background where they are used only as context for the foregrounded objective. Thus game players must keep the big picture in mind as context while they focus on the immediate objectives they face at a given point in the game. When they meet their immediate objective, they do not stop playing; instead, they feel immediately propelled onward to meeting their next objective. Johnson says "talented gamers have mastered the ability to keep all these

©iStockphoto.com/jessicaphoto

▶ Players may get so lost in a game's tasks that they experience a flow state, in which other real-world needs become secondary to achieving the next objective of the game.

varied objectives alive in their heads simultaneously" (p. 54). Telescoping is not the same as multitasking. Multitasking is handling a stream of unrelated objectives, such as talking on the phone, instant messaging friends, listening to music on an iPod, and googling topics. Telescoping focuses more on a sequence of ordered objectives in a hierarchy of priority then moving through them in the correct sequence.

Experiencing flow and telescoping can be very intense and rewarding. It can be like a narcotic that continually draws players back to gaming for a repeat of the experience. And once players feel the experience, they want it to continue uninterrupted. When it is interrupted, they want to get back to it as quickly as possible.

Now that you have been presented with some information about electronic games, let's see how you are able to incorporate this information into your own ways of thinking about these games. Try analyzing some electronic games in Applying Media Literacy 7.2.

Analyzing Electronic Games

1. Think about your exposure to electronic games.

   A. If you do not regularly play electronic games, analyze your needs to identify why not.

   B. If you do regularly play electronic games, go on to #2.

2. Think about your favorite electronic game.

   A. What was it about the game that first attracted you to play?

   B. What were the rewards that kept you playing and kept you coming back?

   C. What features did the producers build into the game that you find so attractive?

   D. Do you typically experience flow when you play the game?

3. Think of other people you know who play this game.

   A. Are they attracted to the game for the same reasons as you?

   B. Are their reasons for playing the game related to how good a player they are?

4. To what extent is your game playing a habit.

   A. How often do you play the game even when it's not enjoyable?

   B. Do you find it hard to stop playing the game?

   C. When you are not playing the game, do you constantly think about playing?

   D. Given your answers to the three previous questions, do you think you are addicted?

INTERACTIVE MESSAGE PLATFORMS

The interactive message platform meta-genre is characterized by producers creating a particular kind of structure that allows individuals to construct their own messages and send them to designated audiences or to disseminate them widely to the general population. Producers of these platforms want to attract certain kinds of users so they tailor the services offered by that platform in a way to offer users the best opportunities to serve their communication goals. Basically, there are two types of interactive message platforms: social contact and sharing.

Social Contact

An SNS is a web-based platform that gives individuals the opportunity to create a public profile, make connections with visitors to their site, and share personal information. Thus, these sites offer tools to allow users to generate all the content—that is, to build their sites easily with text, photos, and video. They also offer easy access through mobile devices and to offer ease of interaction within the platform. These sites offer a sense of community, which is much more psychological than geographic. In fact, geographic limitations are relaxed to the point where interactions can occur with anyone in the world.

The earliest SNS was SixDegrees.com, launched in 1997. In 2003, these sites really expanded with MySpace, Facebook, Bebo, Orkut, and Cyworld. SNSs have grown extremely popular over the past decade. Twitter has more than 500 million users and Facebook has more than 1.2 billion active users worldwide (Smith, 2013). In the United States, there are 170 million users of social media, and they average more than 2.3 hours a day (Statista, 2014).

Social contact can take several forms. Some users want friendship, others want dating experiences, and some want to live in a different world. It is likely the case that many of us want several of these or all three at times. Let's examine each of these in more detail.

FRIENDSHIP Some sites are designed to help users make new friends and more efficiently maintain their existing relationships with friends. The most popular SNS for friendship is Facebook, which was launched in 2004 by Mark Zuckerberg while he was a computer science undergraduate at Harvard University. The website's membership was initially limited to Harvard students but was expanded to other colleges in the Boston area, the Ivy League, and Stanford University. It later expanded further to include any university student; then high school students; and finally, to anyone age 13 and over. By the summer of 2011, Facebook had 600 million users worldwide, and now it has twice that.

DATING While people frequently use the friendship networks from Facebook to move beyond friendships and into dating, there are other forms of social networking that enhance dating. For example, smartphones have apps, such as Tinder, that use GPS to help singles find dates in the vicinity. With your phone, you can search online for photos and profiles of singles in your vicinity, then send instant messages to those people. This helps people meet up in sporting events, shopping malls, and other public places (Li, 2011).

LIVING For people who prefer to keep their contact with friends virtual and not interact in real life, there are virtual friendship sites. One of these is called Second Life; it is described as "A 3D world where everyone you see is a real person and every place you visit is built by people just like you" (Second Life, n.d.).

▶ Mark Zuckerberg launched Facebook as an undergraduate at Harvard University in 2004. The site was originally limited to his campus, then expanded to other colleges, and ultimately went global.

AP Photo/Mark Lennihan

Second Life is an online virtual world—developed by Linden Lab—and was launched in 2003. Anyone 13 years of age and older can join and create an avatar. These avatars, called residents, can explore the world (known as the grid), meet other residents, socialize, participate in individual and group activities, and create as well as trade virtual property and services with one another. As of 2013, Second Life had over 33 million registered user accounts (Second Life Grid Survey, 2013).

Sharing

A second type of interactive message platform is for sharing. These platforms allow people to share their opinions, information, music, and videos.

OPINIONS The most popular way for people to share their opinions in an open forum is on a **blog,** which is a truncation of "web log." These are websites where an individual posts personal opinions and invites responses from readers. Individuals who create a blog must create their own content—textual elements (diary notations, hobbies, quotes, lists of favorite sites, etc.), visual graphic elements (photographs, icons, web links, etc.), and interactive elements (online discussion, e-mails, etc.). Some blogs are focused on the authors themselves while others are focused on issues or interests. Blogs offer the potential for an unlimited size audience, unlimited freedom to talk about anything, and unlimited size of the blog itself. Thus they can address issues outside the mainstream media. Bloggers post their thoughts with the expectation of receiving reactions. Thus, blogs are dialogic—that is, they elicit responses and stimulate conversation.

As of the summer of 2014, there were more than 180 million publicly accessible blogs. While a few of these blogs are very popular and get more than 1 million unique visitors each month, the overwhelming majority are run by single individuals who post their personal opinions about every conceivable topic. The most popular blog is Twitter, which restricts people to messages of 140 characters. By the end of 2012, Twitter had increased to more than 200 million active users, and these people sent an average of 175 million tweets per day (Pingdom, 2014). Tweets are typically impulse messages containing mundane information about their everyday lives (such as what they ate for breakfast) and their opinions about whatever they care about. Other popular blogs are the Drudge Report, with 21 million unique monthly visitors, and the Huffington Post, with 110 million visitors each month ("Top 15 Most Popular," 2015). They are political blogs but have postings on entertainment, business, media, lifestyle, and other topics. Both in the range and quality of their messages as well as their reach among readers, they rival major newspapers.

INFORMATION There are many informational and educational websites, which are open to public participation in an interactive manner. The software technology that allows people to interact with these sites is called a wiki. A wiki is a website that allows any user to add material and to edit as well as delete what previous users have done. The term comes from the Hawaiian word *wikiwiki*, which means fast or speedy. In 1994, a computer programmer named Ward Cunningham developed an initial wiki server designed to be the simplest possible online database. He designed it so that information could be added and edited as easy as possible. Thus, this database is essentially democratic where every user has equal access and equal ability to contribute.

The most well-known wiki so far is Wikipedia, which is a free web-based encyclopedia that does not hire experts to write the content but allows anyone access to add, delete, and edit content. Wikipedia began in 2001. Initially its greatest challenge was generating interest among the general public to volunteer to create articles for the encyclopedia without being paid. It met this challenge and by 2014 had generated over 4.5 million articles and was growing by about 800 articles each day in the English edition (Wikipedia Statistics, 2014). Now its challenge is to check the article writing and editing for accuracy. Also, there is a continuing challenge to ensure that people with certain political or religious orientations do not distort entries for their own purposes. For example, in 2006 Wikipedians noticed that unmet campaign promises of congresspeople were being deleted from articles on those congresspeople. It was discovered that these deletions were coming from web addresses of congressional aides for those Congress people. Also, it was found that the justice department was removing references to certain groups they felt were involved in terrorist activities. And they noticed that supporters of the Church of Scientology were entering a pro-Scientology viewpoint while critics were editing that out in favor of a critical viewpoint. In all of these (and many more instances), Wikipedia had to lock out those people from the editing function (Linthicum, 2009). Now there are an average of 1,000 pages deleted each day for various reasons (Wikipedia Statistics, 2014).

Anyone can create a new article and anyone can edit an existing article. This open editing model is guided by the values of good writing, neutrality, reliable sources, and verifiability. People who create and edit the content are unpaid, and access to the site is free to everyone. The content is created by users for free and belongs to the community, not to the creators of Wikipedia.

What makes this type of interactive platform work is that a large number of knowledgeable people are willing to participate. Whatever errors they make usually receive rapid correction, simply because so many minds are involved. This ensures a much more comprehensive resource than a small group of experts could produce. Also, the great number of people involved contribute to the elaboration of each topic—thus, more detail can be provided because it is coming from many different people. At first, accuracy might seem to be a problem, but the editing function allows errors to be quickly corrected by others. (For more on how the collective knowledge of groups is superior, see *Infotopia* by Cass Sunstein, 2006).

MUSIC People have been acquiring music through social networks since software by the name of Napster became available in 1999. A computer hacker named Shawn Fanning created Napster as a file sharing software program while he was a student at Northeastern University in Boston. It was released in June 1999. Within a year, the software had been downloaded by 70 million users who used it primarily to allow other users to make copies of audio recordings they had stored in their computer memory. Napster used centralized file directories on the Internet to connect users to music files on thousands of individual computers, thus enabling any user to download virtually any recorded music in existence for free.

In December of 1999, the Recording Industry Association of America (RIAA) sued Napster on the grounds that this music sharing service allowed piracy of copyrighted music. The RIAA eventually succeeded in shutting Napster down in July 2001. Since then, many other P2P services (Grokster, LimeWire, Kazaa, Gnutella, BitTorrent) have taken Napster's place in helping people facilitate online sharing and collaboration.

VIDEOS There are many sites where users can access and download videos. Some of these are interactive and allow users to upload videos. The most popular interactive video site is YouTube, which was created in February 2005. The first YouTube video was uploaded in April. Entitled "Me at the Zoo," it shows one of the founders, Jawed Karim, at the San Diego Zoo. The site was opened to the public in November 2005, and it grew rapidly. By July 2006, the company announced that more than 65,000 new videos were being uploaded every day and that the site was receiving 100 million video views per day. By 2007, YouTube consumed as much bandwidth as the entire Internet consumed in 2000 (YouTube, 2009). And by 2014, about 100 hours of video were being uploaded to YouTube every minute of every day, and over 6 billion hours of video are being watched each month, which is about one hour of video for every person on Earth (YouTube, 2014).

Undoubtedly, you have a lot of knowledge about interactive message platforms, but perhaps you have taken some of this knowledge for granted as you have developed your own interactive media habits over the years. Try analyzing some interactive message platforms in Applying Media Literacy 7.3 to see if you can generate some new insights.

▶ Cat videos have grown increasingly popular, with famous feline personalities such as Grumpy Cat, Maru, Lil Bub, and others.

INCREASING MEDIA LITERACY

The key to increasing your media literacy with regard to content begins with an understanding of message formulas. You will also need to work on developing your knowledge structures about the real world, your skills, and your understanding of your personal needs. In addition, you need to pay special attention to the newer major genres of electronic games and interactive message platforms because of their stronger ability to condition you and absorb greater amounts of your time.

Mass Media Message Formulas

As we increase our awareness of media content formulas, we gain greater ability to process the meaning across the incredible wide range of media content as well as develop greater appreciation for the talent of message producers. The most general of all mass media message formulas is the next-step reality. When we understand this, we can move beyond the superficiality of debating whether a message is realistic or fantasy and instead achieve greater depth by analyzing how producers weave together both reality and fantasy elements. This helps us develop a keener aesthetic sense.

Think of the media content formulas as being organized like a tree. The trunk is the one-step reality

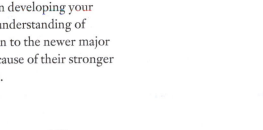

Synthesis

Think about all your favorite elements in all the social contact and sharing platforms you have used. Can you assemble all those elements into a single platform to satisfy all your needs even better?

Analyzing Interactive Message Platforms

1. Think about your exposure to interactive message platforms—both social networking sites (SNSs) and sharing platforms.

   A. If you do not regularly access these platforms, analyze your needs to identify why not.

   B. If you do regularly access these platforms, go onto #2.

2. What is your favorite SNS?

   A. What was it about this SNS that first attracted you to it?

   B. What are the rewards that keep you coming back to the SNS?

   C. What features did the producers build into the SNS that you find so attractive?

   D. Do you typically experience flow when you are on the SNS?

3. Think of other people you know who are on this SNS.

   A. Are they attracted to this SNS for the same reasons as you?

   B. Can you think of personality characteristics these people have that can explain why they spend so much time on this SNS?

4. To what extent is your time on this SNS a habit?

   A. How much time do you spend on this SNS even when it's not enjoyable?

   B. Do you find it hard to sign off?

   C. When you are not on this SNS, do you constantly think about it?

   D. Given your answers to the three previous questions, do you think you are addicted?

formula, and the main branches are the meta-genres of narratives, electronic games, and interactive message platforms. Off of each of these main branches are smaller branches, each representing a different genre of media content and each governed by additional formulas. The more you are able to envision the entire structure of the tree and the more you are able to identify formula from branches down to twigs, the more you will be developing a full picture of the nature of mass media content.

Abstracting

Can you draw a tree diagram on a single page that captures all the information about meta-genres, genres, and subgenres?

Your Skills

We also need to increase our ability to compare the patterns in the media messages with corresponding patterns in the real world. Sometimes there are obvious differences, but more often than not, the differences are subtle. The keener your perceptions in recognizing the differences, the more you can enjoy the fantasy elements while protecting yourself from transporting that fantasy into your own lives as an expectation for how you should live.

In order to perform this task, we need the skills of analysis, which is the tool we use to dig below the surface of media messages and identify the formulas that underlie those messages. We also use analysis to mine through messages to answer a series of questions. How closely do various media messages follow formulas? In what ways do those messages deviate from a formula, and what are the magnitudes of those deviations? How much can a story deviate from a standard formula before audience members become confused and lose sense of what is happening? How closely do the most popular messages follow formulas compared to the less popular messages? What do the actors and actresses in those most popular messages do that makes them so popular?

Look for patterns across various types of messages and make inductions. Use those patterns to group different kinds of messages together; this will help you identify genres. Evaluate how well producers have been using those formulas to attract your attention and program you for repeated exposures.

The more you practice your skills, the more useful they will become. Keep asking questions about these stories. Be skeptical. Take nothing for granted. If you stay active during your exposures, you will be increasing your media literacy skills and thus gain more control over setting expectations for life that are both realistic and special to you.

Stronger Knowledge Structures About the Real World

Entertainment messages depart from the real world when it comes to character portrayals, controversial content, health, and values. The more you know about these discrepancies, the more you can separate your media-world knowledge from your real-world knowledge and thus prevent the media-world distortions from shaping your expectations for the real world. To do this well, you need to have accurate information in your real-world knowledge structures.

With news messages, develop alternative sources of information. In their book *How to Watch TV News*, Postman and Powers (1992) say that for people to prepare themselves to watch TV news, they need to prepare their minds through extensive reading about the world. In short, if individual messages in the media do not provide much context, then you need to search that context out for yourself. With important social, political, and economic issues, this usually means reading books and magazines. But when you do this, make sure you read a variety of viewpoints. Context is more than getting exposure to one perspective on a problem—no matter how in-depth. A fully developed knowledge structure requires in-depth exposure to the issue from as many different points of view as possible. So if you find a detailed article on a topic in a conservative magazine, try to find the same topic treated in liberal, middle-of-the-road, and nonpolitical magazines. Following this strategy will result in your knowledge structure on this topic being much more elaborate, and your resulting opinion will be much sounder.

This is especially important with news from the Internet, where there are so many news services, bulletin boards, and blogs on current events. Often it is not possible to tell who has constructed the stories, how balanced the coverage is, and how accurate the "facts" are. Therefore, it is essential to access information from a wide variety of websites to develop a sense of where the most accurate information and credible contexts are being presented.

Expose yourself to more news and information, not less. Americans have developed a high degree of skepticism about the press. Less than half the population trusts news on TV (Jensen, 2013). Given such high skepticism about journalism, it is not surprising that news exposure is declining, especially among younger people.

Lots of information is available on every topic imaginable. But how good is it? By 2006, Wikipedia offered more than 1 million articles in English—compared to Britannica's 80,000 and Encarta's 4,500, and these were written by more than 20,000 contributors in an "open collective," which allows anyone to contribute an entry or to edit an existing entry. The advantage is that there is almost no topic too small to have its own entry. Also, errors can be quickly spotted and corrected. Anderson (2006) writes, "What makes Wikipedia really extraordinary is that it improves over time, organically healing itself as if its huge and growing army of tenders were an immune system, ever vigilant and quick to respond to anything that threatens the organism" (p. 71).

While blogs do not have a requirement for accuracy like traditional newspapers do, the blogosphere as a whole has better error-correction machinery than the conventional media do. The rapidity with which vast masses of information are pooled and sifted leaves the conventional media in the dust. Not only are there millions of blogs but readers of the blogs get to post their reactions (Anderson, 2006, p. 186).

Periodically examine your existing knowledge structures. Identify faulty information and eliminate it. Identify gaps, and try to fill them with credible information. Look at how the information is organized in your mind. Does it fit together well, or are there inconsistencies causing you dissonance? To be well informed, you need to do more than float along in the flood of information; you need to pay attention to messages and really think about them.

Greater Awareness of Your Needs

The more you are aware of your needs, the more you can use media messages to satisfy those needs. If you are not aware of your needs, the constant flood of messages—especially advertising messages—will create and shape your needs without you knowing it.

One of the biggest dangers concerning the manipulation of our natural needs is with prescription drugs. The number of ads for prescription drugs on TV grows each year until in 2008 the average person was exposed to 16 hours of ads for prescription drugs, which is more time than they spent with their primary care doctors. These ads mislead the public by inflating their claims and by burying their risks in "a sea of unintelligible tiny print" (Foreman, 2009, p. E5). A **content analysis** of these ads found that while most ads (82%) made some factual claims and some rational arguments (86%) for product use, almost all of these ads (95%) used an emotional appeal. Many of the ads urged people to use their drug in order to achieve social approval (78%) and to regain control over some aspect of their lives (85%) (Frosch, Krueger, Hornik, Cronholm, & Barg, 2007). These ads lead people to diagnose themselves then pressure their physicians to prescribe the drugs they see advertised, so they can achieve the wonderful life the drugs depict.

Be careful with persuasive messages that try to tell you what your needs are. Ask yourself the following: Do the producers of those messages really know my needs? Or are those producers trying to convince me of two things instead of one—my needs and the ability of their product to satisfy those needs?

Electronic Games and Interactive Message Platforms

Electronic games and interactive message platforms offer special challenges for media literacy. With messages in these meta-genres, the most important thing to think about is the distinction between opportunity and addiction. If electronic games and SNSs are used by people as opportunities to expand their experience, challenge the limits of their lives, and give them a deeper understanding of who they are, then these games and platforms are useful tools. If people are aware of their own goals and use the platforms as tools to achieve those personal goals, they are acting in a media literate manner. In contrast, if these games and platforms condition people so strongly that those users cannot limit their own use, then these platforms are harmful. Media literacy is reduced to the extent that the platforms take over the person's personal goals and the person slavishly works to achieve the platform's goals beyond the point where the game is bringing excitement or pleasure to the player.

It is also important to consider the nature of people's goals when using these interactive platforms. Prosocial goals are those that help the person function better and more successfully with other people and in society. Thus users who spend time with electronic games that teach business principles, leadership, interpersonal interaction, and the like are learning the value of prosocial behaviors and are developing their prosocial skills. However, many games are available that teach the techniques of fighting, stealing, deception, and even killing people. The players who spend time with these games will learn that antisocial behaviors are successful in resolving conflicts and they will become conditioned to use these behaviors as they build their confidence that they can be successful with such antisocial actions. These games have great potential for teaching all kinds of behaviors, attitudes, emotions, and knowledge. If we use them as tools to help us live a better life for ourselves and other people, then society improves as we improve.

KEY IDEAS

- Mass media content formulas are used by message producers to attract and condition audiences and are used by audiences to process the meaning from those messages.

- The most general formula used by all mass media producers is the next-step reality formula where a message is designed to attract a particular audience by displaying elements that resonate with those audience members' real lives then deepens audience engagement by moving away from reality by adding fantasy elements that appeal to audience members' imaginations and take them beyond their everyday existence.

- There are three meta-genres of mass media content: narratives, electronic games, and interactive message platforms. Each has its own set of formulas.

  o Narratives rely on content formulas in the design of an attractive enough beginning to engage an audience, a middle that drives the audience through the action by heightening

emotions, and an ending that is satisfying enough to stimulate repeat exposures.

  o Electronic games use content formulas to create a competitive experience through the design of goals, rules, settings, reward structures, and feedback that conditions players for continual game play.

  o Interactive message platforms use content formulas to structure a means for people to design their own messages, to disseminate those messages, and to receive replies in an ongoing flow.

- Any media message can deliver a wide variety of experiences to audiences from negative to positive depending on how users engage with the content and construct meaning in a way that achieves their own goals.

- The media literacy perspective offers people a way to make more conscious and more meaningful assessments about the degree to which various platforms are meeting the particular needs of users.

FURTHER READING

Bollier, D. (2008). *Viral spiral: How the commoners built a digital republic of their own*. New York, NY: The New Press. (344 pages with index)

By using the term *viral spiral*, Bollier argues that the way the Internet was designed to be an open networking structure feeds an upward spiral of innovation. The Internet's transformative power comes from allowing people free access to the ideas of other people so they can build on and alter those ideas. Therefore, change is not planned, ordered, or mechanical; rather, change is messy and serendipitous. Threads of thinking radiate dynamically through countless nodes and influence all kinds of people in all kinds of ways to work collaboratively.

Castronova, E. (2005). *Synthetic worlds*. Chicago, IL: University of Chicago Press. (332 pages including index, appendix, and endnotes)

Professor and economist Edward Castronova says that the computer industry is not only producing synthetic worlds in which their games are played but is stimulating the creation of other synthetic worlds by its players. People who use the games are not simply players; they often try to live the games and perform other human activities there, such as looking for friendships, love, employment, social connectedness, power, and prestige. There is much more than gaming going on there: conflict, governance, trade, love.

Dill, K. E. (2009). *How fantasy becomes reality: Seeing through media influence*. New York, NY: Oxford University Press. (306 pages with endnotes and index)

This is a very readable book by a media psychology scholar. In her nine chapters, she explores the various ways the media's use of fantasy leads to real effects among individuals. Topics include violence, beauty, race, gender, advertising, and political coverage.

Essany, M. (2008). *Reality check: The business and art of producing reality TV*. Burlington, MA: Focal Press. (260 pages with index and glossary of TV production terms)

This is an easy-to-read book with a self-help tone. The author is an industry insider who produced and starred in his own reality TV series telecast on E! The book presents a lot of practical information about what goes on during the planning and production of a reality series for American TV.

Henry, N. (2007). *American carnival: Journalism under siege in an age of new media*. Berkeley: University of California Press. (326 pages with index)

This book is written by a journalist who is concerned about how traditional journalism can survive in the new media environment.

Ito, M., et al (2009). *Living and learning with new media: Summary of findings from the Digital Youth Project*. Cambridge, MA: The MIT Press. (98 pages; no index)

This book presents the results of a 3-year ethnographic study that examined how young people use the new media and how they learn from those exposures. They also wanted to find out how the newer digital media were changing "the dynamics of youth-adult negotiations over literacy, learning, and authoritative knowledge" (p. xiv). They focus their attention on four ideas of new media ecology, networked publics, peer-based learning, and new media literacy.

Jensen, C. (1995). *Censored: The news that didn't make the news—and why*. New York, NY: Four Walls Eight Windows. (332 pages with index)

Begun by the author in 1976, Project Censored invites journalists, scholars, librarians, and the general public to nominate stories that they feel were not reported adequately during that year.

From the hundreds of submissions, the list is reduced to 25 based on "the amount of coverage the story received, the national or international importance of the issue, the reliability of the source, and the potential impact the story may have" (p. 15). A blue-ribbon panel of judges then selects the top 10 censored stories for the year.

Jones, J. P. (2004). *Fables, fashions, and facts about advertising: A study of 28 enduring myths.* **Thousand Oaks, CA: Sage. (305 pages, including glossary and index)**

This author is a college professor with 25 years' experience working in a major advertising agency. In this book, Jones confronts more than two-dozen beliefs that the public holds about advertising and shows how each of these is faulty.

Lih, A. (2009). *The Wikipedia revolution: How a bunch of nobodies created the world's greatest encyclopedia.* **New York, NY: Hyperion. (246 pages with index)**

This book tells the story about how the idea for Wikipedia was first conceived in 1995 and then went online in 2001. Within 8 years, it had stimulated people to write 10 million articles across 200 languages for free. How was this made possible? Read the book!

Mindich, T. Z. (2005). *Tuned out: Why Americans under 40 don't follow the news.* **New York, NY: Oxford University Press. (172 pages with index)**

The author clearly documents that the last two generations of Americans have exhibited drastic declines in attention to news in the traditional media. Furthermore, only 11% of young people even attend to the news on the Internet. He develops some explanations for why news has become so irrelevant to the younger generations; then he speculates about how this will impact the political system and society in general.

Paul, R. P., & Elder, L. (2006). *How to detect media bias & propaganda* **(3rd ed.). Dillon, Beach, CA: Foundation for Critical Thinking. (46 pages with glossary)**

This is a short book focusing on critical thinking and the news. It presents a lot of practical advice how to think about news stories critically and thereby protecting one's self from bias, especially from novelty and sensationalism.

Pozner, J. L. (2010). *Reality bites back: The troubling truth about guilty pleasure TV.* **New York, NY: Seal Press. (386 pages)**

The author is a journalist, social critic, and founder of Women In Media & News (WIMN), a media justice group that amplifies women's presence and power in the public debate through media analysis, education, and advocacy. This book presents an extended criticism of so-called reality TV programs.

KEEPING UP TO DATE

News Blogs

There are thousands of news blogs. Many are owned by major news organizations such as CNN (news.blogs.cnn.com) and the *New York Times* (www.nytimes.com/interactive/blogs/directory.html). The most popular news blog is the Huffington Post (www.huffingtonpost.com), which was started by Arianna Huffington independent of any news organization but was bought by AOL in 2011.

Technorati (http://technorati.com/blogs/directory)

Technorati is an Internet search engine for searching blogs. The name Technorati is a blend of the words *technology* and *literati*, which invokes the notion of technological intelligence or intellectualism. Technorati uses and contributes to open-source software. Technorati has an active software developer community, many of them from open-source culture.

WikiLeaks (www.wikileaks.org)

Founded in 2007, WikiLeaks is a not-for-profit media organization that provides a secure and anonymous way for sources to leak information to the public. It relies on a network of volunteers from around the world. Leakers are typically whistle-blowers who work in private businesses and government agencies where they feel their organization is doing something harmful to the public so they steal the private information of that organization and make it available for the public to view.

Wikipedia (http://en.wikipedia.org/wiki/Main_Page)

This is the Wikipedia website's main page. Articles are constantly being added to this web-based encyclopedia. If you have not already done so, check out this amazing resource. Also, you can use this to get more up to date information on almost all concepts presented in this book.

Yahoo Video Games (http://videogames.yahoo.com)

This website allows you to try demonstrations of many of the most popular video games.

Magazines for General Audiences

Entertainment Weekly

TV Guide

Rolling Stone

Hollywood Reporter

Billboard

$SAGE edge™

Sharpen your skills with SAGE edge at **edge.sagepub.com/potterintro**

SAGE edge for Students provides a personalized approach to help you accomplish your coursework goals in an easy-to-use learning environment.

▶ It is critical to recognize how media affects you so you can develop a strategy to handle these effects.

©Stockphoto.com/asiseeit

Test Your Knowledge: True or False

Before reading this chapter, think about which of the following statements you believe to be **true** and which you believe to be **false**.

1. Mass media effects typically occur when one is exposed to a negative message.

2. The easiest media effect to observe is a change in behavior.

3. Media effects can occur even when you don't plan for them.

4. With each media effect, there is usually one factor of influence that is most responsible for it.

Answers can be found on page 247.

8

MASS MEDIA EFFECTS

Most people have a very narrow idea about what a media effect is, and this limits their ability to understand how the media are influencing everyone in many ways every day. People typically think of media effects as happening only to other people. They also think of media effects as changes in that other person's behavior immediately after exposure to a message and things that are negative. Of course it is true that media messages do exert negative effects on the behavior of others, but this is such a narrow idea on media effects that it creates a condition of blinders where people miss seeing most of the effects that are constantly occurring—over the long term as well as immediate, positive as well as negative, and to themselves as well as to other people.

It is the purpose of this chapter to show you how to expand your understanding about media effects by first showing you that those effects are widespread and constant. Then I will help you perceive a greater variety of effects by showing you a four-dimensional perspective on media effects. Finally, I will show you how your expanded perspective on media effects, which will help you become more proactive in enjoying the media much more.

MEDIA EFFECTS ARE CONSTANTLY OCCURRING

Media effects are constantly occurring in a complex process. Perhaps it would be useful to think of this in a metaphorical way (see Box 8.1) to make these ideas more accessible. We

Learning Objectives

After reading this chapter, you will be able to do the following:

1. Distinguish between manifest effects and process effects.

2. Apply the four-dimensional perspective on analyzing media effects.

3. Associate particular factors of influence with particular effects.

4. Develop a personal strategy for dealing with mass media effects in your everyday lives.

Media effects are like the weather in many ways. Weather is always there, but it can take many forms. Sometimes it makes you shiver, sometimes it makes you wet, and sometimes it gives you a painful sunburn—but it's all weather. Weather is very difficult to predict with any precision because the factors that explain the weather are large in number, and their interaction is very complex. Supercomputers are used to try to handle all those factors in highly complex models. They help increase the predictive accuracy on the broad level—that is, they can tell us how much rainfall and how many sunny days a particular locale will have this year. But they cannot tell us with accuracy who will get wet on which days. Although the National Weather Service cannot control the weather, we as individuals can control the weather's effect on us. We can carry an umbrella, use sunscreen, or close ourselves off from elements we don't like. And we can run out to embrace a beautiful day.

Like the weather, the media are pervasive and always around us. Also, like the weather, media influences are difficult to predict because the factors that explain such effects are large in number, and their interaction is very complex. We use powerful computers to examine large sets of variables in trying to make such predictions, and we have learned much about media effects. We know that certain types of messages will lead to certain kinds of opinions and behaviors in general, but we cannot predict with precision whose opinion or behavior will be changed. And as individuals, we do not have much power to control the media, but we have a great deal of power (if we will use it) to control the media's effects on us. To know how to use this power, we must be sufficiently literate about media effects.

are all familiar with the idea that there is always weather and that its effect on us is constantly changing. Also, weather does not occur just to other people; we are all influenced by the weather every day for good and bad.

There is an important difference between the weather and the influence of the media on us. With the weather, we all recognize its different forms and know when they are happening. It is fairly easy to tell the difference between rain, fog, and snow because there is much tangible evidence whenever these occur. But with media influence, the effects are often difficult to perceive until someone points them out. Then they become easier to spot. We need to train ourselves to be able to spot manifestations of media effects—positive as well as negative. And we need to be sensitive to the fact that there are also **process effects** in addition to **manifested media effects.**

Some media effects are easy to spot, because there is an observable change in people's behavior that occurs immediately after their exposure to a media message. For example, if Harry calls a pizza place to order a delivery right after he sees an ad for a pizza or Julie bursts out laughing as she watches a video, we can easily see that media messages have triggered these responses. These are called manifested media effects because they are easy to observe and easy to attribute to a particular media exposure. While it is important that we pay attention to these manifested effects, we also need to be careful that we do not ignore the many other effects that are not so easy to perceive, because there are also other things going on in our minds and bodies due to media influence. The media are constantly in a process of influencing how we think, feel, and act, whether we manifest these things or not. Let's call these other effects *process effects* because we are always in a process of being influenced by mass media messages. If we limit our attention to only the manifested effects, we will greatly underestimate the degree of influence the media exert on us. Just because we do not see an outward manifestation of these things does not mean that the media are without influence. We also need to consider process effects.

To illustrate this distinction between manifested and process effects, let's consider what happened in a situation that occurred when two boys watched the movie *The Deer Hunter*, a fictional film in which American prisoners during the Vietnam War were forced by their captors to play the game of Russian roulette. Russian roulette is a game where one chamber in a revolver contains a bullet while the other chambers are empty. Each player in the game takes a turn pointing the gun at his head and pulling the trigger. If he is lucky and the chamber is empty, the gun does not fire and the player is saved. If he is unlucky, the chamber contains the bullet, which is then fired into his brain, killing him instantly. Several days after watching this movie, two boys were playing in their parents' bedroom and found a revolver under the bed. They began playing Russian roulette, and eventually, the gun fired, killing one of the boys. The manifested effect was the death of the boy who lost the game of Russian roulette. Many people reacted to the death of the boy by blaming the producers of the film. But let's analyze this situation. While the boys watched the movie, they were being influenced by the messages presented there. They felt excitement over the danger of the characters playing Russian roulette. Their attitudes were shaped that this game was a cool thing to play. There may have been no outward manifestation of these changes in emotions and attitudes, but this does not mean that the boys were not influenced by the media message. It was not until the boys discovered a revolver and started playing Russian roulette that there was a manifestation. If a parent had realized there were process effects occurring and did something to reduce those process effects, the boys could have been prevented from proceeding to such a horrible manifested effect.

The public and media critics are fixated on manifested effects. However, if we are to regard media influence from a media literacy perspective, we need to think more in terms of process effects. The more we understand about process effects, the more we can control media influence. This understanding begins with an expansion

Abstracting

Can you explain the difference between manifested and process effects in 25 words or fewer?

of your perspective on media effects. To expand your own perspective, you need to think in four dimensions.

FOUR DIMENSIONS OF MEDIA EFFECTS

The four dimensions of media effects are time, type, valence, and intentionality. Once you understand what these dimensions are, you will have a much more expanded view on media effects.

Timing of Effects

Media effects can either be immediate or long term. The **timing of effects** distinction focuses your attention on *when evidence of the effect starts to show up* more so than on *how long it lasts.*

An immediate effect is one that occurs during your exposure to a media message, and the evidence of that effect is observable during the exposure or immediately after. Immediate effects might last only for a short period of time (such as becoming afraid during a movie), or it might last forever (such as learning the outcome of a presidential election), but it is still an immediate effect because it changed something in you during the exposure. For example, when visiting your friends' Facebook pages, you learn what's new in their lives. Or while reading a website on sports, you immediately feel happy when you learn that your favorite sports team won an important game. And when watching an action/adventure film, you might begin jumping around in your seat and wrestling with your friends. These are all immediate effects, because something happened to you during the exposure.

Long-term effects show up only after many exposures. No single exposure or no single message is responsible for the effect. Instead, it is the *pattern* of repeated exposures that sets up the conditions for a long-term effect. For example, after watching years of crime programs and news reports, you might come to believe that your neighborhood is a high crime environment. No single exposure or event "caused" this belief; the belief is slowly and gradually constructed over years of exposures until one day it occurs to you that you better buy another set of locks for your doors.

Immediate effects are much easier to notice than are long-term effects. There are two reasons for this. First, immediate effects occur during an exposure to a particular message, and this makes it easy to link the effect to the media message as a cause and conclude there was a media effect. By the time people notice a long-term effect, it is well after many media exposures and many other things happening in their lives, so it is more difficult to link the effect to media exposures.

A second reason immediate effects are easier to notice is because they are usually sudden changes. For example, when you are visiting a friend's Facebook page, you see a posting that insults or embarrasses you and immediately you feel anger toward your friend. Or your friend sends you a YouTube clip that makes you laugh. These sudden changes in your emotions are clearly immediate effects from media exposures.

Abstracting

Can you explain the difference between immediate and long-term effects in 25 words or fewer?

Type of Effects

Most of the concern about the media effects focuses on the *behavior* of individuals. For example, there is a belief that watching violence will lead people to behave aggressively, that watching portrayals of sexual activity will make people promiscuous, and that watching crime will make people go out and commit the crimes they witness in media messages. However, we need to expand our focus beyond behavioral effects and also consider cognitive, belief, attitudinal, emotional, and physiological effects. Also, we need to think beyond effects on individuals and also consider effects on more macro things, such as society and institutions. Let's examine each of these in some detail.

COGNITIVE-TYPE EFFECT Perhaps the most pervasive yet overlooked media influenced effect is the **cognitive-type effect**. Media can affect what we know by planting ideas and information into our minds. This happens all the time and may be the most prevalent media effect. We are constantly acquiring information during every exposure to the media. But rarely do people credit the media with this **type of effect** when they are thinking about media effects. Think about all the information you now possess that got into your mind from your exposures to textbooks, magazines, and newspapers.

This cognitive learning is not limited to factual information; we also learn a great deal of **social information** from the media. As children, we learn a great deal about our world by observing role models—parents, older siblings, friends, and so on. Observation of social models accounts for almost all of the information communicated to children up until the time they begin school. The mass media provide an enormous number of role models from which children might learn. Given the large amount of time children spend with the media, pictorially mediated models (especially TV and movies) exert a strong influence on children's learning about social situations.

©iStockphoto.com/youilya

▶ Media can affect what we know. Consider the cognitive-type effect of acquiring information as you read this textbook.

Even as adults, we continue to pay careful attention to social models. When we do not have the social models we need in our real lives, we can usually find them in the media. Some of us want to learn most from social models who are powerful, extremely witty, physically attractive, or very successful in a particular career or sport. We develop a vicarious relationship with a professional athlete, famous actor, powerful politician, or wealthy role model. By observing these role models in the media, we gather lots of social information about what it takes to be successful and happy. Think of all the information you have in your memory about characters in TV shows and movies you have seen; think about all those names, faces, behaviors, witty lines, and emotions they portrayed. Each of those acquired facts is an example of a cognitive-type effect.

BELIEF-TYPE EFFECT A belief is faith that something is real or true. For example, most humans have beliefs about the meaning of life, how we should treat one another, what happens when we die, and the existence of a supreme deity.

The media continually exert a **belief-type effect** by showing us the values used by people in the news and characters in fictional stories. Some of these beliefs are expressed by characters, so it is easy for us to tell what they are; in this case, we simply decide whether to accept or reject them. However, many of our beliefs have evolved over time as we watch what people and characters do in a variety of situations. For example, we might watch a lot of videos about people who have relationship problems with friends so that we can learn how they handle those problems; over time, we develop beliefs about what friendships are and how we can develop the types of friendships we most want. Thus gradually over time media messages can shape our beliefs about important things like attractiveness, success, and human relationships.

ATTITUDINAL-TYPE EFFECT Attitudes are evaluative judgments about things. We compare the thing (like a person, a song, a political position, etc.) to our standard. If the thing meets our standard, we judge it to be okay; if it exceeds our standard, we judge it to be good, very good, excellent, outstanding, or super cool; and if it fails to meet our standard, we judge it to be bad, very bad, terrible, or uncool.

The media can influence our judgments about all sorts of things. This is the **attitudinal-type effect.** We can listen to a political pundit, religious leader, or attractive character express an evaluative judgment and simply accept that attitude as our own. Or we can make up our own minds using a standard that has been shaped by media influence. For example, we might hear a new song on our friend's MP3 player and immediately decide that it is one of the best songs we have ever heard—that is, create a very positive attitude about the song. Or we could read the discussion of a political candidate on some blog and immediately decide that she would be a good leader. In these examples, you might be thinking that these are not illustrations of media influence. But remember that the media can influence our standards so that when we make our own judgments, we end up using their standards. So think about what your standards are for "popular music" or "a good leader," and ask yourself the extent to which the media shaped those standards for you.

Attitudes rely on beliefs because beliefs are often the standards we use when making our evaluative judgments. For example, after years of observing glamorous men and women in Hollywood movies, fashion magazines, and Internet sites, we come to believe that we need to be tall and thin with six-pack abs and thick hair to be considered attractive. While we know this is an impossible standard for everyone to achieve, we still use this standard when evaluating the attractiveness of the people we see as well as what we see about ourselves in the mirror. Few people can live up to this unrealistic standard, so our attitudes about the people around us deteriorate as we come to think that people are getting uglier as we notice that more and more people around us are unable to meet this unrealistic standard.

Media influence on attitudes has been found to be stronger on people's attitudes at a more general level—like opinions about society—than on more specific level attitudes—like opinion about one's friends, one's own experiences, and oneself (Chock, 2011).

EMOTIONAL-TYPE EFFECT The media exert an **emotional-type effect** by making us feel things. They can trigger strong emotions such as fear, rage, and lust. They can also evoke weaker emotions such as sadness, peevishness, and boredom. Emotional reactions are related to physiological changes. In fact, some psychological theoreticians posit that emotions are nothing more than physiological arousal that we label (Zillmann, 1991). If a character on a YouTube video triggers a very high level of arousal, we might label this feeling love or we might label it hate; it depends on whether we are positive or negative about the character.

©iStockphoto.com/killerb10

We have all experienced emotional changes while exposing ourselves to media messages. Horror movies trigger extreme fear, bloggers can make us feel outrage, magazine pictures can make us feel lust, and calm music can help us feel more peaceful.

The media also exert long-term emotional effects. One long-term emotional effect is **desensitization.** Over years of watching violence in the media, which rarely show victims suffering and instead focus on the perpetrators of the violence and how attractive they are, we gradually come to lose the ability to feel sympathy for victims both in media portrayals

▶ Have you ever cried while watching a sad movie? Then you've experienced an emotional-type effect.

and in real life. We might regard the homeless as people who are victims of their own bad judgment and don't deserve much sympathy from us.

PHYSIOLOGICAL-TYPE EFFECT Media can influence our automatic bodily systems, which is a **physiological-type effect.** These are usually beyond our conscious control, such as the contraction of the pupil of the eye when we look at a bright light. We cannot control the degree to which the pupil contracts, but we can look away from bright lights and thus prevent the iris from contracting.

With the media, there are many physiological effects that usually serve to arouse us. A suspenseful mystery serves to elevate our blood pressure and heart rate. A horror film triggers rapid breathing and sweaty palms. Hearing a patriotic song might raise goose bumps on our skin. Viewing erotic pictures can lead to vaginal lubrication, penile tumescence, and increased heart rate. A farce might make us laugh so hard that we are unable to stop, even when laughing becomes painful. Or listening to music can calm and relax us by reducing our heartbeat and bringing our rate of breathing down to a regular, slow rate.

Over time, our physiological responses to particular media messages can change. For example, when we see our first horror movie, our heart rate might go through the roof. But if we keep watching horror movies, we might find that it takes more and more gore to trigger any increase in heart rate. Gradually over many exposures to horror films, our physiological responses wear down.

BEHAVIORAL-TYPE EFFECT Media can trigger actions. This is the **behavioral-type effect.** For example, after seeing an ad for a product, we might get on a website and order the product. Or we read about some disturbing event on a news site on the Internet and call a friend to talk about it.

There are also long-term effects to our behavior. For example, think about when you first got access to a computer to surf the Internet. Initially, you might have visited a lot of sites for a few minutes each. But over time, you developed a pattern of going to a few favorite sites and spending more and more time on particular sites. Perhaps you have gotten to the point where you spend almost all your waking hours playing certain games or connecting with friends on a social networking site (SNS). Perhaps your Internet behavioral habit is displacing other activities, such as exercising, hanging out with friends in real life, or going to class. Perhaps this behavioral habit has moved into an addiction.

MACRO-TYPE EFFECT The five types of effects presented previously are all effects on individuals. The media also exert their influence on larger units such as organizations, institutions, and society; this influence results in **macro-type effects.** Some institutions, such as politics, have fundamentally changed due to the direct influence of the media, especially TV and now the Internet. Other institutions—such as the family, society, and religion—have changed because of many different social pressures, and the media have served to heighten these pressures.

To illustrate this point, let's consider the institution of family. In the span of a few generations, the makeup of the American family has changed radically. The number of traditional two-parent families has shrunk, eclipsed by childless couples, single parents, and people living alone. During the 40-year period starting in the early 1970s to 2009, the percentage of American households made up of married couples with children dropped from 45% to under 21%. Marriage has also dropped from 75% of all adults in 1972 as being married to 48% (U.S. Bureau of the Census, 2013).

One argument for the cause in the decline of the traditional family is that the rates of divorce are very high in the United States, and they have been climbing since TV first penetrated our culture. In 1960, approximately 16% of first marriages ended in divorce, and that figure is now 50% (U.S. Bureau of the Census, 2013). Critics claim that the rise of the divorce rate and the portrayals of broken families on TV are not a mere coincidence; they claim that the TV portrayals have socialized people to believe that divorce and having children out of wedlock are acceptable. Critics point out that TV too frequently portrays divorce, single-parent households, and alternative lifestyles. These portrayals, presented over many different kinds of shows and over many years, tend to be internalized by viewers. Over time, people become dissatisfied with their own marriages and seek adventure with other partners. Also, many popular TV series have been portraying married life in a negative manner, thus giving young people the idea that marriage is an unattractive lifestyle.

The media have the potential to bring the family together to share a common experience. Families can build a bonding ritual around shared media behaviors and use those exposures as a chance to talk and bond. For example in the 1970s, many households had only one TV, and viewing was a common family activity (Medrich, Roizen, Rubin, & Buckley, 1982). However, few families now use TV or other media in this way. Family members rarely share viewing time. Instead, family members are likely to watch very different shows at different times on different platforms, like laptops, smartphones, and iPods. And the content different family members expose themselves to is fragmenting so that family members rarely share the same media experiences.

▶ Some families bond by consuming media together, but family members may also consume media on their own devices, without a shared experience.

©Photodisc/Photodisc/Thinkstock

Also, parents have reduced the time they spend with their children—40% less time from the 1950s to the 1990s (Pipher, 1996), and that time is even less today. Pipher argues, "Rapidly our technology is creating a new kind of human being, one who is plugged into machines instead of relationships, one who lives in a virtual reality rather than a family" (p. 92). "When people communicate by e-mail and fax, the nature of human interaction changes" (p. 88). The conveniences of technology serve to cut us off from others. We depend less and less on others (at least face-to-face). People are things or services, not human beings. Pipher says that 72% of Americans don't know their neighbors, and the number of people who say they have never spent time with the people next door has doubled in the past 20 years.

Even if we accept the argument that TV has influenced the trend toward the breakdown of the traditional family, we must realize that there are also other influences, such as economic ones. For example, it takes more money to support a family. The median household income is now about $50,000 (U.S. Bureau of the Census, 2013), so both adults are likely to work, and this makes it harder for them to have children and raise them at home. The percentage of women in the labor force has been steadily climbing, until now about 60% of all women 16 and older in the United States work outside the home (U.S. Bureau of the Census, 2013).

Another reason that family structure and family interaction have changed is that careers have become more important to many people than their families. Wage earners work longer hours, and this takes them away from the home for a higher proportion of their waking hours. There are strong stressors of time, money, and lifestyle, which make people regard the home as a place to recover from the workplace, not a place where they have high energy. No longer is family of paramount importance in most people's lives (Pipher, 1996). The irony is that perhaps people are working longer hours so they can afford more of the things advertised on TV and thereby achieve a happier life as promised by advertisers, but by spending less time with our loved ones, we are steadily becoming less happy.

Clearly, family structures and interaction patterns have been changing over the past four decades. There are many reasons for this. Media influence is a key element, but not the only one, in this change. The additional elements of economic demands, the rise in the importance of careers, and changes in lifestyle preferences have all contributed to the probability of change in the institution of family.

Valence of Effects

The effect can be in a positive or negative direction. These terms are value laden. Who is to decide what is positive and negative? The answer can be approached in two ways: the individual and society.

From the individual perspective, a positive direction is one where the effects help you achieve your personal goals. In this situation, you are usually aware of your goals, and you use the media strategically to achieve those goals. For example, if your goal is to get some information to satisfy your curiosity, then finding facts in a book, in a newspaper, or on the Internet is a positive cognitive effect. This can move you toward a goal of having more information and achieving a higher level of knowledge. However, the media are constantly trying to use you and your resources to achieve their own goals, and when their goals are in conflict with your goals, this results in negative effects for you. For example, advertisers want you to spend more and more of your money on their products. If you do this, you may be going bankrupt trying to solve problems you really don't have.

We can also look at the **valence of effects** from a broad societal point of view. If the media teach people how to commit crimes then trigger that criminal behavior, then the media are exerting a negative influence. However, the media also make a great deal of information available, which can serve to make the public more informed and therefore choose better leaders and support the best solutions for social problems. When this happens, society is stronger, and therefore, this is a positive effect.

Intentionality of Effects

Oftentimes, we intend for an effect to happen, so we consciously seek out particular messages in the media to get that effect. For example, we may be bored and want to feel high excitement. To satisfy this conscious need, we go to a movie that presents a great deal of action and/or horror. During the movie, our blood pressure and heart rate go way up, and we are on the edge of our seat with fear. We have satisfied our need. Also, when we seek out factual knowledge in the media, we are consciously trying to achieve a positive cognitive effect. For example, you visit a sports site on the Internet to learn about which teams won their games yesterday, you watch a cooking show to get ideas for new menus, or you access an **app** on your smartphone that tells you which groups will be appearing in concerts around your area. The information does not need to be extremely important, and it need not be remembered for more than a few minutes for an effect to have occurred. Every day, there are dozens of examples where you intentionally use the media to pick up a fact that you can use or trigger a feeling you want to experience.

Many times, we expose ourselves to the media for one reason, but other effects that we were not seeking also occur. To illustrate, you get on an SNS to connect with friends and find out what is new in their lives. We want to laugh at their jokes and funny

▶ Analyzing and evaluating media messages actively helps you gain control over unintentional media effects.

pictures, and we want to celebrate their successes. During these exposures, we will usually have our intended effects occur—that is, we will laugh and get some information about our friends. But other effects are also occurring—effects we did not seek out and perhaps effects that we are not even aware of until someone later points them out. For example, our behavior is being conditioned for repeated exposures so that we spend more and more time each day on these platforms, and this can lead to unintended effects like Internet addiction.

Unintentional effects can be both long term and immediate. They can be cognitive, belief, attitudinal, emotional, physiological, and behavioral. For example, after years of watching exciting movies, you develop a belief that the real world should be much more exciting. Also, your emotional and physiological reactions may have become desensitized—that is, it takes more excitement to make you happy. You did not intend for this to happen, but it happened anyway.

Even when you are experiencing an intentional effect, you may be subjected to unintended effects at the same time. For example, you watch a violent movie solely for the excitement, and the movie does deliver the excitement you wanted. However, the movie may also be delivering other effects with the excitement. You may be experiencing an emotional desensitization effect. Also, you have the elements forming to generalize to a belief that the world is a mean and dangerous place, which is a long-term cognitive effect.

Unintentional effects frequently occur when you are in the state of automaticity because your defenses are not engaged. You are not aware that any learning is taking place; hence, you are not actively evaluating and processing the information. However, even when you are trying to be an active viewer, unintended effects can occur. For example, let's say you watch a news program or read a current affairs blog. You understand that the pundits are spinning the story in a way to reach their own particular goals. They are not there to inform you about the complexity of the situation; they do not want to reach a compromise or a synthesis of a higher realization on the issue. Instead, they dumb down the issue and present their polarized position in a way to get viewers to agree with them. If you actively process this information, you can protect yourself from their influence by evaluating the credibility of their information then discounting their arguments. This is much better than simply accepting their polarized position. By analyzing and evaluating the messages actively, you gain control over your opinion formation and this is good. But a negative effect may still occur as you develop a mistrust of political figures.

FACTORS INFLUENCING MEDIA EFFECTS

Now that you are developing a broader perspective on media effects, you need to know something about the influences that lead to those effects. Because there are so many different effects, I cannot give you a list that would show you all the influences that go into each of those many effects, but I can present a list of things that are generally related to just about any media effect (see Table 8.1). These are organized as characteristics about the person who is exposed to those media messages and the characteristics of the messages themselves. The more of these characteristics that are in evidence in a situation, the greater the probability of an effect occurring.

Induction

When you next watch several hours of TV shows, look for a pattern in the producers' intentions. Can you see a pattern where several producers all have the same intentions?

INCREASING MEDIA LITERACY

The more you understand about media effects, the more you can be proactive and not just reactive. When we are only reactive about media effects, all we can do wait for effects to happen. This reactive perspective does not give you much control over the effects. In contrast, media literacy helps you to develop a more proactive perspective so that you can exercise some control over the probability of different media effects occurring. The more you understand about how the media exert their influence, the better you can help yourself avoid the negative effects and also increase the occurrence of positive effects.

The power to control media effects on one's self begins with an understanding about the wide variety of effects and how media influence works in combination with other influences.

With media influence, it is important to keep in mind three ideas. First, media effects are constantly occurring because we are constantly being influenced directly and indirectly by media messages. Second, the media work with other factors in our lives in exerting their influence. And third, you can control the effects process in your own life—if you understand how the process works.

Deduction

Can you think about a particular media effect then logically reason which factors of influence are likely to have been present to account for that effect?

By now, you should have a basic knowledge structure about the wide variety of media effects and the major factors about yourself and the media messages that

Table 8.1 Influences on the Media Effects Process

Characteristics About the Person

- *Developmental maturities.* As we develop cognitively, emotionally, and morally, we are able to process more information and to apply more sophisticated skills well.

- *Cognitive abilities.* The two most important cognitive abilities for media literacy are field dependency and conceptual differentiation.

- *Existing knowledge structures.* People with the largest amount of knowledge learn most from media.

- *Sociological factors.* People who have been consistently socialized with particular values for a long period of time will have stronger values that are more resistant to change.

- *Lifestyle.* People who have active lifestyles where they interact with many people and institutions are generally less affected by the media.

- *Personal locus.* People who have a strong personal locus have more awareness of the effects process, so they exercise more control over the effects process.

- *Media exposure habits.* In general, people who spend more time with the media are likely to be more influenced by them.

- *Motivations.* When we have a conscious need for a particular kind of information, we will actively seek out this type of information in the media, and the chance of us learning from this experience is high.

- *Arousal.* When we are aroused, our attention is more concentrated, and the experience is more vivid for us. We will remember the portrayals more and will be more likely to act while aroused.

- *Degree of identification.* We typically pay more attention to those characters with whom we identify.

Characteristics About the Messages

- *Type of content.* If you watch a film with a great deal of violence, you will be influenced differently than if you watch a film with humor or romance.

- *Context of portrayals.* The meaning of the messages arises from the *way* they are portrayed, especially social lessons.

- *Cognitive complexity of content.* When the message makes few cognitive demands on viewers, people can process its meaning easier.

Credits from top: ©iStockphoto.com/Nixken; ©iStockphoto.com/HerminUtomo

Thinking About Media Effects

1. Pick a child with whom you have spent a fair amount of time. Can you think of any effects that child exhibited that could be regarded as a media effect?

_____

_____

_____

2. Pick a friend about your own age. Can you think of any effects that friend exhibited that could be regarded as a media effect?

_____

_____

_____

3. Pick an adult with whom you have spent a fair amount of time—perhaps a parent or a neighbor. Can you think of any effects this adult has exhibited that could be regarded as a media effect?

_____

_____

_____

4. Now think about yourself. Can you think of any effects that you exhibited that could be regarded as a media effect?

_____

_____

_____

influence that effects process. Now it is time to practice using this information. Start with the people around you (see Applying Media Literacy 8.1). Have you noticed any examples of mass media effects on those people? Any obvious effects? Can you infer some process effects?

Recognizing Immediate Effects

1. Think about the differences among cognitive, belief, attitudinal, emotional, physiological, and behavioral effects. Then think about what has happened to you in your life after particular media exposures.

2. On a blank sheet of paper, divide the page into six rows, labeling them cognitions, beliefs, attitudes, emotions, physiology, and behaviors.

3. For each row, see if you can list at least two effects that have happened to you immediately after being exposed to the media. Name the immediate effect and then describe a specific example of how the media have affected you or someone you know.

Use the following list to guide your thinking.

    a. Cognition: Media can immediately plant ideas and information.

    b. Belief: Media can illustrate beliefs that we accept.

    c. Attitude: Media can influence our evaluative judgments.

    d. Emotion: Media can trigger an immediate emotional reaction, such as fear, attraction, sadness, and laughter.

    e. Physiology: Media can arouse or calm you.

    f. Behavior: Media can trigger behavior.

Now concentrate on effects that are likely to happen during an exposure to a particular media message or soon afterward (see Applying Media Literacy 8.2). Once you have completed that exercise, take on the more challenging exercise of seeing if you can identify any long-term effects (see Applying Media Literacy 8.3 and 8.4). I must warn you that it is more difficult to identify long-term effects compared to the easier task of identifying immediate effects, but use your imagination. Once you start to think creatively about long-term effects, you will likely discover many examples of how the media have shaped your beliefs about all sorts of things and have created standards you use to evaluate many things in your everyday life. As you work through each of these exercises, think about the factors of influence listed in Table 8.1, which was earlier in this chapter; this will likely trigger ideas for effects.

Recognizing Long-Term Effects

1. Think about how the media may have exercised a subtle effect on you over the long term.

2. On a blank sheet of paper, divide the page into seven rows, labeling them cognitive, beliefs, attitudes, emotions, physiology, behaviors, and macro.

3. For each row, see if you can list two long-term effects. Next to each effect, describe specifically how long-term exposure to media has led to that effect on you.

Use the following list to guide your thinking.

Long-term effects: Slow accumulation of information, attitudes, and images leads to beliefs about the real world.

 a. Cognitive: Think about patterns that you have noticed across lots of facts or large bodies of information that you have acquired over a long time.

 b. Beliefs: Think about the values you hold and the standards you use to make evaluations. Where did they come from and how have they been shaped over time?

 c. Attitudes: Have any of your existing attitudes eroded away or become stronger over time?

 d. Emotions: Have you noticed any lessening of the intensity of your emotional reactions to particular kinds of media messages over time? (Less freaking out during horror shows, less feeling of anger over news stories, less feeling of joy when listening to your favorite recording artists, etc.)

 e. Physiology: Look for evidence of increased tolerance for certain content; physiological dependency on a medium or certain content.

 f. Behaviors: Have your behavioral patterns changed over time? Examine your media habits. Examine other ways you spend your time and money.

 g. Macro: Have you noticed a change in an institution that can be attributed to media influence? If not, perhaps you can make an argument that the institution has remained stable and not changed because of media influence.

Now that you have been exposed to the perspectives in this chapter and worked on exercises to internalize this information, you are off to a good start on being able to recognize a wider range of mass media effects in a way that can help you increase the probability that good effects will occur with greater frequency to you and others around you. This proactive perspective on mass media effects will also help you take actions early to prevent the eventual occurrence of negative effects.

What Have You Internalized From the Media Culture?

1. When you are driving and listening to your car radio, do you switch the channel, looking for something else, even when you are satisfied with the song you are currently hearing—thinking maybe a better song is on another station now? Do you flip through the TV channels looking for something better? When you surf the web, do you continually look for new websites?

2. In romantic relationships, which is more important to you: commitment or perfection? When you are in a romantic relationship, are you happy when you make a lasting, strong commitment to the other person? Or do you worry that this person may not be the absolute best one for you and perhaps there is someone a little better out there?

3. In college, do you value learning or efficiency more? Do you make a commitment to each course, attend every session, and try to get all you can from them? Do you take a wide range of courses (some you know nothing about) to expand your experience?

   Or do you look for ways to spend your time better during class, such as going on a job interview, finishing a term paper for another course, or catching up on sleep? Do you look for courses on the basis of which ones require the least amount of work for the highest grades?

4. In your career, which will be more important to you: loyalty or success? Will you find a job and build your entire career there to pay back your employer for your first big opportunity? Or will you take the first job as a stepping-stone to something better and leave as soon as you have learned all you can in that job?

5. When you have a major problem, are you upset when you cannot solve it in a short period of time?

KEY IDEAS

- Media effects are constantly occurring. Some of these are easy to observe because they are manifested as behaviors and occur during exposures. But others—the process effects—are more difficult to observe because they typically occur inside a person's mind.

- When you expand your view on media effects along the four dimensions of timing, type, valence, and intentionality, you will be able to perceive a greater variety of media effects

  o Timing refers to how long it takes for the effect to show up—either immediately during exposure to the media content or a long time after many exposures.
  o Type refers to how the individual experiences the effect—as a cognition, belief, attitude, emotion, physiological, or behavioral reaction.

- o Valence is a judgment about whether the effect is positive or negative.
- o Intentionality refers to whether the sender and/or receiver planned for the effect to occur as it did.

- There are many factors about the person as well as the message that can be used to assess the probability of an effect occurring.

- When we take a proactive perspective on media effects, we can do the following:

  - o Continually assess the probability of various effects occurring and take steps to avoid potentially negative effects as well as enhance potentially positive effects.
  - o Gain control over the effects process in our own lives.

FURTHER READING

Johnson, S. (2006). *Everything bad is good for you*. New York, NY: Riverhead Books. (250 pages including end notes)

Steven Johnson is a best-selling author who argues that the popular opinion that the media are harmful to us is wrong. Instead he says that exposure to media, especially TV and video games produce more net good than harm. He explains that media messages are getting more complex, not more simple over time. This makes exposure more challenging and hence more rewarding. The story lines of TV shows are much more complex and involved now than they were several decades ago. And today's video games are far more challenging than were early video games. He says the culture is getting more intellectually demanding, not less.

Nabi, R. L., & Oliver, M. B. (Eds.) (2009). *Media processes and effects*. Thousand Oaks, CA: Sage. (643 pages with index)

This edited volume includes 37 chapters that focus on a wide variety of media effects topics. It is organized into six sections: conceptual and methodological issues; society, politics, and culture; message selection and processing; persuasion and learning; content and audiences; and medium issues.

Potter, W. J. (2012). *Media effects*. Thousand Oaks, CA: Sage. (377 pages with index)

In this book, I more fully develop the ideas that I am introducing in this chapter. I also present many more examples of media effects.

KEEPING UP TO DATE

There are perhaps several hundred scholarly journals that publish research examining how media messages affect individuals and institutions. The seven journals listed next are the ones that account for most of that type of research published each year.

Communication Research

Journal of Advertising

Journal of Advertising Research

Journal of Broadcasting & Electronic Media

Journal of Communication

Journalism & Mass Communication Quarterly

Media Psychology

$SAGE edge™

Sharpen your skills with SAGE edge at **edge.sagepub.com/potterintro**

SAGE edge for Students provides a personalized approach to help you accomplish your coursework goals in an easy-to-use learning environment.

▶ Each person is affected differently by media, so it is important for each to have a personal media literacy strategy when engaging with media.

Test Your Knowledge: True or False

Before reading this chapter, think about which of the following statements you believe to be **true** and which you believe to be **false**.

1. Increasing your media literacy requires constantly analyzing media messages.

2. Increasing your media literacy requires that you develop a broad perspective on the media industries, how they view audiences, how they develop and market content, and how that content affects you and society at large.

3. Increasing your media literacy requires that you develop a clearer understanding of your personal goals.

4. Increasing your media literacy requires you to stay away from negative content.

Answers can be found on page 247.

9

SPRINGBOARD

By now, you should have a fairly good awareness about what it means to be media literate. You have developed the beginning of good knowledge structures on the mass media industries, audiences, content, and effects. And you have begun to internalize much of this information as you have worked through the Applying Media Literacy exercises.

The next step is to develop a useful strategy to continue building on what you have learned and continue applying it. The purpose of developing a personal strategy for media literacy is to gain control over the process of influence that the media currently dominate. This is not to say that you forsake all automatic processing of information. That is an unrealistic expectation. Instead, your strategy should be focused on helping you gradually improving your awareness of the process of influence and gradually exercising more and more control over it.

In this chapter, I will help get you started on this task, but I cannot give you *The Strategy*. You must develop that for yourself so that it fits your particular needs. This chapter begins with 12 guidelines to remind you about what is most important to think about as you develop your own personal strategy for media literacy. Then I will present some illustrations of levels of media literacy.

Learning Objectives

After studying this chapter, you will be able to do the following:

1. Describe the ideas in the 12 guidelines for increasing your media literacy.

2. Apply the 12 guidelines to develop your own proactive perspective on the media.

3. Incorporate the information presented in previous chapters into your proactive perspective.

TWELVE GUIDELINES

1. Strengthen Your Personal Locus

This is the most important guideline, because if your personal locus is weak, then the other guidelines become irrelevant. Remember that your personal locus is a combination of an awareness of your goals along with the drive energy to search out information and experiences to attain those goals. Therefore, your primary task is to strengthen your personal locus.

Analyzing

Can you identify your most important goals for today, for this week, and for the long term?

Begin by analyzing your goals. What really makes you happy? What kind of people make you most happy? How do you most enjoy spending your time? What do you really want to achieve in life? Sometimes the answers to these questions are obvious to you, but sometimes they require a lot of thought over weeks and even months.

Once you have a clear articulation of your goals, think about where those goals came from. To what extent do you think they have been shaped by the media? What role models have been most influential in shaping your goals? Are those role models real people (parents, relatives, friends, teachers, authority figures, etc.) or media portrayals (characters in your favorite shows, news accounts of public figures, avatars in games, etc.)? Think about how comfortable you are with your goals given how they have been shaped.

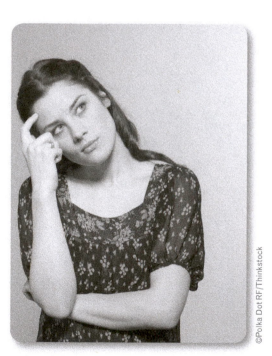

©Polka Dot RF/Thinkstock

▶ What are your personal goals for increasing media literacy?

Now, think about your general willingness to expend mental effort to satisfy your needs. Have you developed habits that typically focus on easy to achieve goals so that you don't have to work very hard to satisfy each need? Or have you developed a pattern of seeking out more difficult challenges as you progress through life?

Think about your expectations for the mental effort that is necessary to read a book, listen to a lecture on an iPod, play a video game, or watch a TV program. Each medium requires a different amount of mental effort; each medium also requires a different kind of cognitive engagement. When a message meets our expectation, we typically continue our exposure but do so in an automatic state. However, when a message requires more effort than we expect, we might stop our exposure to that message and look for another message that requires less mental effort. This is a natural reaction, but sometimes it is helpful to stay with challenging messages and try to figure out why the message is so challenging. The greater the mental effort expended, the higher the comprehension, learning, and eventual recall.

2. Focus on Personal Usefulness as a Goal

As you expose yourself to media messages, ask yourself: Whose needs am I serving most? If you are aware of a personal need and have sought out this media message as the best way to meet your particular need, then you are maximizing your exposures to meet you own personal needs. But if you instead engage in habitual exposure patterns with no personal goals, then you are clearly a tool of the mass media—that is, they have successfully conditioned you to serve their needs.

3. Develop an Accurate Awareness of Your Exposure

Periodically (maybe once a year), keep a diary of media usage for a week. By repeating this exercise, you can monitor your changing interests in media, vehicles, and messages. As you monitor changes, ask yourself the following types of questions:

* Am I broadening my exposure to different media, or am I staying primarily with only one or two?

* Am I broadening my exposure to different vehicles? (If you used to watch mainly sports and action/adventure on TV, are you now spreading your viewing around to a wider range of genres?)

Explore a wider range of websites, new musical artists, new kinds of TV shows, and different magazines. You don't have to like all these exposures; in fact, you are likely to hate many of them. But by trying new vehicles, you are giving yourself the opportunity to find even better messages than those delivered through your habitual exposures. And you are likely to discover new messages that you might like even better than the messages you usually get in your habitual patterns of exposure. If you do not occasionally explore the range of media messages, you will likely default to a narrower and narrower media habits over time.

Evaluating

Compare your personal goals to your willingness to work on them. Can you make a judgment about which will require more work than you are willing to undertake?

Grouping

Can you divide your personal goals into three groups: those that are really your own personal goals, those that have been imposed on you by other people (friends, family, religious leaders, political leaders, etc.), and those that have been imposed on you by the media?

4. Acquire a Broad Base of Useful Knowledge

The key to knowledge is that it is useful; acquiring knowledge that is not useful does not help you. This means we must be continually aware of our needs for knowledge and then focus on satisfying those needs.

There is always a gap between the knowledge we already have and the knowledge we need to understand the world better. We can close the knowledge gap for ourselves. But we must do this on a topic-by-topic basis. The means for closing the knowledge gap on a topic is in our control because the knowledge gap is influenced more by our interest in a topic than by our general level of education (Chew & Palmer, 1994). If we have high interest on a topic, we will search out information from many different media and many different sources. But when we have low interest on a topic, we allow the media to determine for us how much information we get.

In this book, I have given you enough information in four areas—media industries, audiences, content, and effects—to get you started with four useful knowledge structures. To see how well you have absorbed that information, do Applying Media Literacy 9.1.

▶ Broaden your horizons by actively seeking out different types of media messages.

5. Think About the Reality–Fantasy Continuum

Continually ask yourself the degree to which something is real or fantasy; this is a continuum. Some programs will be easy to spot as fantasy, such as *Looney Toons*. But other programs may not be so obvious. Some have a realistic setting and some realistic situations but are still fantasy, such as *Scandal* or *Two and a Half Men*. Others may have a fantasy setting but deal with situations in a realistic manner, such as *Star Trek*. Distinguishing reality from fantasy in the media is often a difficult task that requires you to think about the many different characteristics of a message. So you must think analytically and break a message down into its component parts, then assess which parts are realistic. Do not try to categorize

Induction

As you experience a wider range of media messages, can you recognize patterns that you can use as guides as you continue to explore new kinds of messages?

Testing Awareness of Your Knowledge Structures

Here is a list of chapters in this book. Each one presents a knowledge structure on its topic.

1. For each chapter in the book, try to recall the structure of the content.

   a. Can you remember the key ideas that appeared at the end of each chapter? Can you remember major ideas or sections of the chapter?

   b. Then go back to each chapter to check your recall. Give yourself 1 point for each key idea you remembered correctly. Thus, your score should be somewhere between 0 and 5 for that chapter.

   c. Enter your score in the left column, which is labeled "Book."

   Book   AdExp

   _____ _____ Chapter 1: Why Increase Media Literacy?

   _____ _____ Chapter 2: How to Think About Media Literacy

   _____ _____ Chapter 3: Mass Media Industries: Historical Perspective

   _____ _____ Chapter 4: Mass Media Industries: The Economic Game

   _____ _____ Chapter 5: Mass Media Audience: Industry Perspective

   _____ _____ Chapter 6: Mass Media Audience: Individual Perspective

   _____ _____ Chapter 7: Mass Media Content

   _____ _____ Chapter 8: Mass Media Effects

   _____ _____ Chapter 9: Springboard

2. Next, think about additional reading you undertook after studying each chapter.

   a. For each book or article you read from the Further Reading list or from the reference list, give yourself 2 points.

   b. For each additional book you have read relevant to the topic since studying the chapter, give yourself 1 point.

   c. For each significant experience you have had concerning that topic since studying the chapter, give yourself 1 point. (A significant experience is an extended conversation you had with someone on the topic of the chapter, consciously trying to apply the principles in that chapter, etc.)

   d. Record your point totals for each chapter in the column labeled "AdExp" for Additional Experiences.

(Continued)

(Continued)

3. Look at the pattern of numbers across the chapters. What does this tell you about the state of your current knowledge structures?

  a. Look down the Book column. If you have mostly 4s and 5s, you have a very strong set of knowledge structures. If you have mostly 3s, you have a good beginning set of knowledge structures. If you have some zeros, you need to go back and reorient yourself to the structure of information in those chapters.

  Remember that having strong knowledge structures does not necessarily mean you have a great deal of knowledge on that topic, but it does mean that you are aware of the main ideas, and this will help you acquire additional knowledge much more efficiently.

  b. Look down the AdExp column. If you have 3s or above, you are showing a strong commitment to extending your knowledge and elaborating your knowledge structures. Look where you have zeros, and ask yourself why you were not willing or able to extend your knowledge.

  c. Look at the total pattern of numbers. Were you stronger on certain chapters than others? It is understandable that you may have more interest in particular topics than others. But remember that balance is important. Be proud of your accomplishments—now build on them to overcome your weaknesses.

messages as simply being either real or fantasy; media messages always have elements of both.

Being aware of the reality–fantasy continuum is especially important now, when there are so many so-called "reality" programs on TV. Although all of these programs have reality elements, they also contain many fantasy elements. And some of these reality shows may have a mix of elements that make them less real than some fictional programs. The distinction between shows that are labeled as reality and those that are labeled as fiction is not a sharp, clear line. Be careful about accepting the simple labels for messages. The important thing is to recognize the fantasy elements so that you can process them differently—that is, enjoy them but don't let them influence your standards you use to evaluate your real life.

Do not go on a quest to avoid fantasy merely because fantasy elements are dangerous to use in real-world expectations. There is a place for fantasy in the enjoyment of the media. Fantasy messages can be very entertaining because of their imaginative or humorous

Deduction

Can you clarify your own distinction between reality and fantasy so that you can use it as a general principle to make conclusions about the relative mix of reality or fantasy as you watch TV shows?

appeal. They can stimulate our thinking creatively; however, we must realize that fantasy is a tool to stimulate our imagination and is not a model to imitate.

6. Examine Your Mental Codes

As you engage in your habits of media exposures, periodically ask yourself why your habits are the way they are. To what extent have you programmed your habits to serve your needs? And to what extent have the mass media programmed your habits to meet their needs? After you consider answers to these questions, rethink your mental code then reprogram your code to satisfy your own needs better. After this reprogramming, you can return to your routine exposures in a state of automaticity, but this time the code will be delivering on your goals rather than the media's goals.

7. Examine Your Opinions

Ask yourself the following: Are my opinions consistent with one another and with my behavior? If they are not, then it is likely that you hold some faulty opinions. If you are honest in this analysis, you will find some inconsistencies, because we all have them.

One area of inconsistency is between our opinions of TV programs and our exposure behavior—that is, we often complain about particular shows but them watch them anyway. For example, The Roper Center for Public Opinion Research, under the sponsorship of NBC in the early 1980s, had respondents in a national survey express their reactions to 17 particular TV shows—16 of which had been the targets of complaints about sex and violence from religious organizations. Only 13% of respondents said there was too much violence on *The Dukes of Hazard*, and 10% said there was too much sex on *Dallas*—these were the most negatively rated shows! But when asked about TV in general, 50% of the respondents said that there was too much sex and violence on TV (The Roper Organization, 1981). While this study was conducted before you were born, are the findings still valid for you? Do you systematically gather valid information before constructing your opinions? Then do you back up your opinions with behavior?

8. Change Behaviors

To what extent do your behaviors correspond with your beliefs? For example, if you think society is too materialistic, do you avoid buying many material goods? If you do keep your consumption of material goods at a minimum, then there is a match between your behaviors and your beliefs. But there are people who continually complain about waste in our materialistic society,

Grouping

Can you arrange your opinions (about school, courses, professors, classmates, etc.) in three groups: well-informed opinions, opinions where you need more information, and opinions that you simply accepted from others without gathering any information of your own?

then go out and buy lots of new things they don't need. In a recent survey, 82% of Americans agreed that most of us buy and consume far more than we need. And 67% agreed that Americans cause many of the world's environmental problems because we consume more resources and produce more waste than anyone else in the world. And yet we in the United States continue to consume nearly 30% of the planet's resources and services each year, although we account for less than 5% of the world's population. We can choose from more than 40,000 supermarket items, including 200 kinds of cereal. Do we really need all these material products?

Another example of a disconnect between beliefs and behavior is with pollution and cleaning up the environment. The media have put the issue of pollution on the public agenda as the prominence and length of these stories have increased dramatically from the 1970s to the 1990s (Ader, 1995). During that same period, air pollution went down about one third, but solid waste went up about 25%. This shows us that as Americans become more concerned about pollution, they have put pressure on the government to clean up the air by regulating manufacturing plants and requiring emission controls on cars. But solid waste, which is under the control of individual citizens through voluntary recycling programs, has not been so successful. This means that individuals are not cutting back on their waste through lower consumption or recycling. Again, many people are looking to the government or someone else to solve their problems.

Changing your behavior to correspond with your beliefs demonstrates commitment to a moral responsibility of following through on your beliefs rather than simply blaming someone else and doing nothing, which has become a popular strategy for many of society's problems. The first step in behavioral change is a realistic assessment of the match between your beliefs and existing behaviors.

You could boycott advertisers, cancel subscriptions, and write letters when you see something you don't like in the media. This action, of course, will have almost no effect on the media themselves, unless large numbers of other people feel as you and do the same things. However, that is not a reason to stop yourself from doing these things. By taking action, you give yourself a sense of gaining control over the media, and this new sense of power will make a difference in your personal life.

9. Make Cross-Channel Comparisons

Although media literacy is a generic concept that spans across all media, there are some special challenges presented by different channels. For example, reading a magazine article requires some skills not required when watching a situation comedy on TV. This point, of course, is obvious. But the nature of the differences themselves is not so obvious. To illustrate this, read about a news story on an Internet site, and then look for that story in your local newspaper or local TV newscast. Analyze those similarities and differences. Are they important?

These differences are especially clear when we consider the interactive media, such as social networking websites and video games. The obvious difference is that with interactive sites, you are not just the receiver of a message but you are also actively engaged in creating the messages. But there are also other more subtle differences. The more you engage with these sites while you are in the self-reflexive state, the more you will appreciate these differences and even begin to use them better to enhance your media experiences.

▶ Compare a news story across different media channels to find similarities and differences in the messages.

10. Become More Skilled at Designing Messages

Many media now not only offer you the chance to create your own messages but they require it. The best example of this is when you create a Facebook account, you must design your own pages, and you are expected to update your site continually. How does your Facebook page compare to those of your friends? How well designed is it aesthetically? Do you have photos and graphics with your text? Would people want to visit your page just to see how well designed it is?

How well designed is your Facebook page from an information point of view? What have you decided to reveal about yourself? How is the information on your page likely to affect your friends? Your parents? Future employers?

11. Do Not Take Privacy for Granted

In past generations, an individual's use of the media was a relatively private thing. However, today your media exposures are tracked in meticulous detail, and that information is sold to advertisers or to anyone else interested in your media use habits. When you post a message on your own webpage, a blog, or send a tweet, you initially have some control over who will see your message. But you soon lose that control when the webpage server, web browser, blog owner, or Internet service provider can make copies of your messages, repackage them, and sell them to other users of the Internet. Once your message is sent in digital form, it can be endlessly copied, stored, and distributed to anyone. Therefore, before you digitize a message and put it out on the Internet, think about all potential audiences who could read that message—marketers,

Evaluating

Can you make insightful judgments about the elements that you like most on the Facebook pages of other people?

Synthesizing

Can you redesign your own Facebook page to incorporate all the elements you like best from the Facebook pages of others?

potential employers, friends, future spouse, children, parents, government officials, and on and on. What impression are you likely to create among all those audiences?

12. Take Personal Responsibility

This may be the hardest to do. We as Americans are fond of placing blame on others, because it allows us to feel that the problem lies elsewhere and therefore it is someone else's problem to fix. For example, let's consider the problem of overeating. The American Medical Association tells us that one third of Americans are obese and another one third are overweight. This would seem to be a personal problem, but most people continue to eat too much and exercise too little. They wait for a government to impose some solution. In the spring of 2002, the California legislature was considering the California Childhood Obesity Prevention Act. This act would have essentially banned the sale of carbonated beverages in public schools (Bartholomew, 2002). By the summer of 2002, there were already eight states restricting junk food sales in some form, and another dozen states were considering their own legislation. Furthermore, people were filing lawsuits against fast-food chains (Tyre, 2002). Are people really that weak willed that they need the government to ban something before they will stop consuming something harmful? Many people are that weak. Are you one of them?

EXAMPLES OF LEVELS OF LITERACY

There are many different reasons why people expose themselves to different kinds of content, and there are many different benefits people can get out of any particular message. Because of this, it is not possible to analyze a message and assume that all those who are exposed will extract the same meaning or have the same experience from it. Next, we explore several examples to illustrate this point.

Deduction

Think about what how much privacy is important to you. Can you compare that general principle to your Internet practices to arrive at conclusions about the consequences of your practices?

Reality Series on TV

Reality series as a genre can appeal to viewers of all levels of media literacy. At a low level of literacy, people feel that the characters are real and that the situations actually happened as presented. They cannot explain why they like the characters or the show.

At a bit higher level of development, people will watch reality series because they feel a personal identity with the characters and enjoy their parasocial interactions with those characters in their world, which is more exciting than their own existence that they consider boring and limited. This leads to a strong emotional reaction. Other people will watch reality shows because they want to learn how attractive characters dress and act; this leads to some cognitive processing and evaluation of how characters look and act.

At a higher level of media literacy, people share the media experience with others. They view reality series in groups so they can discuss the action as it unfolds. Or they will call their friends later and use the action as an important topic of conversation. These people use the viewing to maintain a community of friends that they would not have without the reality series. This requires a considerable amount of cognitive processing and emotional attachment. This also illustrates how they are using the media as a tool to achieve their own personal social goals.

At a higher level still, the viewing takes on an in-depth analysis of the aesthetic and moral elements displayed there. Viewers marvel at the editing that focuses their attention on the most exciting parts of the participants' lives and overdramatizes their mundane problems by blowing them up into huge moral dilemmas. This illustrates the using of media messages to increase their appreciation of things around them and to construct a deeper understanding of their world.

Facebook Page

At a low level of media literacy, creating a Facebook page entails uploading snapshots that a user thinks are cool. The user adds elements and sends messages to maximize the list of friends. Then the user spends a lot of time monitoring the growing list of friends and sending them all short, superficial messages to maintain contact.

At a higher level, users try to improve the artistic quality of their images and sounds so as to impress visitors to their page. They take pride in the increases in hits and friends who are attracted by their updates.

At the highest levels of media literacy, users are very strategic in using Facebook as a tool to create and maintain a personal image to satisfy specific goals, such as reinforcing a few key friendships, attracting a specific kind of romantic partner, or showing off web skills to a prospective employer. They are very conscious of what they reveal about themselves and make sure those revelations contribute substantially to constructing a positive image over the long term.

Remember that it is not the type of messages you watch or create that makes you media literate. Instead, literacy is keyed to what you think and how you feel while you are engaging with the media. The more active and aware you are during those engagements, the more you will get out of the media and the more those experiences will help you achieve your personal goals.

KEY IDEAS

- Media literacy is a perspective. To build a media literacy perspective that is most useful to satisfy your everyday needs, you need a proactive strategy.

  o In order for this strategy to be useful, it needs to be based on your personal needs.
  o This chapter has provided you with a dozen guidelines to follow in crafting and executing your personal strategy.
  o The proactive perspective gives you the power to redirect your habits and ways of thinking away from negative directions and toward the satisfying of your real needs.

- The more you incorporate this information from this book into your perspective on the media, the more you will be able to appreciate all the wonderful advantages your selected exposures will provide and the more control you will be able to exert over avoiding faulty ways of thinking and behaving.

- Only you have the power to increase your own level of media literacy.

FURTHER READING

Frechette, J. D. (2002). *Developing media literacy in cyberspace: Pedagogy and critical learning for the twenty-first-century classroom.* New York, NY: Praeger. (185 pages)

This book offers a vision of learning that values social empowerment over technical skills. The author argues that media literacy offers the best long-term training for today's youth to become experienced practitioners of 21st-century technology. The author provides guidelines to help educators develop and provide concrete learning strategies that enable students to judge the validity and worth of what they see on the Internet as they strive to become critically autonomous in a technology-laden world.

Jenkins, H., Purushotma, R., Weigel, M., & Clinton, K. (2006). *Confronting the challenges of participatory culture: Media education for the 21st century.* Cambridge, MA: MIT Press. (128 pages)

Funded by the John D. and Catherine T. MacArthur Foundation, this book focuses on the skills that are most important for dealing with the new media culture, which is characterized by interactive media making it possible for people to participate in society in ways not available before.

Macedo, D. P., & Steinberg, S. R. (Eds.). (2007). *Media literacy: A reader*. New York, NY: Peter Lang. (710 pages)

The editors say the purpose of this book is to help students develop the ability to interpret media as well as understand the ways they themselves consume and emotionally invest in media. The book is an extensive collection of essays written primarily for people who are not expert in media literacy and want more of an introduction to the topic rather than a scholarly treatment.

Mackey, M. (2007). *Literacies across media* (2nd ed.). New York, NY: Routledge. (224 pages)

This book describes an 18-month-long project that was designed to study how a group of boys and girls, aged from 10 to 14, made sense of narratives in a variety of formats, including print, electronic book, video, DVD, computer game, and CD-ROM. The author's analyses reveal how those children developed strategies for interpreting narratives through encounters with a diverse range of texts and media.

Potter, W. J. (2013a). *Media literacy* (7th ed.). Thousand Oaks, CA: Sage. (452 pages plus glossary and index)

This book is the basis for *Media Literacy Essentials*; it contains more detail and covers a greater number of topics. This *Essentials* text is an introduction level treatment of almost all the ideas presented in the seventh edition, so if you want more details (especially about the media industries, content, or issues), you should check out *Media Literacy*.

Tyner, K. Ed. (2010). *Media literacy: New agendas in communication*. New York, NY: Routledge. (243 pages with index)

The 10 chapters in this edited volume deal with how media literacy initiatives have taken place in the past and what they should emphasize going forward. These initiatives are organized into four contexts: community-based settings, K–12 classrooms, higher education, and virtual environments.

KEEPING UP TO DATE

There is a good deal of information about media literacy that is made available by various groups on their websites. While some of this information is offered for sale in the form of books, reports, CDs, and DVDs for a nominal price, a lot of this material is available for free. I recommend the following websites for media literacy organizations:

Center for Media Literacy (www.medialit.org)

Children Now (www.childrennow.org/index.php)

Citizens for Media Literacy (www.main.nc.us/cml)

Media Education Lab (mediaeducationlab.com)

Media Watch (www.mediawatch.com)

National Association for Family and Community Education (www.nafce.org/home-overview.html)

National Association for Media Literacy Education (http://namle.net)

Parents' Choice Foundation (www.parents-choice.org)

$SAGE edge™

Sharpen your skills with SAGE edge at **edge.sagepub.com/potterintro**

SAGE edge for Students provides a personalized approach to help you accomplish your coursework goals in an easy-to-use learning environment.

INTRODUCTION TO APPENDICES

Analyzing Media Literacy Issues

In these appendices, we will analyze four prevalent criticisms of the media. Appendix A deals with a criticism of sports, which is that the salaries paid to professional athletes have gotten too high. In Appendix B, we will analyze the primary criticism of media ownership patterns—specifically that there is too much concentration of ownership of media businesses. In Appendix C, we will analyze the typical criticism of news—that too often the news is not objective. Finally in Appendix D, we take on the criticism that there is far too much violence in the media.

The purpose of the analyses in each of these four appendices is to illustrate how to use the media literacy perspective to dig below the surface of these popular criticisms of the media so that we can uncover problems with a lack of factual basis and faulty reasoning. The appendix does not try to resolve any of these issues. To the contrary, the appendix is designed to show you that each of these issues is much more complex than is reflected in superficial arguments so that the resolution of any of these issues requires more than a quick fix.

It is not my intention to argue that your existing opinions are wrong or to try to change your opinions. Instead, I want to show you how to examine your own opinions to greater depth and thereby either (1) come to appreciate your existing opinions in a more informed manner or (2) resolve to make particular changes so that your opinions become more useful to you.

With each of these issues, I start with the key criticism that is typically made by the public. Then I break the criticism down into its key components and analyze each of those components. Some of these components have a factual basis, so we examine whether or not the facts presented in support of the criticism are valid or not. Some of these components do not have a factual basis; instead, they rely on beliefs expressed by experts or the public.

To help you work through these issues on your own, each appendix presents an extended exercise. As you work through the steps in an exercise, you will be applying the skills and knowledge structures of media literacy that you read about in previous chapters. The more you work at applying the skills and knowledge, the more you will be using the media literacy perspective. This practice will then transfer to the experiences you have with the media for the rest of your life. You will be able to perceive more things in those experiences and will be able to make more informed decisions about how to use those experiences to achieve your own goals.

The four issues I have chosen for these appendices are not the only issues that relate to media literacy; however, they are arguably four of the most salient and most important. There are many more issues about the media that warrant discussion and debate. The process you learn to use in these appendices will help guide you through a systematic thinking procedure when you encounter those additional issues about the media.

The value of media literacy lies in helping you think better for yourself, rather than substituting one opinion for another. Learn how to engage important issues by avoiding superficial arguments and unchallenged factual claims to dig below the surface so you can more fully appreciate the nature of complex issues. This will help you reframe the issue and suggest more realistic avenues for solving the problems that are embedded in these issues and continue to frustrate people.

APPENDIX A

ANALYZING MEDIA ISSUES
Are Professional Athletes Paid Too Much?

An increasingly prevalent criticism of sports is that the money paid to professional athletes has increased so much over the past five decades that athletes are now being paid way too much. Critics argue that these dramatic increases in pay cannot be sustained and that these overpaid athletes are ruining professional sports.

Let's analyze this criticism and its supporting arguments. There appear to be four components: (1) increase in pay, (2) pay now too high, (3) non-sustainability, and (4) ruining sports. Let's examine each of these four points.

INCREASE IN PAY

This first claim is a factual one—that is, we can examine the facts of the situation to determine if the claim is true or false. When we do this, it is clear that the claim is accurate—there has been a dramatic increase in payments to professional athletes over the past five decades.

To illustrate how dramatically the pay to professional athletes has increased, let's go back to the 1950s when Major League Baseball (MLB) was the premier sport in the United States and one of its superstars and highest paid athletes was Ted Williams. In 1959, the Boston Red Sox offered Williams a new contract for $125,000, but Williams returned his contract unsigned to management. He rejected their offer because he felt it was for *too much money*. Williams argued that he was not worth that much money because he was coming off a year in which he hit "only" .259, which was a bad year for Williams, although it would be a better than average year for almost everyone who ever played professional baseball. Williams asked for a pay cut of 25%, which was the maximum pay cut.

Since the days of Ted Williams, salaries for MLB players have been increasing rapidly. For example, in 2013, the New York Yankees paid Alex Rodriguez $28 million, which worked out to about $173,000 per game or $19,000 per inning (Baseball Player Salaries, n.d.). Thus, in 2013, Alex Rodriguez was paid more to play six innings than Ted Williams was paid for playing an entire season. In that same year, the highest paid pitcher was CC Sabathia, who was paid a salary of $23 million by the New York Yankees; this works out to about $100,000 per inning pitched.

▶ Ted Williams, left, earned less money playing an entire season for the Boston Red Sox in 1959 than Alex Rodriguez, right, made by playing just a single game for the New York Yankees in 2013.

As for the National Basketball Association (NBA), Michael Jordan was earning $4 million during the 1995–1996 season, when he led the Chicago Bulls to their fourth championship in professional basketball in 6 years. He was named the most valuable player of the year, and many basketball fans still regard Jordan as the best basketball player of all time. A year later, he was a free agent and signed a new contract for $18 million, making him the highest paid player in the league—temporarily (Rhodes & Reibstein, 1996). Now there are seven players being paid more than $18 million per year in the NBA, and if you wanted to be the highest paid player, you needed to beat out Kobe Bryant at $27.8 million ("NBA Player Salaries, 2012–2013"). Salaries for players in the National Football League (NFL) have also escalated dramatically. For example, the median earnings of the 2,000 NFL players in the 1999 season were $430,000, and a decade later, it had increased to $770,000. In 1999, if you earned $6.2 million, you would be in the elite top five of players, but by 2012, there were 40 NFL players paid more than that (Spotrac.com, 2012).

There have been two reasons behind this dramatic increase in player salaries. One has been the increasing support from TV networks, who bid up prices to televise the games. The second reason is that since the 1980s, there has been free agency for players. Up until the 1970s, the team owners and leagues were much more in control of players' contracts and salaries. When a player signed a contract to play for a team, that team owned his playing rights—that is, the player had to play only for that team unless the team traded him. If a player was traded to a team he did not want to play for, his only choice was to play for that team or not play at all. During the 1970s, players in all professional sports challenged this model, and they won the right to become free agents and allow any team to bid for their services. Thus, the competition for athletic talent greatly increased and continues to this day.

When we think about payments to professional athletes, we need to look beyond the salaries their teams pay them and also consider the money that companies pay them to endorse their products. Companies are willing to spend huge fees to athletes who endorse their products because such endorsements work to increase sales. For example, Nike pays LeBron James $93 million for a 7-year endorsement deal, which is $13.3 million per year. Adidas pays Derrick Rose $185 million for 13 years, which is $14.2 million per year (Saporito, 2012).

While top professional athletes earn very large salaries from playing their sports, many earn much more money by endorsing commercial products (see Table A.1).

Table A.1 Top Earning Athletes in 2014 (ranked by endorsements)				
2014 Income in Millions of Dollars				
Name	Sport	From Sport	From Endorsements	Total
Tiger Woods	Golf	$6.2	$55	$61.2
LeBron James	Basketball	19.3	53	72.3
Roger Federer	Tennis	4.2	52	56.2
Phil Mickelson	Golf	5.2	48	53.2
Kobe Bryant	Basketball	30.5	31	61.5
Rafael Nadal	Tennis	14.5	30	44.5
Cristiano Ronaldo	Soccer	52	28	80
Mahendra Singh Dhoni	Cricket	4	26	30
Usain Bolt	Track	200 K	23	23.2
Lionel Messi	Soccer	41.7	23	64.7
Maria Sharapova	Tennis	2.4	22	24.4
Novak Djokovic	Tennis	12.1	21	33.1
Rory McIlroy	Golf	4.3	20	24.3
Derrick Rose	Basketball	17.6	19	36.6
Li Na	Tennis	5.6	18	23.6

Source: The World's Highest-Paid Athletes (2014).

PAY NOW TOO HIGH

Now that we know that there have been dramatic increases in payments to players (salaries as well as product endorsements), we move on to the next argument that the money paid to professional athletes is too high. This claim is not a factual one but a personal judgment. In order to arrive at such a judgment, people compare the current salaries of professional athletes to a standard for what they believe those athletes should be paid and conclude that the payments are much higher than the standard. So the key to understanding this judgment is to look at people's standards for pay. Because there is no objective standard for pay, people must use their own personal standard that is based on their feelings about what is equitable. The two feelings that we are likely to see most in such standards is jealousy and appreciation.

As for the jealousy standard, many people resent that others are able to make more money than they do. They reason that just because other people have been lucky to have been born with more athletic talent, it's not fair that they are given more rewards. They are jealous that those other people are given more rewards. Other people realize that they have their own talent but that talent is in another area besides athletics where the rewards are not as high, so it is unfair that they got the "wrong" kind of talent.

As for the appreciation standard, many people marvel at what some professional athletes can do. They believe that certain athletes perform at such a high level that only 1 out of 100 million people could attain, so they should be paid well for such extraordinary performances. Also, many people are such dedicated fans to a professional team and crave winning so much that they feel any salary is worth paying if players continue to win.

What is your personal standard? If you haven't thought much about this issue, then your standard is probably a fuzzy subjective one based primarily on emotion. In the case of the level of pay for professional athletes, it is not likely that we will find an objective standard; instead, we are stuck with subjective standards based on feelings. Therefore, the key to thinking about this issue in a literate manner is to recognize what our standard is and to think about how reasonable it is.

NON-SUSTAINABILITY

How much longer can teams afford to pay these astronomical salaries? Is this increase sustainable? This component to the criticism has a factual basis. It appears that these increases have not harmed the sport thus far. The major professional sports leagues are all very profitable despite paying out huge sums for player salaries (see Table A.2).

Table A.2 The Big Four American Professional Sports Leagues

	NFL	MLB	NBA	NHL
Number of teams	32	30	30	30
Games per season	16	162	82	82
Attendance per game	67,413	29,950	17,273	17,455
Average value per team	$1.04 billion	$605 million	$393 million	$240 million
Annual revenue per league	$9.5 billion	$7.7 billion	$4.3 billion	$3.0 billion
Average operating income	$979 million	$432 million	$175 million	$30 million
Salary paid by teams				
Highest team salary	$138.4 million	$198.0 million	$116.9 million	$70.1 million
Lowest team salary	$81.8 million	$55.2 million	$32.2 million	$29.7 million
Median team salary	$106.5 million	$85.0 million	$76.2 million	$56.0 million

Source: Adapted from Plunkett Research (2013) and USA *Today* Salaries Databases (2013).

Team owners and leagues have been trying to control this growth in player salaries by creating salary caps for teams. However, many owners have routinely ignored the caps for years. For example, in the 1995 NFL season, the salary cap was $37.1 million per NFL team, and 26 of the 30 teams in the league went over that maximum with the Dallas Cowboys spending $62.2 million ("NFL Teams," 1996). By the 2009–2010 season, the salary cap had been increased so high (to $127 million) that only one team (New York Giants at $138.4 million) was over the spending cap ("National Football League 1999 Salaries," 2000). Now the leagues levy a heavy tax on teams that overspend, so all teams find creative ways to pay players as they struggle to stay under the spending cap.

All salary caps have loopholes. For example, in the 1996 basketball season when the Chicago Bulls had a spending cap of $24.3 million and wanted to pay Michael Jordan $18 million, they found a loophole that permitted the team to avoid counting Jordan's salary against the salary cap. Owners and players' agents who are determined to make a deal can find a way around any limits on salaries and bonuses.

Despite the rising salaries of athletes and the ineffectiveness of salary caps, professional teams are still profitable, because they generate an even larger sum of money than they pay out. Their income depends on a money cycle that involves not just the owners and leagues but also TV networks, advertisers, and the millions of us in the public.

The increases in player salaries has been made possible in large part because of dramatic increases in fees leagues receive from TV. Without a TV contract, no sports league could survive. The American Football League got started in the early 1960s with a TV deal of $1.7 million. Although this does not seem like much money today, it made the difference in whether the league survived in the early 1960s. In 1965, CBS paid $14.1 million to broadcast NFL games. By the mid-1990s, the NFL was charging $500 million per year for broadcasting rights, and this sum was so large that it had to be shared by five networks: ABC, NBC, ESPN, Fox, and TNT. By 2014, the NFL was expected to generate more than $7 billion per year from broadcasting rights. The TV networks are willing to spend these large sums of money because the NFL generates strong TV ratings. In the fall of 2012, 31 of the top rated 32 TV shows in the United States were NFL games (Eichelberger, 2013).

▶ Networks pay for a game's broadcasting rights and maximize return on the investment by using announcers and color commentators to fill airtime before, during, and after a game, when more advertising can be sold.

Where do TV networks get their money to pay these huge fees to sports leagues? The answer is from advertisers who want access to these sports audiences. Advertisers pay huge fees to TV networks to get their messages to their target audiences. During the first Super Bowl in 1967, the time to broadcast a 30-second ad cost advertisers $42,000; by 1995, the cost had increased to over $1 million. Then in 2001, the cost broke through $2 million, and in 2013, the cost was $4 million for a single 30-second ad (Stampler, 2013).

Why do advertisers pay so much to place their messages before sports audiences? The answer is because sports audiences are so valuable as consumers to these advertisers. Almost everyone watches some kind of sports. We also buy the products advertised there. This stimulates advertisers to spend more on ads in sporting event telecasts, which generates more money for TV, which makes TV more willing to bid up contracts to televise games, which generates more money for leagues and team owners who then have the means to pay higher salaries to their players. This is the money cycle.

As fans, we also contribute to the money cycle when we buy tickets to games, souvenirs, parking, etc., at the games. We buy sports apparel and equipment. The money cycle accelerates as it pulls in more fans each year and conditions them for more commitment to teams and games so that those fans spend even more time watching the games, going to the stadiums, buying the team merchandise, and supporting all the advertisers.

The media offer the public a great variety of sporting events, and people expose themselves to these messages. In 1998, researchers estimated that there were more than 8,000 sporting events televised that year (Kinkema & Harris, 1998). That sounds like a huge number until you realize that this is an average of 22 events per day and that today this number is likely to be much larger. With long tail marketing, there are many niche audiences for a much greater variety of sporting events, and with interactive technologies we have instant access to all kinds of sporting events beyond what the traditional media offer.

Not only does the money cycle depend on continued support from fans but it requires support from non-fans also. This is most clearly seen in the building of new sports stadiums across the country. The major sports leagues have been successful in getting local municipalities to finance a large part of these stadiums through public financing and taxes. From the summer of 1998 to the summer of 2003, there were 12 new NFL football stadiums that were opened—many in cities with existing football stadiums. Each of these new stadiums had between 82 (Seattle) and 208 (Washington, D.C.) premium skyboxes that the owners of the NFL teams could rent out to wealthy clients and businesses. But the sweetest part of most of these deals was that the NFL got the cities to pay for most of the construction costs. Only one owner (Daniel Snyder, owner of the Washington Redskins) paid for at least half of the construction costs, and with three of the stadiums (Raymond James Stadium in Tampa, Florida; Reliant Stadium in Houston, Texas; and the Coliseum in Nashville, Tennessee), the NFL saw to it that the cities paid the entire cost of the stadiums. Therefore, if you use an airport, rent a car, or pay for a hotel room in a city with an NFL team (or a major league baseball team or NBA team), you are likely paying a tax that helps that city finance its stadiums (Metropolitan Sports Facilities Commission, n.d.).

iStockphoto.com/Stockbyte/Thinkstock

▶ The Staples Center is home to the Los Angeles Lakers and Los Angeles Clippers NBA teams, the Los Angeles Sparks WNBA team, and the Los Angeles Kings NHL team. Privately financed for $375 million, it is part of a larger retail, residential, and entertainment complex called L.A. Live.

Most cities feel that it is important to have major sports teams. Cities with such teams are willing to spend a great deal of public money to keep them, and those cities without such a team are willing to spend a great deal of public money to attract such a team away from another city. In the mid-1990s, four teams left their home NFL city to get a better deal. For example, the Los Angeles Rams went to St. Louis when St. Louis offered a brand-new stadium, plus guaranteed $16 million per year in gross ticket sales along with other financial considerations (Bellamy, 1998). After Los Angeles went several years without a football team, the NFL was getting pressure from advertisers that there was no team in the nation's second largest media market. In 1999, the NFL put pressure on Los Angeles to build a stadium and other facilities (parking lots, training areas, etc.) so the NFL could put a team back in that city. A Los Angeles billionaire put together an ownership group, and the city put in $150 million in state revenue bonds to build parking structures around an existing facility—the Los Angeles Coliseum. But the NFL commissioner, Paul Tagliabue, objected to the deal, saying that the municipality was not putting in enough taxpayer money, and because of this, the team would not be profitable for its owners—projecting an annual profit of only $25 to $28 million per year. The city of Houston offered $200 million in public money for a new stadium plus private investment in an adjacent football museum. When the city of Los Angeles would not put more taxpayer money into its offer, the NFL awarded the franchise to Houston, which is also a very important media market (Flanigan, 1999). Since that time, the NFL has continued to pressure Los Angeles to invest hundreds of millions of dollars of taxpayers' money to build a state of the art stadium so that it can award an NFL franchise to the country's second largest media market.

By this point in our analysis, you should be realizing that there are many benefits to the money cycle and its acceleration. Owners use salaries to compete for the best talent so they can make their teams more competitive and successful, which attracts more revenue from fans, the media, and advertisers, which makes their businesses more valuable as investments. The media benefit from being able to present more competitive contests with more superstars, and this attracts more fans. The advertisers benefit by having more access to their consumer niches, which stimulates more purchases of their advertised products. All of these businesses greatly benefit from the acceleration of the money cycle.

But what about us, the consumers? Do we also benefit? Our costs are certainly rising. We have to pay more to attend those games as far as tickets, parking, concessions, etc., are concerned. When we watch those games on TV, we have to endure a greater number of commercials, and when we buy the advertised products, the costs are higher to pay for those increased advertising fees. Instead of taking our participation for granted, we need to evaluate how much pleasure we are getting by being a fan of professional sports.

RUINING THE GAMES

Is the accelerating increase in player salaries ruining the games? The answer to this question depends on who's asking—the players, the owners, or the fans.

Players

It should be obvious that players benefit from the increasing payments to them. Until salaries began increasing five decades ago, many professional athletes could not support themselves on their playing salaries alone, so they needed to work another job during the off season. Now professional athletes are paid enough so they do not need a second job and can devote full time to training. This helps increase their potential to deliver on their talent which will lead to higher salaries, more fame, and chances to endorse products.

Owners

From the business perspective, team owners have the same goal as do the owners of any business, which is to increase the value of the business over time. The value of a team over time increases when the team is highly competitive. Team competitiveness starts with the acquisition of top talent. So owners regard the increasing salaries as an unavoidable cost of doing business.

There are generally two ways to build a competitive team. One way is to go after established talent when their contracts run out, pay those athletes more money, and attract them to your team. In baseball, this is what the teams in big cities do, such as the New York Yankees and Los Angeles Dodgers, which have the largest salary expenditures. The other way is to get really good at scouting for new talent and signing those players to contracts before they become well known and are recruited by the richer teams. This is what teams like Oakland do (for more detail on this, read *Moneyball* by Lewis [2004], or see the movie that was made from his book). However, while this second strategy works well in the short term, it does not deliver a consistently competitive team because not all promising talent develops to their full potential.

When owners consistently field competitive teams, not only do their yearly revenues increase with greater fan support but the value of their franchises greatly increases. Thus they regard the paying of huge salaries to top athletes as an essential investment in their businesses. For example, the Chicago Bulls NBA franchise was valued at $17.5 million in 1985—Michael Jordan's rookie year. In 1996, after the Bulls won their fourth NBA title, the franchise was valued at $178 million. The owner had a huge yearly income from broadcast rights, merchandising, and ticket sales. The Bulls play at the United Center, where there are 216 suites each selling for $175,000. In 1996, all games were sold out, and there was a waiting list of more than 17,000 fans for season tickets (Rhodes & Reibstein, 1996). Now the Bulls have been valued at more than $800 million (Badenhausen, Ozanian, & Settimi, 2013).

Fans

Are the escalating player salaries ruining professional sports for fans? This question is impossible to answer in a general way because fans have different standards for what the sports should be. For many fans, professional sports has been ruined for them because they are no longer able to afford to go to the games due to the very high cost of tickets, parking, concessions, etc. And some fans now have reached a point where they can no longer watch the games on TV because there are too many commercial breaks interrupting the games. In contrast, there appear to be enough fans still available to go to games and watch them on TV. Therefore, we must conclude that for most fans, the benefits of watching professional sports have been increasing each year in proportion to the increasing costs.

It is important to consider that fans are likely receiving benefits from professional sports beyond the pleasure they get in watching the professional games. That is, the professional sports games and fabulously talented athletes are so attractive that they have increased the attractiveness of all sports at all levels. The "Big Four" professional leagues of the NFL, NBA, the National Hockey League (NHL), and MLB are the most visible and as such provide role models for all other athletes at the college, high school, and Pee Wee league levels. They also stimulate us to participate in amateur leagues or even backyard games that bring us pleasure and a higher degree of physical fitness. So when we think of benefits, we need to look at the big picture of sports. The total sports industry in the United States generates $435 billion annually in revenue. Of this total, less than 6% ($24 billion a year) is generated by the Big Four sports (Plunkett Research, 2013). This means that we as fans are spending a lot of money on sports and that over 94% of these expenditures are not going to support the increasing salaries of professional athletes in the most visible sports. Instead, almost all that money is going to support college, high school, and amateur athletes in addition to supporting ourselves by purchasing our own sporting equipment. If we think of professional athletes as serving as role models to stimulate widespread participation in all sports, then their influence is enormous.

CONCLUSIONS

Sports is now dominated by the money cycle that keeps accelerating each year. Athletes demand higher salaries to play for particular teams that need to buy their talent to be competitive and eventually win championships. Owners of those teams and their leagues generate huge revenues—mostly from TV contracts. TV networks bid up the rights to telecast games so their commitment to sports grows each year. Advertisers pay higher fees to show their ads because the drive to get their messages before these sports audiences is so strong. Why? Because we the fans are willing to buy the advertised products at higher rates each year; we also buy a great deal of sporting equipment and paraphernalia.

The money cycle is generated by us—the fans. If we stopped watching sports, advertisers would stop paying huge fees in sporting telecasts, TV networks would stop bidding up the rights to televise the games, and the leagues and owners would see a big drop in their revenues and would need to cut salaries of their players. So if you believe that athletes are being paid too much, then examine your own contribution to their increasing salaries. Have you been spending more of your time and money supporting sports?

Resolving this issue for yourself starts with examining your own standard for sports salaries. When you change your standard, you will likely change the result of your evaluation. Find a standard that makes the most sense to you.

FURTHER READING

Lewis, M. (2004). *Moneyball: The art of winning an unfair game.* **New York, NY: Norton. (288 pages)**

The author writes the story of Billy Bean, who was able to make the Oakland Athletics baseball team competitive most years even though he had a much lower payroll for player salaries than almost every other team in professional baseball. He was able to field a competitive team by being great at scouting new talent and developing that talent to a high degree while paying the players low salaries.

Raney, A. A. (2009). The effects of viewing televised sports. In R. L. Nabi & M. B. Oliver (Eds.), *Media processes and effects* **(pp. 439–453). Thousand Oaks, CA: Sage.**

This chapter presents a relatively current review of the empirical literature on the effects of exposure to sports in the media.

Raney, A. A., & Bryant, J. (Eds.). (2006). *Handbook of sports and media.* **Mahwah, NJ: Lawrence Erlbaum. (633 pages including index)**

This edited volume contains many chapters written by experts on sports in the media. It is organized into four sections of the development of sports media, the coverage and business of sports media, sports media audiences, and critical perspectives on sports media.

Wenner, L.A. (Ed.). (1998). *MediaSport.* **New York, NY: Routledge. (336 pages with index)**

This edited book contains 17 chapters in four parts: playing field, institutions, texts, and audiences. Although this book is now a bit dated, with most of its research coming from the early to mid-1990s, it still presents valuable insights into how sports have developed primarily in the United States to become such a powerful economic and social force.

ESPN (http://espn.go.com)

The cable TV network devoted to sports has a website that presents a great deal of current information about players, teams, and contests.

Plunkett Research (http://www.plunkettresearch.com/Industries/Sports/SportsStatistics/ tabid/273/ Default.aspx)

This is the website of a company that conducts and reports research on a wide variety of topics. It is a valuable resource for information on sports statistics, such as players' salaries, value of different sports franchises, attendance at games, etc.

USA Today Salaries Databases (http://content.usatoday.com/sportsdata)

This website presents a lot of detail about the salaries of professional athletes and teams in America's major sports.

APPLYING MEDIA LITERACY A.1

Analyzing Criticism of Sports

By applying the skill of abstracting, we can show that there are four main ideas in this appendix:

A. The income of professional athletes has increased dramatically.

B. The pay of professional athletes is now too high.

C. The dramatic increase in pay is not sustainable.

D. The dramatic increase in pay is ruining professional sports.

Let's apply the other skills to the ideas in this appendix.

I. Analysis

1. Examine the standard you use for making judgments about the credibility of arguments.

   * Do you consider accuracy of facts?

   * Do you consider amount of information that supports the argument?

   * What else do you consider?

2. Examine the standard you use for making judgments about fairness.

   * Do you define fairness in terms of your personal experience?

   * Do you use some societal or legal perspective?

II. Evaluation

3. Evaluate the first statement (A) using your standard for credibility—that is, make a judgment about how credible this claim is.

4. Evaluate the second statement (B) using your standard of fairness—that is, make a judgment about how fair it is to pay professional athletes their current salaries.

III. Induction

5. The third statement (C) makes a claim about what will happen in the future. You can test this claim by using the skill of induction. First, take a close look at the increase in salaries up until this book was written to determine the rate of increase, which is your observed pattern. Then, second, test to see whether this observed pattern is generalizable—that is, does the pattern continue to hold with each new year.

IV. Grouping

6. Compare and contrast across sports to see if they all follow the same pattern or different patterns.

V. Deduction

7. Consider the following syllogism, and do some research to see if the conclusion holds:

   College sports are strongly influenced by the money cycle.

   My college has sports programs.

   Therefore, my college sports program is strongly influenced by the money cycle.

VI. Synthesis

8. By now, you have a good understanding of the money cycle, how it has changed sports, and the role of the mass media in the money cycle.

   * Is there something in this issue that really bothers you so much that you would like to see a change? If so, develop a strategy to try to bring about this change.

   * If instead you like the way things are going in sports, then develop a strategy to ensure that things will continue as they have been.

9. Use the skill of synthesis to develop your strategy.

   * Begin with listing all the insights that you experienced while reading this appendix and doing the exercise up to this point.

   * Divide all those insights into two groups: (a) those things you do like and would like to preserve, and (b) those things you do not like and would like to change.

(Continued)

(Continued)

* Make some recommendations to preserve the things you think are good.

* Make some recommendations about how to change those things you think are bad.

* Assemble all your recommendations into a single system—your proposed strategy—so that all the recommendations work together and support one another.

* Analyze the viability of your proposed strategy by thinking about which kinds of people and groups would oppose your strategy.

— What are you asking the opposition to give up?

— Can you show the opposition that they have more to gain than to lose by your proposed strategy? If not, how viable is your strategy?

APPENDIX B

ANALYZING MEDIA ISSUES

Is Media Company Ownership Too Concentrated?

A persistent criticism about the ownership of media businesses is that too few companies own too many media properties. Critics argue that this consolidation of ownership is harmful because it concentrates power too much, reduces competition, limits access, and changes content in a negative way—all of which makes the owners more wealthy at the expense of everyone else.

Let's analyze this criticism and its supporting arguments. There appear to be six components: (1) consolidation of ownership, (2) concentration of power, (3) reduction of competition, (4) limitations on access, (5) changes in content, and (6) enrichment of only a few people. Let's examine each of these six claims.

CONSOLIDATION OF OWNERSHIP

The claim that there has been consolidation of ownership of media properties is a factual one. When we examine this claim, we find that it is accurate. There has indeed been a great many mergers and acquisitions in the media industries, especially over the past three decades. During the 1980s, there were 2,308 mergers and acquisitions involving media companies for a total of $214 billion (Ozanich & Wirth, 1993). During the 1990s, mergers became even more popular, because they are so profitable. Merger activity shows no signs of slowing down; to the contrary, it appears to be increasing. The number of mergers among media related companies more than doubled from 2011 to 2012 with over 1,350 mergers with a total value of almost $75 billion. However, 90% of these mergers were considered relatively small—that is less than $50 million each (BtoBonline, 2013).

Five Generations of Kindle

AP Photo/Reed Saxon

▶ Jeff Bezos, CEO and founder of Amazon, purchased the *Washington Post* in August 2013, adding to a long list of investments such as IMDB, Zappos, and Audible.com.

This trend toward consolidation of ownership of media properties is most clearly highlighted in the work of Ben Bagdikian, who began conducting an analysis of media ownership patterns in 1983 and found that the control of the media was essentially in the hands of 50 people—these were the CEOs of the largest media companies that, in combination, controlled more than half of the revenues and audiences in their media markets. Less than a decade later, Bagdikian (1992) found that the number had shrunk to 23 CEOs of corporations that control most of the business in the country's 25,000 media businesses. Eleven companies controlled most of the daily newspaper circulation. In magazine publishing, a majority of the total annual industry revenues went to two firms. Five firms controlled more than half of all book sales. Five media conglomerates shared 95% of the recordings market, with Warner and CBS alone controlling 65% of that market. Eight Hollywood studios accounted for 89% of U.S. feature film rentals. Three TV networks earned more than two thirds of the total U.S. TV revenues (Bagdikian, 1992). By 2004 when Bagdikian published the seventh update of his analysis, he claimed that five companies (Bertelsmann, Disney, News Corporation [or News Corp], Time Warner, and Viacom) owned most of the newspapers, magazines, book publishers, motion picture studios, and radio and TV stations in the United States as well as many other media properties all over the world.

CONCENTRATION OF POWER

So far we have seen that there has been a great deal of consolidation of ownership of media properties, but does this automatically mean that there is *too much* concentration of power? The answer to this question requires a judgment that reveals a standard. There appear to be two values that can serve as standards for such a judgment—the value of localism and the value of efficiency. Localism values the sharing of power among as many people as possible; a person who values localism will judge this trend as resulting in too much concentration of power. In contrast, efficiency values the concentration of power in the hands of a few people who can make decisions well and quickly; a person who values efficiency more will judge this trend as not resulting in too much concentration of power. Let's examine each of these values in more detail.

Value of Localism

Localism is a populist value. It is exhibited by the belief that control of important institutions should be spread out as much as possible so that many people share the power. Thus, a considerable amount of power should exist at the local level, which is closest to individuals. It is based on the ideal that each person is a rational being, so each person should have an equal say in the political and economic arenas. This maximizes the freedom of each person. It also empowers all people by keeping them involved in as many important decisions as possible.

Localism is a part of the American tradition. The Founders of the United States followed this value when creating a democratic form of government rather than a more efficient totalitarian one (such as a monarchy) at the national level. They believed that the individual is more important than are institutions or governments. When government is necessary, it should be decentralized so as to be closer to the people's needs and more accountable to them, so they dispersed power by restricting the federal government from some areas and left decisions in these areas up to state and local governments. Thus, political power was structured so that it was spread out over many layers. America now has 18,000 municipalities and 17,000 townships. Within these, there are 500,000 local governmental units directly elected by local residents, and 170,000 of them have the power to impose taxes. Over time, the American public has retained its value for dispersion of power and has continued to support the overlapping, multilayered structure of government, even if it often seems inefficient.

Concerning the mass media, there is also a strong feeling by many that the media voices should be kept local if they are to serve best the needs of individuals and society. The media started as innovations at the local level. When a government was called upon to regulate them, the governmental agencies often favored this localism ethic in their policymaking. A good example of this is how the federal government handled the development of the broadcasting industries. If you want to broadcast a radio or TV signal, you must send your signal out on a frequency. If you and I wanted to use the same frequency to broadcast our different signals, then our signals would interfere with each other, and radio listeners would receive a garbled signal. Because there were only a limited number of frequencies made available for radio broadcasting on something called the **electromagnetic spectrum,** someone had to decide who got to use which frequencies. The federal government decided that it was the one to make the assignment of radio broadcasting frequencies, reasoning that the electromagnetic spectrum belonged to all Americans much like a national park or any other resource that should be shared by all citizens.

In the early days of radio broadcasting, the federal government decided to require individuals to apply for a broadcast frequency with the **Federal Communications Commission (FCC).** The FCC was immediately flooded with applications for

AM radio frequencies. But the AM band on the electromagnetic spectrum allowed for only about 117 broadcast frequencies. The FCC could have chosen 117 applicants and awarded each of them their own frequency. This would have led to 117 AM radio stations, with each using their frequency to broadcast their signal to the entire country. But that is not what the FCC did. Instead, the FCC divided the country into many local market areas and awarded some frequencies to each market. Also, each radio station was limited in the amount of power it could use to broadcast its signal so that the signals would not go beyond their local markets. This allowed the FCC to assign the same frequency to many different markets without having to worry about signals interfering with one another. The FCC chose this alternative because it wanted to spread the limited resource of broadcast frequencies around to as many different people as possible.

By keeping ownership of radio licenses at the local level, the FCC believed it was setting up a system whereby the stations would be operated in the best interests of their local communities. Private businesses were allowed to broadcast on these frequencies, provided they operate "in the public interest, convenience, and necessity." Therefore, the rationale for regulation in broadcasting was based on the following points: spectrum scarcity, localism, public interest, and promoting a diversity of ownership.

When TV came along in the 1940s, the FCC used the same procedure of allocating broadcasting licenses to local TV stations in the 215 local markets across the United States. Now we have more than 6,800 broadcast TV stations and 13,000 radio stations.

In an effort to preserve localism and prevent monopolies, the FCC for decades limited the number of broadcasting properties one company could own. Their early rules prevented one company from owning more than seven AM, seven FM, and seven TV stations in total, with no two being in the same market.

Value of Efficiency

Straining against this value of localism is a very strong trend toward concentration, consolidation, and centralization. This value of efficiency can also be seen in the formation of the United States. While the Founders preserved states rights and the formation of many local governmental bodies, they also created a powerful centralized national government.

▶ Protestors outside City Hall in New York oppose the possible merger between Comcast and Time Warner Cable, fearing that this would give too much control to one megacompany.

Bloomberg via Getty Images

The value of efficiency can also be seen in the development of the media industries. Although almost every media company began as a small, local operation, they take on the characteristics of big business as they grow. Big businesses are complex organizations that market many different products and services but do so under a strong centralized system to achieve a more efficient operation. Big businesses grow by claiming a larger share of the markets in which they compete. They accomplish this by acquiring control of more resources, and this often leads to buying—or at least investing in—other companies.

General industry-wide trends show that fewer and fewer people control more and more of the media. And this trend will probably continue as the cost of buying and operating a media voice keeps going up and as entry into the industry becomes more difficult. Today, a person needs a great deal of money and expertise to attempt to buy a business in one of the established media industries. Because of this, only companies that already own media businesses are successful in acquiring new businesses. Entrepreneurs can still start a media business in the magazine, book publishing, and Internet industries, but those businesses begin as very small enterprises. Either those small companies go out of business quickly, or they grow successful and are usually bought by one of the big media **conglomerates**.

Broadcasters have lobbied the FCC to relax its limits on ownership of broadcasting licenses. In the 1980s, the rules were relaxed to 12 AM, 12 FM, and 12 TV stations. Then the Telecommunications Act of 1996 further relaxed the limits to a significant extent in the guise of opening up competition. Also, the ban was lifted prohibiting a company from owning a TV and radio station in the same market. This deregulation triggered many mergers among media companies. During the 1990s, there was more than a total of $300 billion worth of major media deals in which companies bought multiple TV and radio stations (Croteau & Hoynes, 2001). Since that time, the FCC has periodically held public hearings and continued to move in the direction of allowing more concentration of ownership. Now a single company can own as many TV stations as it wants as long at the coverage of that set of stations does not exceed 39.5% of viewers; it can also own more than one TV station in a TV market. As for radio, a company can own as many stations as it wants, including three to eight stations within a single radio market depending on the size of that market. Now one company—iHeartMedia (formerly Clear Channel)—owns 850 radio stations in the United States without violating the current "restrictions" on ownership.

Why does the FCC continually deregulate the broadcasting industry? The answer is that broadcasters put a great deal of pressure on the federal government to deregulate. Broadcasters have argued successfully that they were being unfairly limited in their rights to own multiple businesses. They pointed out that there were no ownership limits for magazines, book publishers, newspapers, and Internet sites; also, the previous limits on film studios had been relaxed. Consumer groups, who argued against relaxing the ownership rules, could present no convincing evidence that multiple ownership of broadcasting businesses caused harm to the public. In contrast, broadcasters showed that when businesses are consolidated, they are more efficient and that this efficiency benefits consumers.

Cable operators have also been fighting to have limits relaxed so that they can expand. In 2009, the FCC had limited cable systems from servicing more than 30% of the U.S. population. Comcast, the nation's largest cable company at the time with almost 25% of the nation's cable homes as subscribers, sued the FCC to raise their limit and won in a federal court of appeals, which reasoned that the restriction must be lifted to reflect the changing realities of the dynamic video marketplace where consumers have lots of alternatives to cable and therefore cable should not be regarded as a monopoly (Flint, 2009).

In summary, the debate on this issue can be traced to a clash of these two values, which have served as the standards when critics have made their judgments about "too much." This debate between the values of localism and efficiency dates back to the founding of this country. Some Framers of the U.S. Constitution wanted to limit the power of government and tried to spread power out over as many people as possible. Other Framers of the Constitution wanted a strong federal government so that decisions could be made quickly and so that a single entity could be held accountable for those decisions. In a compromise, the Constitution created a strong federal government that was assigned certain powers but it also reserved other powers for state and local governments. This debate also has influenced the development of the mass media industries.

REDUCTION OF COMPETITION

Some people regard concentration of power in an industry as a good thing, because it leads to economic efficiencies, which are then passed on to customers in the form of lower prices. For example, huge companies such as Walmart and McDonald's can consistently offer lower prices because they are so big and efficient.

Other people regard anything that reduces competition as bad and should be prevented. They reason that business monopolies are bad, because monopolies concentrate too much power in the hands of one business, which is then free to raise prices and degrade service because there are no competitors. Those who argue that ownership is too concentrated point to the fact that seven conglomerates now control well over half of the mass media audience exposures (see Table B.1). But does this necessarily mean that competition is reduced?

This criticism that concentration of ownership reduces competition in a market seems valid on the surface, but it breaks down when analyzed. To illustrate, let's say a city has two newspapers. A chain buys one of those newspapers. The chain-owned newspaper cuts subscription costs and ad rates. Readers and advertisers switch to the chain newspaper because it is less expensive. Eventually, the other newspaper goes out of business. The degree of concentration in that market goes up, because now there is only one newspaper. Critics will point out that with this elimination of newspaper competition, the remaining lone newspaper will be able to raise its advertising rates and subscription fees while degrading its service. But this reasoning is too shortsighted. Just because a local market has only one newspaper does not mean that this newspaper has no competition for audiences and advertisers. That newspaper must still compete with other news services (from radio, magazines, TV, and websites) for audiences. Its sales staff competes with other media for advertisers. And the newspaper must compete for journalistic talent. If the newspaper reduces its competitive edge, its news product will be reduced, and readers will turn to other sources of news. With lower circulation rates, the newspaper will need to drop the rate it charges advertisers, and this will produce less revenue. With less revenue, the newspaper will need to lay off reporters, and the news product further degrades. This downward cycle continues until the newspaper is out of business. Of course, we must recognize that newspapers that are owned by large conglomerates experience a lot of pressure to increase profits. They try to achieve this through cutting costs but they also know that if the cost cutting degrades their product to a point where there audience shrinks, then they will lose not only subscription revenue but more importantly, advertising revenue. Newspapers remain in a highly competitive environment even when there is only one newspaper in a market.

There is no media market where one media business has a monopoly and can avoid competition. All media markets are highly competitive for audiences, advertisers, and talent.

LIMITATIONS ON ACCESS

Critics argue that as concentration increases, the individual's access to the media is reduced. *Access* here can mean two different things: access to ownership and access to using the media to get one's voice heard.

Ownership Access

Does media consolidation reduce access to ownership? Because most media companies are public corporations, any individual can buy a share of any publicly traded company. So the limits to ownership of one of the big media conglomerates is keyed to the financial resources of an individual, not to consolidation.

With most mass media industries, there are relatively low barriers to entry—that is, it is relatively easy for an individual to start a magazine, newspaper, video

	Company Details	Book Publishing	Magazine Publishing	Newspapers	Television	Cable/ Satellite Networks	
Bertelsmann ($17.8 billion)	Founded in 1835 Home office: Gütersloh, Germany 112,000 employees	Random House Knopf Doubleday			Owns the most television stations in Europe		
Comcast/ NBC Universal ($64.6 billion)	Founded in 1963 Home office: Philadelphia, Pennsylvania 139,000 employees				NBC Broadcasting Network Telemundo 28 television stations	Nation's leading cable television operator MSNBC CNBC Bravo Syfy SportsNet	
Disney ($48.8 billion)	Founded in 1923 Home office: Burbank, California 180,000 employees	Hyperion Books Disney Publishing Worldwide	*Discover* *Biography* Marvel Comics		ABC Television Network 8 ABC affiliates	Disney Channel ESPN A&E ABC Family Lifetime	
News Corporation (36.3 billion)	Founded in 1979 Home office: New York 64,000 employees	HarperCollins Zondervan	Several Australian magazines	275 newspapers internationally, including: *The Wall Street Journal* *The New York Post*	Fox Network 25 television stations	Fox News Channel Fox Sports FX Network National Geographic Golf Channel	

Recordings	Movie Studios and Distributors	Radio	Cable/ Internet/ Phone Services	Online Properties	Sports Teams	Other
BMG (Bertelsmann Music Group) operates in 54 countries 200 labels in the United States		Owns the most radio stations in Europe				
	Universal Studios		Major high speed provider with more than 17 million customers	Hulu Fandango	Philadelphia 76s Philadelphia Flyers	
Several recording companies, including: Walt Disney Records Buena Vista Records	Walt Disney Pictures Touchstone Pictures Buena Vista Pixar Marvel Entertainment Dreamworks	ABC Radio Network Over 277 radio stations			Anaheim Angels Mighty Ducks of Anaheim	Theme Parks The Disney Store
	21st Century Fox	Fox Sports Radio Network		DirectTV AmericanIdol. com	Colorado Rockets	

(Continued)

	Company Details	Book Publishing	Magazine Publishing	Newspapers	Television	Cable/ Satellite Networks	
Sony ($75.5 billion)	Founded in 1964 Home office: Tokyo, Japan 140,900 employees				Columbia TriStar		
Time Warner ($29.8 billion)	Founded in 1990 Home office: New York 25, 600 employees	Little Brown DC Comics	Largest U.S. magazine publisher, including: *Time* *Life* *People* *Fortune*	7 dailies	CW Network	HBO CNN WTBS TNT Drama Turner Classic Movies Cartoon Network	
Viacom and CBS ($28 billion)	Founded 1971 (as Viacom International) Spit into two separate corporations in 2006	Simon & Schuster			CBS Television Network (approximately 30 stations)	Viacom Stations Group Comedy Central MTV VH1 BET	

Table B.1 (Continued)

Sources: Compiled from Albarran (2001); Baker, Falk, and Manners (2000); Bettig and Hall (2003); CBS Corporation. (N.d.); Chmielewski & Fritz (n.d.); Polman (2003); Sony Corporation (n.d.); The Walt Disney Company (n.d.); Time Warner (n.d.); Verrier and James (2003); Viacom (n.d.).

production company, recording company, or website. With several thousand dollars, a desktop computer, and a strong initiative, anyone could begin a business in one of these media industries. Of course, he or she should be prepared to face very stiff competition to gain the attention of an audience and the confidence of

Recordings	Movie Studios and Distributors	Radio	Cable/ Internet/ Phone Services	Online Properties	Sports Teams	Other
More than 50 recording labels, including: Sony Music Entertainment CBS Records Columbia Records Tri-Star Music	Sony Pictures Columbia TriStar Motion Picture Group Columbia TriStar Television Group					Sony PlayStation Sony Ericsson
Warner Bros. Music Group Atlantic Elektra	Warner Bros. DC Entertainment Castle Rock Entertainment New Line Entertainment Hanna-Barbara Cartoons			AOL America Online	Atlanta Braves Atlanta Hawks Atlanta Thrashers	
Famous Music	Paramount Pictures MTV Films Nickelodeon Movies	Infinity Broadcasting CBS Radio Network				Paramount Theaters Famous Players Theaters

(2009); Comcast. (n.d.); Croteau and Hoynes (2001); Flanigan (2003); Free Press (2012); NBC Universal (n.d.); News Corporation

advertisers. But it is possible to create one's own media voice in those industries. In contrast, barriers to entry are much higher in the radio, broadcast TV, and cable TV industries, but these barriers to entry are keyed less to consolidation of ownership than to government regulations.

Voice Access

Access can also mean the ability to get your particular point of view heard through a media property. As media companies grow larger and more centralized, there is a reduction in the proportion of voices that will get heard. For example, if you send a letter to the editor of a newspaper with a circulation of 1,000, there is a good chance that your letter will get published. But if you send that same letter to a newspaper with a circulation of 1 million, your chance of being published is much smaller. Thus, the larger and more powerful the media company is, the less access you have for using that media property to get your voice heard. Larger companies must filter out more requests, but it is a mistake to equate the lower proportion of letters to the editor published with a reduction in the range of voices. To the contrary, newspapers value controversy in their stories and on their opinion–editorial pages, so a person with a different opinion would seem to be more likely to get her letter to the editor published than would someone who expresses the same opinion as many other people.

There is also another flaw in the reasoning that the large media conglomerates automatically reduce the number of voices they disseminate. The large media conglomerates own many different media properties in order to attract the attention of many different kinds of audiences. While the editorial focus within one media property might be narrow in order to maximize its appeal to a specific audience, the conglomerate is likely to own a variety of media properties that would appeal to audiences across the full range of interests.

Media conglomerates acquire media properties not to limit content but to increase their revenue streams. Rupert Murdock's News Corp owns the book publisher HarperCollins, which in 1988 bought Zondervan, which publishes more than 500 bibles and controls 35 of the best-selling books in the Bible market. Beal (2011) explains the following:

> Rupert Murdoch didn't acquire Zondervan because he wanted to spread the Word any more than he acquired MySpace because he wanted to expand his friends list. As owner of HarperCollins, he also published occult classics like *The Satanic Bible* and *The Necronomicon*. Getting into Bible publishing is simply good business. (pp. 24–35)

Some researchers have examined the diversity of media content to determine if reductions in diversity were associated with increases in concentration of ownership. For example, Einstein (2004) points out that "in study after study, scholars have determined that there is no proven causality between media ownership and programming content" (p. vii). Einstein argues that the reduction in the number of program choices is not due to consolidation but to TV's reliance on advertising as its primary source of revenue. Because of this reliance, there are severe limits on content, which include timelines for length of program, the "lowest common denominator" mentality, and an avoidance of controversy. In an analysis of the TV industry over the past four decades, Einstein reveals that as the industry became more concentrated, programming became more diverse. She said that diversity was at its peak in the late 1960s and then declined when the FCC imposed regulations about sharing programs through syndication. Then, when those syndication rules were relaxed and broadcasters could keep the programs they produced to themselves, diversity increased sharply.

CHANGE IN CONTENT

Critics argue that as competition among media companies decreases, the content of messages changes in a negative way. They argue that as companies grow larger, their content decreases in quality and that the messages are more likely to harm the public.

Has the quality of the media products declined? There is no evidence that it has. For example, Lacy and Riffe (1994) looked at the news content of radio stations and compared group ownership effects. They found that group ownership had no impact on the financial commitment or the local and staff emphasis of news coverage. Also, a study done on newspaper content could find no change in content after a newspaper was bought by a chain (c.g., see Picard, Winter, McCombs, & Lacy, 1988). No evidence of change was found with the stories, the range of opinions on the editorial page, or the proportion of the newspaper displaying news. Crider (2012) conducted a content analysis of news stories on radio station websites to determine the amount of local news, which was covered by journalists at the local stations, and syndicated content, which was imported from other news agencies. While it was found that local programming was less prevalent on smaller-market stations, there was no relationship between large corporate ownership and diminished local programming.

Has the trend toward concentration of ownership led to an increase in harmful content? This has not yet been tested directly, but there is indirect evidence that concentration of ownership in the radio industry is associated with an increase in negative speech and obscenity. One research study found that as big broadcasters buy more radio stations, shock jock programming often replaces local content. From 2000 to 2003, the nation's four largest radio companies racked up 96% of the fines handed out by the FCC although their stations accounted for only about half the country's listening audience (Hofmeister, 2005).

The danger presented by so much consolidation is not in lost quality in the production of messages. The media companies have a huge stake in attracting and holding audiences, whether they have competition or not. The danger instead is that the messages become too slick and too commercial in their quest to attract audiences. The argument then shifts to criticizing the media for providing content that is too slick, but this is rather a disingenuous line of argument because the media businesses are producing content that proves itself in terms of attracting audiences. If there is indeed a movement toward more slick content, then it must be viewed as a response to audience needs. Instead, shouldn't we be examining why audiences allow themselves to be attracted by slick, commercial news stories rather than news stories with more substance and that require more mental effort from audience members?

When we analyze this criticism, it appears that changes in content—if they have occurred—are more likely to be attributable to audience tastes than to ownership conglomeration. Therefore the resolution to this "problem" would lie more with changing public taste than with limiting media business ownership. Thus, relying on government regulations to protect us from our own poor habits is a roundabout solution at best.

ENRICHES FEW PEOPLE

Critics complain that consolidation of media ownership has led to the formation of huge conglomerates that generate ever-larger profits so that the owners of these conglomerates are enriching themselves at the expense of the many. This criticism evokes an image of a few "robber barons" getting fabulously wealthy by exploiting the public. However, media companies—especially the very large ones—are overwhelmingly publically traded corporations. They issue stock that can be bought by anyone. Furthermore, much of this stock is owned by insurance companies, banks, and retirement funds, so the number of people who benefit from one of these companies doing well financially runs into the tens of millions. Thus, critics who want to break up ownership will likely harm the efficiency of these companies and thus reduce their economic value, which ripples outward to millions of people. For example, Disney has 1.7 billion shares of stock that are publically traded on the New York Stock Exchange. About 64% of these shares are owned by institutions such as banks, insurance companies, and mutual funds.

CONCLUSIONS

Media critics are wary of the degree of concentration in the media industries. Their concern is focused on the central issue of which is more important: efficiency (brought about by industry integration and economics of scale) *or* localism (diversity of content and easier entry into the market, leading to a range of alternative voices). If you side with localism, you will conclude that media ownership is too concentrated. If you side with efficiency, you will conclude that the concentrated ownership of mass media businesses is a good thing.

This is an issue about which you likely have an opinion. But to construct an informed opinion, you need to build it up from an analysis of the situation. In building your informed opinion, think about all the harms to you of the current situation. Then think of all the advantages. If you are proposing a change, think about the advantages that such a change would deliver, but also factor in the costs. On balance, do you think your proposed change would deliver enough additional advantages to warrant all the costs it will entail?

FURTHER READING

Bagdikian, B. H. (2004). *The new media monopoly*. **Boston, MA: Beacon. (299 pages with endnotes and index)**

Since 1983, Bagdikian has been conducting an economic analysis of the media industries to track the degree of concentration. With each new edition, the number of powerful companies shrinks as their media (as well as nonmedia) holdings dramatically grow. This book is a must-read for anyone concerned about how much power is being concentrated in the hands of a few CEOs of media holding companies.

Bettig, R. V., & Hall, J. L. (2003). *Big media, big money: Cultural texts and political economies.* **Lanham, MD: Rowman & Littlefield. (181 pages with bibliography and references)**

In this book, two professors at Penn State University argue that the media have been unfettered in their drive for greater profits and control over constructing meaning in our culture. They present a great deal of detail in support of this thesis in their six chapters. The authors demonstrate that the result of this media consolidation is that a few very powerful companies are becoming even more invasive in our lives and are successfully supplanting family, friend, religion, and education as the controlling source of constructing meaning.

Einstein, M. (2004). *Media diversity: Economics, ownership, and the FCC.* **Mahwah, NJ: Lawrence Erlbaum. (249 pages, including references, appendices, and indexes)**

The author examines the issue of whether the consolidation in the media industries has led to a lessening of diversity. This book offers strong historical and economic perspectives on the issue. She concludes that despite a clear consolidation of ownership of media properties and the narrowing in the number of people making decisions about media content, there is even more diversity in messages now than there was four decades ago.

Maney, K. (1995). *Megamedia shakeout: The inside story of the leaders and the losers in the exploding communications industry.* **New York, NY: John Wiley. (358 pages, including index)**

This is a well-written description of the major players in the technologies landscape in the mid-1990s. There are lots of anecdotes and stories about what has been happening in the telephone, cable, computer, wireless, and entertainment industries. The book is full of facts and personal descriptions of the personalities involved. However, things are happening so fast in these industries with new rollouts and buyouts that the book is likely out of date.

McChesney, R. W., Newman, R., & Scott, B. (Eds.). (2005). *The future of media: Resistance and reform in the 21st century.* **New York, NY: Seven Stories Press. (376 pages with index)**

This edited volume of 19 chapters plus an introduction was written by scholars who have been very concerned about the conglomeration of American media and the FCC not only allowing it to occur but actually encouraging it. The authors document the increasing level of concentration in ownership of media properties by fewer and fewer companies and argue that this trend is harmful for consumers and citizens.

Columbia Journalism Review (www.cjr.org/resources)

This website allows you to check all the media holdings of many major conglomerates.

Vault (www.vault.com/wps/portal/usa)

This is a website that provides lots of useful information about various industries, particularly relevant to media literacy are the industries of publishing, newspapers, Internet and new media, music, broadcast and cable, advertising, and public relations.

APPLYING MEDIA LITERACY B.1

Analyzing Criticism of Media Ownership

By applying the skill of abstracting, we can show that this appendix focuses on six arguments that people use when arguing the issue of media ownership:

A. The consolidation of ownership

B. Too much concentration of power

C. The reduction in competition

D. The limiting of access

E. Negative changes to media content

F. Enriches only a few people

Let's apply the other skills to the ideas in this appendix.

I. Analysis

1. Examine the standard you use for making judgments about the credibility of arguments.

   * Do you consider accuracy of facts?

   * Do you consider amount of information that supports the argument?

   * What else do you consider?

2. Examine the standards you use for ownership of companies.

   * Do you favor the principle of localism more and therefore believe that there should be a great many owners of media businesses?

   * Do you instead favor the principle of efficiency more and therefore believe that concentration of ownership is good because it allows for greater efficiencies?

II. Evaluation

3. Evaluate the statements A, C, and D using your standard for credibility—that is, make a judgment about how credible each of these claims is.

4. Evaluate the second statement (B) using your standard for ownership of media businesses—that is, make a judgment about whether the ownership is **too** concentrated.

III. Induction

5. The third statement (E) makes a claim about there being negative changes in content because of concentration of ownership.

   * Begin by looking for patterns in the content of the media and vehicles you typically use. Do you see examples of what you would consider "negative" content? If so, are these isolated examples or a pattern?

   * Find out which company owns the media vehicles you are examining, and then identify other media vehicles that this company also owns and look for more examples of negative content in those other vehicles. Keep examining additional vehicles to see how widespread this pattern of negative content is.

IV. Grouping

6. Compare and contrast ownership patterns across types of media in terms of how much access you feel you have. Are there some media where you feel excluded from providing content or even feedback while there are other media where you feel you have open access?

V. Synthesis

7. By now you have a good understanding of the issue of media ownership.

   * Is there something in this issue that really bothers you so much that you would like to see a change? If so, develop a strategy to try to bring about this change.

   * If instead you like the way things are going with media ownership trends, then develop a strategy to ensure that things will continue as they have been.

8. Use the skill of synthesis to develop your strategy.

   * Begin with listing all the insights that you experienced while reading this appendix and doing the exercise up to this point.

   * Divide all those insights into two groups: (a) those things you do like and would like to preserve and (b) those things you do not like and would like to change.

   * Make some recommendations to preserve the things you think are good.

   * Make some recommendations about how to change those things you think are bad.

(Continued)

(Continued)

* Assemble all your recommendations into a single system—your proposed strategy—so that all the recommendations work together and support one another.

* Analyze the viability of your proposed strategy by thinking about which kinds of people and groups would oppose your strategy.

 — What are you asking the opposition to give up?

 — Can you show the opposition that they have more to gain than to lose by your proposed strategy? If not, how viable is your strategy?

ANALYZING MEDIA ISSUES

Is News Objective?

We often hear people complain that the news is not objective. They argue that in a democracy the public needs a continuous flow of accurate information about their society and its political environment in order for people to make good decisions when they vote for issues and leaders. Therefore, it is the job of journalists to present the most credible facts on all sides of an issue. When journalists distort the truth in any way, they are violating the public trust and exploiting audiences. Thus, news needs to be objective so that the public can be well informed.

The challenge in assessing whether this criticism is valid lies in determining what critics mean by "objective."

ANALYZING THE IDEA OF OBJECTIVITY

There is a strong ethic of objectivity in journalism (Parenti, 1986). But what does this mean? From a philosophical point of view, objectivity means that journalists have achieved an omniscient view on events they are covering so that they can see everything completely; then they present that picture of the events in an accurate, undistorted manner. In short, they are holding a mirror up to the events and simply reflecting their reality to the public.

This standard of pure objectivity, however, is unattainable in journalism because news workers are not capable of achieving an omniscient point of view where they can see everything about an event. Instead, journalists are human beings who construct the news through the decisions they make about what to cover and what to ignore. What gets covered is called news. Journalists also make decisions about how to tell their stories—that is, what facts to put in the story and how to sequence those facts.

News Is a Construction

If you were to ask someone how the news differs from entertainment programming, most people would say that entertainment is fiction and therefore made up by writers, whereas news presents actual events that happened. Therefore, we think of news as a reflection of the events of the day— that is, the media are simply holding a mirror up to reality.

As you have seen in the previous section, journalists do not simply hold a mirror up to reality and reflect it back to the public. Instead, journalists construct the news, and this construction is limited by many constraints. News coverage is triggered, of course, by actual occurrences. But what we see presented as news by the media are not the events themselves. Instead, the media present us with stories *about* the events, and those stories are constructed by journalists who are significantly influenced by a variety of constraints, especially the constraints of deadlines, resource limitations, and the news perspective.

Journalists are constantly subjected to many influences that limit the construction process and shape the news. Even when they strive to provide the most accurate information to convey the full picture of an event, they fall short of this goal. Let's examine some of these influences.

DEADLINES The most obvious limitation on journalists is the deadline. Deadlines often prevent journalists from gathering all the facts and presenting a complete and accurate story about the event. For example, daily newspapers have a deadline every single day. Morning newspapers usually have a deadline about 11:00 p.m. the night before. Let's say a fire breaks out in a well-known building at 2:00 a.m. on a Wednesday morning and firefighters battle the blaze until 4:00 a.m. when the fire is out and the building is gone. People reading their Wednesday morning newspaper over breakfast would want to learn about the fire, but no report of it will be in the Wednesday morning paper. The editor of the newspaper must then decide whether to print a story of the fire in the Thursday morning edition, which would make the story old news. The deadline constraint has prevented the newspaper from reporting the fire as "news." Deadlines are even more troublesome for weekly newspapers and newsmagazines; by the time their readers get their stories, the stories seem less like news because much time has elapsed between the event occurring and the "news" story being made available to the audience.

On the surface, it might appear that journalists working for radio-, TV-, or Internet-based news organizations are not constrained by deadlines, like journalists working for print-based news organizations. However, this perception would be false, because all journalists have deadlines. To illustrate, let's say there are several **developing news events** where the action is ongoing. Newspaper journalists have a deadline every day and must write a new story every day that brings readers up to date as much as possible on those developing events. Radio journalists might have a deadline every hour if the radio station has a mini-newscast each hour. All news TV channels, such as CNN and Fox News, might expect their reporters to file updates on continuing stories every 30 minutes. A reporter on a news blog might be expected to post an update every 10 minutes. All of these journalists have deadlines, and once they have submitted their news story of an ongoing event, it is already out of date because the events keep unfolding. Thus, deadlines are a limitation—that is, by the time someone sees a news story about an ongoing event in a newspaper, on TV, or on a blog, that story is already missing key elements.

RESOURCE LIMITATIONS Although the news-gathering departments of the major media organizations—especially broadcast networks, major daily newspapers, and well-funded websites—are very large and have considerable resources, there are still limits to those resources. There are never enough resources to be able to cover all the events that happen in a given day, and assignment editors must decide which stories will get covered and which will not. Editors must be highly selective in their filtering process; therefore, what we see presented as news is never the complete reporting of all the important events of the day.

To make matters worse, editors do not always allocate their resources well. For example, the Associated Press news service has more than 100 reporters in Washington, D.C., alone, and many of them are trying to develop the same contacts at the White House. Every 4 years, the two major political parties hold nominating conventions to select their party's candidate for president. News organizations send a total of about 16,000 journalists to these "nonevents." These are non-events because the person who is nominated is usually known months in advance of the "nominating" conventions, so the news value of the convention is very small. If those journalistic resources that were assigned to the convention were instead directed to other locations, the news audiences would likely receive a much wider and richer span of news from those same limited resources. This same principle applies every day on smaller scales in every town of the United States, with several newspapers, magazines, radio stations, and TV stations all sending reporters to the same police stations, city halls, and athletic contests.

© Nancy Kaszerman/ZUMA/Corbis

▶ Despite 24 hours of airtime and sizable budgets, CNN tends to offer sustained focus on a few stories each day rather than covering brand-new stories every hour.

NEWS PERSPECTIVE Perhaps the most subtle—but still very important—influence on the construction of news is what has been called the "news perspective" (Altheide, 1976). The news perspective is a way of thinking about what is news and how it should be best presented. Journalists learn that if they want to get more of their stories published and if they want their stories to be featured more prominently, they need to follow the news perspective. While informing the public is an important purpose for news organizations, this purpose is secondary to the more primary purpose of attracting audiences and conditioning them for repeat exposures. This news perspective is influenced by the factors of commercialism and **marketing orientation.** If news organizations were not commercial businesses and funded by a different method (such as by government support or philanthropy), then these factors would be far less influential.

News organizations are in the business of constructing audiences so they can rent those audiences to advertisers. The larger the audience, the higher the rent and the more revenue the news organization generates. Therefore, the ultimate goal of news is a commercial one, and journalists are driven to construct stories that will attract large audiences. Therefore, news organizations must be careful not to run hard-hitting stories that would offend audiences. Also, news organizations must be careful not to offend their advertisers (Lee & Solomon, 1990). For example, the harmfulness of tobacco has been greatly underreported because tobacco advertising is so important to the survival of many magazines and newspapers. TV has also been affected, even though no tobacco products have been advertised on TV for over three decades. The tobacco companies are large conglomerates that sell and advertise many nontobacco products. A TV news show that offends a tobacco company is in danger of losing advertising of other brands controlled by the large tobacco conglomerates.

National Archives and Records Administration

▶ The news value of reporting on the *Titanic* is clear when it occurs one day after it sank on April 15, 1912, but questionable when it happens more than 80 years later and in advance of a related TV mini-series.

Also, journalists will write stories that are not strictly news but that instead have the value of promoting other commercial products being marketed by the organization that owns the news organization. For example, Kaniss (1996) criticized news shows in the Philadelphia area by pointing out that during the November 1996 sweeps month, the local CBS affiliate on its evening news show ran nine stories on the *Titanic*, a ship that sank 84 years prior to those "news" stories but was the subject of a CBS miniseries. The Philadelphia ABC affiliate was cited as frequently running "news" stories about Mickey Mouse because the ABC network is owned by Disney. Local affiliates in many TV markets are also found to frequently run news stories about stars on their network series, and they often run soft news stories on topics of made-for-TV movies appearing that night on the network.

One of the core debates in newsrooms has been whether to give news audiences what journalists think they need or to give audiences what they want. This debate is essentially about who holds more power in determining what is news. Some journalists take a **professional responsibility orientation** and argue that they are experts in what is most important, and therefore, they should determine what is news. Journalists regard themselves as having a responsibility to inform the public about the most important and significant events of the day, and they believe they are more expert in determining this than is the public. For example, journalists operating within this perspective would strive to provide in-depth information on candidates and issues during a campaign so that voters can make a more informed decision. These journalists would also try to present clear explanations about economic conditions, implications of government policies, the patterns of changes in society, and other broad-scale issues so the public is exposed to the context behind individual issues. But there is a danger of providing such in-depth coverage of complicated issues—that is, such coverage is likely to bore most audience members.

In contrast, the business managers of news organizations take a marketing orientation and argue that their job is to satisfy public wants. If there is a market for a particular kind of story, the managers need to find journalists who can provide those kinds of stories. For example, journalists who work from a marketing orientation are more likely to present stories that grab the attention of large audiences by highlighting the unusual so as to shock people. This marketing perspective has led news workers to believe that the public wants more soft news items than stories about the government, the economy, and political matters. In a content analysis of 13,000 items in 12 daily newspapers, it was found that newspapers with a strong market orientation publish fewer items about government and public affairs and more items about lifestyle and sports than do newspapers with a weak market orientation.

> Today, the newsrooms of hundreds of U.S. newspapers, magazines, and TV stations have embraced, to greater or lesser extents, this approach to making news. Typically a market-driven organization selects target markets for its product, identifies the wants and needs of potential customers in its target markets, and seeks to satisfy those wants and needs as efficiently as possible. (Beam, 2003, p. 368)

Also, Schudson (2003) reports that the amount of soft news increased dramatically throughout the 1980s and 1990s in TV networks, major news magazines, and leading national newspapers.

The influence of commercialism has moved the news away from the professional responsibility orientation and placed it squarely under the marketing orientation. As a result, the news has attempted to be more entertaining. The stories are shorter. There is more focus on personalities than genuine leaders. There is more focus on celebrities than on people of substance. And there is more focus on gossip than news.

This ambivalence between social responsibility and entertainment is evident in public opinion polls. For example, when Americans were asked whether TV stations should broadcast live coverage of a hostage being held at gunpoint, only 22% said yes. But when those same people were asked whether they would watch such coverage, 59% said yes (Luntz, 2000). Most of us know that it is not responsible for certain events to be broadcasted. However, we are attracted to such events and would watch if we could.

In summary, news can never be fully objective because it is always a construction by journalists who are influenced by all sorts of limitations. However, this does not mean that all news has the same value to audiences. News can vary by quality.

ANALYZING THE IDEA OF QUALITY IN NEWS

What does a standard of quality for news entail? This is a question you must answer for yourself. In this section, I will present six elements of quality that are relevant to news stories. As you read through each of these six, think about whether each is reasonable, and if so, then incorporate those elements into your standard for news.

Avoiding Fabrication

For most people, the minimum standard for quality is the requirement that journalists should avoid fabrication and not make up facts or sources of information, like fiction writers do. While news can be entertaining and evoke strong emotions like fictional stories, news stories need to have a solid factual basis.

Fabrication is always a threat because sometimes journalists do not have enough time or are too lazy to get all the facts they need, so they make some up or accept some facts without checking them out fully. Also, sometimes journalists are tempted to tell a good story and ignore facts that get in the way of telling that story (Jamieson & Waldman, 2003).

Fortunately, there are not many examples of fabrication, but the few major instances that have been revealed have really damaged journalism's credibility. In an article published in the *American Journalism Review*, Lori Robertson (2001) highlighted almost two dozen high-profile acts of ethical violations that resulted in the firing of journalists. The problem seems to be in all kinds of print vehicles, including well-known magazines (*Time, New Republic, Businessweek*), large newspapers (*Wall Street Journal, New York Times, Boston Globe*), and small newspapers (*Sun News* [Myrtle Beach, South Carolina], *Press Enterprise* [Bloomsburg, Pennsylvania], *Messenger-Inquirer* [Owensboro, Kentucky]), and cuts across all kinds of reporters, including sports, business, general news, columnists, and art critics.

Perhaps the most publicized ethical problems were perpetrated by Jayson Blair, a 27-year-old reporter on the fast track at the *New York Times*. In order to enhance his career, he tried to write stories that would be so interesting that they would be selected for publication in the most prominent places in the newspaper. However, in order to write such stories, he liberally embellished the facts, even going so far as to make up whole stories. When *Times* editors finally began checking his stories, they found many fabrications and quickly fired Blair. But the damage to the credibility of the *Times* was done, and the editors felt compelled to publish a 14,000-word apologia on its front page (Wolff, 2003).

Sometimes newsmakers will fabricate facts and present them to journalists who must then decide whether to publish the fabricated facts or to expose them as being false. This is especially the case in political campaigns where the public relations staffs of candidates often manufacture "facts" to strength the position of their candidate. The 2012 presidential campaign was a good one for fact-checkers like PolitiFact and FactCheck.org, which uncovered many instances of bending the truth as well as outright lies and brought these to the attention of the public. However, this exposure seemed to have had little effect on either voters or the campaigns. For example, the Romney campaign claimed that Barack Obama was ditching welfare work requirements. This was found to be false and reported as false by the fact-checkers. However, when this campaign lie was exposed, it did not harm Romney's campaign. Either the electorate did not hear that it was a lie or did not care, because polling numbers were found to increase support for Romney as a result of the claim. When Romney pollster Neil Newhouse was confronted with the lie, he replied, "We're not going to let our campaign be dictated by fact-checkers" (Poniewozik, 2012).

Avoiding Bias

Another criterion of quality is the avoidance of bias as much as possible. Uncovering bias requires interpretation, and this makes it a more difficult to document than fabrication. Assessing whether a fact was fabricated requires relatively little interpretation, but with bias, we must infer whether the story has essential elements that the journalist failed to report because those elements supported a side of the issue that the journalist did not want supported. Therefore, bias—like fabrication—is a willful distortion on the part of a journalist, but it is difficult for audiences to recognize when this is occurring. If you agree with the journalist, you conclude that there has been no bias; in contrast, if you are a critic of the journalist, you are likely to argue that bias exists in all stories from that journalist. Let's examine two ways bias can influence journalists' decisions: bias in ignoring stories and bias in the writing of a story, particularly political stories.

BIAS IN IGNORING IMPORTANT STORIES News organizations cover only a tiny fraction of the occurrences on any given day. Does bias influence how they decide what to cover? Some people make a strong case that bias is a major influence. For example, let's look at the findings of Project Censored, which was a yearly analysis that compares happenings in the real world with events covered by the news organizations (Jensen, 1997). This project began in 1976 to monitor news coverage in the mass media and determine if there were major events or issues that were not being covered. Jensen (1997) says the following:

> The essential issue raised by the Project is the failure of the mass media to provide people with all the information they need to make informed decisions concerning their own lives. Only an informed electorate can achieve a fair and just society. The public has a right to know about issues that affect it and the press has a responsibility to keep the public well-informed about those issues. (p. 10)

Jensen (1997) argues that the media are biased in the way they select which events they choose to cover:

> The media are more concerned with their next quarterly profit than with the unique opportunity given them by the First Amendment. And most journalists are more concerned with keeping their jobs and increasing their income than with fighting for the public's right to know. . . . America's mainstream mass media basically serve three segments of society today—the wealthy, politicians, and the sports-minded. The news media have done an exceptional job providing full and, on the whole, reliable information to those who are involved in or follow the stock market and to those who are involved in or follow politics and to those who are involved in or follow sports. (p. 12)

Jensen (1997) says that there is no conscious conspiracy among journalists to censor the news:

> News is too diverse, fast-breaking, and unpredictable to be controlled by some sinister conservative eastern establishment media cabal. However, there is a congruence of attitudes and interests on the part of the owners and managers of mass media organizations. That non-conspiracy conspiracy, when combined with a variety of other factors, leads to the systematic failure of the news media to inform the public. While it is not an overt form of

censorship, such as the kind we observe in some other societies, it is nonetheless real and often equally as dangerous to the public's well being. (pp. 14–15)

In his book *Censored: The News That Didn't Make the News—And Why,* Jensen (1995) describes many seemingly important stories that did not receive much, if any, coverage by the news media. For example, in 1985, the National Institute for Occupational Safety and Health (NIOSH) found that more than 240,000 people were in danger in 258 work sites around the United States. Although it is the purpose of NIOSH to monitor safety in the workplace and to inform workers when they are in serious danger of contracting life-threatening diseases from exposure to chemicals and other hazardous materials in the workplace, NIOSH had informed less than 30% of the people who it had found to be in daily danger a decade earlier. Thus, NIOSH knew that 170,000 people were working in highly risky environments every day and let 10 years go by without telling them. The news media ignored this governmental negligence for more than a decade.

A more recent example is the lack of adequate news coverage in the lead up to the Iraq War. News organizations simply accepted the Bush administration's claim that Iraq had weapons of mass destruction that threatened the security of the United States and the world—a claim that was later found to be groundless.

BIAS TOWARD PARTICULAR POLITICAL VIEWS Those who follow the media closely often complain about a liberal or a conservative news bias or they say that there is too much negativism. In an analysis of Gallup public opinion data, it was found that more than half of Americans felt that the media were influenced by advertisers, business corporations, Democrats, the federal government, liberals, the military, and Republicans (Becker, Kosicki, & Jones, 1992). The newspaper industry itself has found the same thing in its own surveys. For example, a survey by the American Society of Newspaper Editors (ASNE) found that most people believe the media have political leanings (Jeffres, 1994).

What is interesting is that conservatives feel that the media have a general liberal leaning, whereas liberals feel that the media are conservative. Conservatives complain that most news reporters are liberal in their own views, and these liberal journalists show their bias when they present their stories. In contrast, liberals feel that conservative commentators have too much power and have redefined the American agenda to stigmatize liberals.

In the early days of the United States, most newspapers were founded by men who had a clear political viewpoint that they wanted to promote. Towns had multiple newspapers, each one appealing to a different niche of political thinking. Newspapers were biased politically, and the bias was clearly labeled. But by the late 1800s, newspapers had shifted from a political focus to a business focus, with the goal of building the largest circulation. To do this, newspapers lost their political edge so as to avoid offending any potential readers. This business focus still underlies the mass media. Decisions are made to build audiences, not to espouse a political point of view. Sometimes, arguing for a particular political point of view can be used as a tool to build an audience, but these instances are usually found within those media with a niche orientation. Instead, the large national news organizations such as the TV networks and the large newspapers try to present both sides of any political issue so as to appear objective and balanced because they want to appeal to all kinds of people across the political spectrum. This conclusion has been supported by D'Alessio and Allen (2000), who conducted a meta-analysis of 59 quantitative studies of news bias in presidential campaigns since 1948. They found no evidence of bias with newspapers or magazines and only an "insubstantial" bias in network TV news.

It is important to be sensitive to whether particular news vehicles present either a liberal or conservative bias. But it is far more important to be sensitive to the broader bias underlying all news vehicles—that is, the bias of commercialism, entertainment, and superficiality. If all we do is debate the liberal–conservative issue when it comes to news bias, we are in danger of missing the larger picture that the news media are providing us with a worldview that determines not only what we think about (as in agenda setting) but also what we think, how we think, and who we are.

Using the Best Sources

News is shaped by the sources that journalists use to gather information; therefore, we need to consider news sources when we are selecting criteria for quality in news. At minimum, journalists need to name their sources. While unnamed sources of news might be highly credible, it is not possible for audiences to make this judgment unless they are named. But just because a source is named does not mean that the source is the most credible one the journalist could have used. Credibility would seem to require two characteristics: expertise and trustworthiness. Expertise refers to the source's ability to know the facts. Trustworthiness refers to the source's willingness to tell those facts honestly to the journalist.

How do journalists know who is an expert? Most journalists don't. They lack the experience or education to evaluate the credentials of many people who could serve as experts in news stories, so they chose people not on the basis of knowledge but on their *appearance* of expertise and their willingness to tell a good story. This is why the dominant sources of news are public information officers in businesses and governmental units. Most companies and institutions have public relations departments whose sole job is to establish themselves as experts and feed information to journalists. Once a person is established as an expert source, he or she is called by journalists when they want an expert opinion on that particular issue. This point is illustrated by Steele (1995), who examined how TV news organizations selected and used expert sources to interpret the news. She found that news organizations chose expert sources that reflected journalists' understanding of expertise. Experts were selected according to how well their specialized knowledge conformed to TV's "operational bias," which places its emphasis on players, policies, and predictions of what will happen next. Steele concluded that these processes undermine the ideals of balance and objectivity as well as severely limit how news is framed.

The major news organizations all use the same sources—many of whom are unnamed—so the same type of stories always get covered. This is a clear conclusion of two journalists—Lee and Solomon (1990)—who wrote a book titled *Unreliable Sources: A Guide to Detecting Bias in News Media*, in which they expressed strong criticism of American journalistic practices. These journalists observed that over time, reporters become close friends with their sources and stop looking for other points of view. This makes their jobs easier because these reporters do not have to continually develop new and better sources of information. But the problem with this practice is that the sources have their own agendas. Frequently, the sources are public relations people for various governmental agencies, businesses, or political action groups. Thus, these sources are not trying to provide unbiased expertise to help journalists understand the issue better; instead, these people are paid to present only their one side of the issue and to make their side appear as the only valid position on the issue. For example, the military establishment has always had a sophisticated public relations operation that works to maintain strong public support for its goals and its need for increasing funding. In the 1960s, when the Soviet Union had 100 long-range missiles and the United States had 2,000, the Pentagon convinced the American people that the United States lagged far behind Russia in weapons, and the public ended up supporting greater defense budgets. During the Reagan administration, the Pentagon had an annual public relations budget of $100 million and employed 3,000 staff people.

AP Photo/Pablo Martinez Monsivais

▶ White House press secretary Josh Earnest interacts with the White House Press Corps, a group of journalists dedicated to covering White House news, at a daily briefing where he represents the president and others within the administration.

Sources often have incestuous relationships with journalists. Many journalists go into government and serve as press secretaries or public information officers. Also, press secretaries go into journalism. Over time, the two professions converge, and this revolving door homogenizes the coverage. Schudson (2003) observes, "Political institutions and media institutions are so deeply intertwined, so thoroughly engaged in a complex dance with each other, that is not easy to distinguish where one begins and the other leaves off " (p. 154). Bennett (2003) argues that this close relationship leads to what he calls indexing. By this, he means that journalists take their direction from the government when deciding the range of public opinion. What the government recognizes as the range of public opinion, journalists accept and limit their reporting to that range.

Avoiding Imbalance

Balance in news stories refers to the perception that the viewpoint of all sides in a controversy has been presented equally. Because most news stories present simple conflicts, there are usually two sharply differing sides, so it is relatively easy to tell if both sides are being presented equally. However, in reality many conflicts have more than two sides, and this makes it much harder to determine balance.

Are news stories balanced? Fico and Soffin (1995) looked at balance in newspaper coverage of controversial issues such as abortion, condoms in schools, and various governmental bills. Balance was assessed by examining whether both sides of an issue were illuminated in terms of sources interviewed for both sides and whether assertions for both sides were in the headline, first paragraph, and graphics. They found that 48% of stories analyzed were one-sided—that is, a second side was not covered at all. They counted the number of story elements that illuminated the different sides of each issue and found that, on average, one side received three more elements compared to the other side—therefore, the average story was imbalanced. Only 7% of stories were completely balanced. The authors concluded that professional capability and/or ethical self-consciousness are lacking in many journalists.

Complete Story

Another criterion of quality is to consider whether journalists are telling us only part of the story. This type of distortion is not usually regarded as bias because there does not seem to be an intention by the journalist to mislead the audience. Instead, the journalist has run out of time or does not have enough sources or ability to tell the entire story. Even though the journalist is not trying to mislead the audience, people exposed to a partial story are still shown a distorted picture of the occurrence, and therefore, the story cannot be regarded as being of high quality.

One form of a partial story is when a major story stops getting covered, even though important events continue to occur. An example of this is the $21 billion settlement by the tobacco industry that was covered during negotiations. But then the press stopped covering the story as the tobacco companies began paying billions of dollars to state governments between 2000 and 2002. Why would it be important to cover how the money was used? The settlement specified that states should spend the money for health care and to educate people, especially children, about the health risks of smoking. But only 5% of this total payout went toward antismoking efforts as it was intended. Instead, it got funneled to all sorts of pork barrel projects across the 50 states, and in North Carolina, much of it went to subsidize tobacco farmers. These subsidies did not go to help tobacco farmers transition to other crops; instead, much of it went to modernize their tobacco farms (Mnookin, 2002). Also, the press did a poor job of educating the public about where the money for the payout was coming from. Most people know that it is from the major tobacco companies, but most people do not know where the tobacco companies get much of their revenue that they use to make their payments to states in the tobacco settlement. Each of the major tobacco companies now controls hundreds of brands of all kinds of food products in supermarkets. So the payout was likely financed by a rise in prices of crackers, cereals, peanut butter, dog food, soups, and so on.

Another type of partial story is when a journalist will tell a story from a single point of view. American journalists typically will tell their stories from the point of view that America is always justified in its military actions, and those we aggress against are not justified. For example, Fishman and Marvin (2003) analyzed 21 years of photographs appearing on the front pages of the *New York Times*. They focused on violence and found that non-U.S. agents were represented as more explicitly violent than U.S. agents and that the latter are associated with disguised modes of violence more often than the former. The recurring image of non-U.S. violence is that of order brutally ruptured or enforced. By contrast, images of U.S. violence are less alarming and suggest order without cruelty. Thus, violence is associated more with out-group status than with in-group status.

Providing Full Context

Perhaps the most demanding criterion of quality is that the story present a full context. This is the concern over how much background-type information to present to help readers make sense of the event. Without context, the story has ambiguous meaning. For example, a story could report that Mr. Jones was arrested for murder this morning. That fact can convey very different meanings if we vary the context. Let's say that the journalist put in some historical context that Mr. Jones had murdered several people a decade ago, was caught and convicted, served time in prison but was recently let go because of a ruling of an inexperienced and liberal judge. In contrast, let's say that Mr. Jones, one of the candidates running for mayor, was arrested despite the fact that police had in custody another man who possessed the probable murder weapon and who had confessed. The fact of the arrest takes on a very different meaning within different contexts.

Bagdikian (1992) argues that the most significant form of bias in journalism appears when a story is reported with a lack of context. The fear is that context is only the journalist's opinion, and opinion must be avoided in "objective reporting." Bagdikian continues, "But there is a difference between partisanship and placing facts in a reasonably informed context of history and social circumstance. American journalism has not made a workable distinction between them" (p. 214). He says that "there are powerful commercial pressures to remove social significance from standard American news. Informed social-economic context has unavoidable political implications which may disturb some in the audience whose world view differs" (p. 214). So the media report undisputed facts about things but ignore the meaning behind the facts and, in so doing, severely limit our ability to see that underlying meaning.

Although contextual material is very important, many stories present very little context (Parenti, 1986). For example, the many stories about crimes that we see reported every day are each limited to the facts of that one crime. Rarely is there any context about crime rates or how the particular crime reported in the story matches some kind of a pattern—historical, social, economic, and so forth. Crime stories are like popcorn for the mind. Each story is small, simple, and relatively the same. They give our mind the sense that it is consuming information, but those stories have little nutritional value. After years of munching on this information, we have come to believe that most crime is violent street crime and that it is increasing all around us. But the real-world figures indicate that most crime is white collar (embezzlement, fraud, forgery, identity theft, etc.) and property crimes (larceny, shoplifting, etc.) rather than violent crime (murder, rape, armed robbery, etc.). But it is the more rare violent crime that gets reported because it is more deviant and thus more likely to capture the attention of the news audience.

Asking journalists to build more context into their stories presents two problems. First, journalists vary widely in talent, and it takes a very talented and experienced journalist to be able to dig out a great deal of relevant contextual information on deadline. Second, when journalists have the responsibility of constructing the context, they may be manifesting a lot of power to define the meaning of the event for the readers. Journalists can substantially change the meaning if they leave out (whether intentionally or through an oversight) an important contextual element.

Let's examine an example of a story reporting facts that are accurate but that leads readers to a wrong conclusion because the reporter does not provide an adequate context for those facts. In 2004, *Los Angeles Times* reporter Larry Stewart wrote a story from a report by a group calling itself the Institute for Diversity and Ethics in Sport. In his newspaper story, Stewart (2004) reported that the report said that it found six of the schools in the 2004 National Collegiate Athletic Association (NCAA) basketball tournament Sweet 16 had graduation rates no higher than 50%. This leaves the reader with the impression that universities (at least six) were exploiting their athletes. But what the reporter did not put in the story is that, nationwide, only about 50% of students who enter a 4-year program as a freshman end up graduating with a bachelor's degree. Therefore, the problem is not with basketball teams having unusually low graduation rates, which is what the story implied. The real issue is the relatively large dropout rate of all college students. Also, the reporter said that the report complained that only 3 of the 16 teams had an African American head coach. Why is this number bad? What should the number be? If the number should be proportional to the number of African Americans in the United States, then we should expect 12% of coaches to be African American, and that would make it two coaches. Or instead, should the number of African American coaches be proportional to the number of African American players on NCAA basketball teams? This would be a much larger percentage, but then this begs the question that perhaps African Americans are overrepresented on these basketball teams and that the problem is that there needs to be better representation from non–African Americans on NCAA basketball teams: Why are there not many more Hispanic or Asian American players? The determination of adequate representation is a complex issue. If news organizations see themselves as having the function of informing their audiences so those people can make good decisions, then journalists must provide more detailed contexts. If, instead, a journalist writes a superficial story that features only a controversy, then this serves to stir up negative emotions instead of educating audiences.

In summary, you can see that objectivity is a complex concept with many layers of meaning. This makes it difficult to understand what people really mean when they use the term. Thus, it is useful to move past objectivity and focus on a combination of other indicators of journalistic quality.

CONSIDERING STANDARDS FOR NEWS

Recall that the process of evaluation requires the comparison of some element—in this case, news stories—to some standard. The key to understanding our attitudes is to examine the standards we used to make our evaluations that led to our attitudes. In this section, we will first examine the standards of journalists then shift to the standards of audience members.

Journalist Standards

In 1922, the ASNE adopted its Canons of Journalism that contains six articles: responsibility, freedom of the press, independence, truth and accuracy, impartiality, and fair play. These articles were revised in 1975; they were renamed the Statement of Principles. The idea of objectivity appears nowhere in the document, but the general public still thinks of this as the fundamental criterion of journalism.

Instead of objectivity, journalists use the standard of credibility and balance. They try to present their sources as experts so that they appear credible. And they attempt to present more than one side of an issue.

Audience Standards

For us as audience members, what standards should we use? It appears that we use credibility, balance, and usefulness. The problem with these first two is that they are difficult to test—that is, we cannot simply expose ourselves to one news story and make a good judgment about credibility and balance; instead, we need to either have a well developed knowledge structure already on the topic of the news story, or we need to do a good deal of research on the topic on our own. This is why knowledge structures are so important.

The criterion of usefulness is an easier standard to apply because all we need to know is what our motivation for exposing ourselves to a particular news story is. If we are simply trying to keep up to date and a news story presents us with something current that interests us, then we are likely to conclude that the story is useful. This reinforces our exposure and makes it more likely that we will habitually return to this provider of news in the future.

CONCLUSIONS

Think about your criteria for news, and ask yourself the following: Are my criteria realistic? The criterion of objectivity is not realistic, but the criteria of accuracy, avoidance of bias, balance, use of good sources, and presentation of a complete story with full context are.

Then ask yourself this question: Who set these criteria for me? If the answer is the mass media, then you might want to examine the nature of those criteria—that is, are the criteria serving the purpose of the media organizations more or are they satisfying your own needs more? Make adjustments to your criteria so that they serve your purposes more. Then evaluate the usefulness of the news stories you typically expose yourself to in your everyday habitual exposures. If you typically expose yourself to stories from providers of news who are not covering the stories you find most useful or if they are not providing you with enough information, then think about why you expose yourself to these news providers.

FURTHER READING

Henry, N. (2007). *American carnival: Journalism under siege in an age of new media*. Berkeley: University of California Press. (326 pages with index)

This book is written by a journalist who is concerned about how traditional journalism can survive in the new media environment.

Jensen, C. (1995). *Censored: The news that didn't make the news—and why*. New York, NY: Four Walls Eight Windows. (332 pages with index)

Begun by the author in 1976, Project Censored invites journalists, scholars, librarians, and the general public to nominate stories that they feel were not reported adequately during that year. From the hundreds of submissions, the list is reduced to 25 based on "the amount of coverage the story received, the national or international importance of the issue, the reliability of the source, and the potential impact the story may have" (p. 15). A blue-ribbon panel of judges then selects the top 10 censored stories for the year.

Mindich, T. Z. (2005). *Tuned out: Why Americans under 40 don't follow the news*. New York, NY: Oxford University Press. (172 pages with index)

The author clearly documents that the last two generations of Americans have exhibited drastic declines in attention to news in the traditional media. Furthermore, only 11% of young people even attend to the news on the Internet. He develops some explanations for why news has become so irrelevant to the younger generations and then speculates about how this will impact the political system and society in general.

Paul, R. P., & Elder, L. (2006). *How to detect media bias & propaganda* (3rd ed.). Dillon Beach, CA: Foundation for Critical Thinking. (46 pages with glossary)

This is a short book focusing on critical thinking and the news. It presents a lot of practical advice on how to think about news stories critically and thereby protect one's self from bias, especially from novelty and sensationalism.

Postman, N., & Powers, S. (1992). *How to watch TV news*. New York, NY: Penguin. (178 pages with index)

These authors argue that what TV news says it is presenting and what it actually presents are two different things. The authors say that TV presents the important happenings of the day that all citizens should know. But what it really presents is superficial constructions designed to create large audiences for advertisers. The authors say that for people to prepare themselves to watch TV news, they need to prepare their minds through extensive reading about the world.

Schudson, M. (2003). *The sociology of news*. New York, NY: Norton. (261 pages, including endnotes and index)

Schudson sharpens and clarifies many points in the argument that journalists "not only report reality but create it" (p. 2). He digs deep into the issue and offers explanations about how the news construction occurs and the effect those constructions have on the public. After providing a brief history of journalism, he identifies two criticisms as being especially salient today. The first is that news coverage of politics is critical and this promotes cynicism in the public. Second, news itself has gone soft—that is, it is a mix of information with entertainment rather than a legitimate effort to explain complex situations.

Shoemaker, P. J., & Reese, S. D. (1996). *Mediating the message: Theories of influences on mass media content* (2nd ed.). White Plains, NY: Longman. (313 pages)

In this book, the authors review research on media content and build toward a theory with assumptions, propositions, and hypotheses.

The strength of this book is its broad look at research on news. It includes much empirical social science work, many industry examples and anecdotes, and an entire chapter on a cultural approach to ideology. It has two shortcomings. First, its span purports to be all media content, but it focuses almost exclusively on news. Once we get to Chapter 5, there is almost nothing on entertainment content. And nowhere is there anything on ad content. Also, the focus is limited to the media of TV and newspapers. A second limitation is that there is really nothing new here. Their "theory" is really several lists.

KEEPING UP TO DATE

Journal of Broadcasting & Electronic Media (http://beaweb.org/jobem.htm)

Journalism & Mass Communication Quarterly (www.aejmc.org/home/publications/jmc-quarterly)

These are scholarly journals that publish research that examines how news is presented in the content of the mass media, particularly newspapers and TV.

WikiLeaks (www.wikileaks.org)

Founded in 2007, WikiLeaks is a not-for-profit media organization that provides a secure and anonymous way for sources to leak information to the public. It relies on a network of volunteers from around the world. Leakers are typically whistle-blowers who work in private businesses and government agencies where they feel their organization is doing something harmful to the public so they steal the private information of that organization and make it available for the public to view.

News Blogs

There are thousands of news blogs. Many are owned by major news organizations such as CNN (news .blogs.cnn.com) and the *New York Times* (www.nytimes.com/interactive/blogs/directory.html). The most popular news blog is the Huffington Post (www.huffingtonpost.com), which was started by Arianna Huffington independent of any news organization but was bought by AOL in 2011.

Technorati (http://technorati.com)

Technorati is an Internet search engine for searching blogs. The name Technorati is a blend of the words *technology* and *literati*, which invokes the notion of technological intelligence or intellectualism. Technorati uses and contributes to open source software. Technorati has an active software developer community— many of them from open-source culture.

Analyzing Criticisms of News

I. Analysis

1. This appendix presented some influences on the news construction process that shape the news. Can you think of any additional constraints on news construction that were not mentioned in this appendix?

2. Analyze a print news story—from a newspaper, magazine, or website.

   a. Identify shortcomings in those stories due to deadlines.

   b. Identify shortcomings in those stories due to limited resources.

   c. Identify shortcomings in those stories due to the news perspective.

3. Analyze your standard for quality in news.

   a. Which of the quality components discussed in this appendix are the most important to you personally?

   b. Which of the quality components discussed in this appendix are unimportant to you personally?

   c. Are there other components you would like to add to your standard for quality?

II. Evaluation

4. Using your own personal standard, evaluate the print news story for quality.

5. Find a nonprint news story—from radio or TV—and evaluate its quality.

III. Induction

6. Look for patterns of problems across the news stories you have analyzed and evaluated.

   a. Can you see any evidence for fabrication of facts?

   b. Can you see any evidence of reporter bias?

   c. Do you think the journalists used the best sources?

   If not, which sources do you think are weak?

   If not, which sources should the journalist have used?

   d. Do you regard the story as balanced—that is, is there an important point of view that is missing from the story?

   e. Do you think the journalist did a complete job with this story?

   If not, what facts were missing?

   f. Do you think the journalist provided a full context—that is, was there enough background material to help you understand the event that made this story news?

(Continued)

(Continued)

7. Given the conclusions you reached previously (in #6), how generalizable do you think those conclusions are? Test the generalizability of those conclusions by analyzing more news stories to see if the patterns hold up.

IV. Abstracting

8. Go to a public meeting or event and take notes about what occurs. Then write up your notes in the form of a news story of 100 words maximum.

   a. How did you decide what to leave out?

   b. How did you decide what to emphasize in the story?

   c. Do you feel you captured the essence of the event so that someone who did not attend could experience the event from your news story?

ANALYZING MEDIA ISSUES

Is There Too Much Violence in the Media?

The public continually complains that there is too much violence in the mass media. This criticism flares up whenever a high-profile violent event happens in real life, like a school shooting. The argument is based on the belief that the media's presentation of so much violence exerts a dangerous influence on certain groups of people, particularly children and criminals, which increases the probability that these people will behave violently in real life. So to protect society from this harmful effect, the media need to reduce the amount of violence it presents.

Let's analyze this criticism and its supporting arguments. There appear to be three components that form a syllogism: (1) There is a great deal of violence in the media; (2) certain types of people are vulnerable to media influence; and, (3) therefore, reducing the amount of violence in the media would decrease the influence on these vulnerable people and make society safer. Let's examine each of these claims in detail.

HIGH AMOUNT OF VIOLENCE IN THE MEDIA

The claim that there is a lot of violence in the media is a factual one. When we search for evidence supporting this claim, we find that it is fairly accurate. While we do not have much of an information base about how much violence there is in many of the mass media, we have a good research literature that has analyzed the amount of violence on TV (see Potter, 1999, 2003). Since the early days of TV, the scientific analysis of that content has repeatedly shown that over half of all primetime and weekend morning shows aimed at children present some violence and that on average there are about a half dozen acts of violence per hour on TV across all types of shows.

While the public is accurate in its perception that there is a great deal of violence on TV, the irony is that the public greatly *under*perceives the amount. That is, the public's definition for what they regard as media violence is narrow, and this leads them to filter out a great many acts that they should regard as violent. Furthermore, it is those acts that the public is ignoring that are likely to create greater harm to the public. Let's examine the implications in these two shortcomings in public perceptions.

The Public's Narrow Conception of Violence

The public uses a conception of violence that is narrower than the conception used by researchers who conduct careful analyses of the amount of violence in TV content. This difference is an important one. To illustrate this point, look at the questions posed in Box D.1 and answer each of those eight with a yes or a no. If you answered yes to all eight, then you have a very narrow definition of violence and are likely to perceive very few acts of violence when you watch TV. In contrast, if you answered no to all eight questions, then you have a very broad definition of media violence and would likely perceive about 30 acts of violence per hour on average when you watch TV.

A broader definition of media violence is more useful than a narrower one because it includes many different kinds of violence, and each of these kinds has its own risk of leading to negative effects. So if our concern over media violence is keyed to a concern

Key Elements in Definitions of Violence

1. Does the act have to be directed toward a person? Gang members swing baseball bats at a car and totally destroy it. Is this violence?

2. Does the act have to be committed by a person? A mudslide levels a town and kills 20 people. Do acts of nature count? Remember that nature does not write the scripts or produce the programming.

3. Does the act have to be intentional? A bank robber drives a fast car in a getaway chase. As he speeds around a corner, he hits a pedestrian (or destroys a mailbox). Do accidents count?

4. Does the act result in harm? Tom shoots a gun at Jerry, but the bullet misses. Is this violence? Or what if Tom and Jerry are cartoon characters and Tom drops an anvil on Jerry, who is momentarily flattened like a pancake? A second later, Jerry pops back to his original shape and appears fine.

5. What about violence we don't see? If a bad guy fires a gun at a character offscreen and we hear a scream and a body fall, is this violence, even though we do not see it?

6. Does the act have to be physical (such as assaults), or can it be verbal (such as insults)? What if Tom viciously insults Jerry, who is shown through the rest of the program experiencing deep psychological and emotional pain as a result? What if Tom embarrasses Jerry, who then runs from the room, trips, and breaks his arm?

7. What about fantasy? If 100 fighting men "morph" into a giant creature the size of a 10-story building, which then stomps out their enemies, does this count as violence?

8. What about humorous portrayals? When the Three Stooges hit each other with hammers, is this violence?

about harm to the audience, then it is much better to use a broader definition in order to inventory all the different types of media violence and their subsequent harms. Therefore, the public's narrow definition is faulty because it ignores many of the portrayals of violence that could lead to negative effects.

The public's conception of media violence focuses on graphicness. For example, people might not think an action/adventure movie with wall-to-wall car chases and gunfire is more violent than a drama in which one character is unexpectedly shot and we see the bullet tearing through flesh and bone. A single highly graphic scene in a movie is much more likely to trigger the perception that the movie is violent compared to a movie with a constant stream of car chases, gunfights, and explosions where the victims were never shown in a graphic manner. When a violent act is portrayed with a high degree of graphicness, this typically offends audience members and this offense triggers the criticism. Thus, producers avoid offending audience members by sanitizing the violence. Producers know that if they remove the graphicness of violence by rarely showing harm to victims, that audiences are much less likely to be offended. Research studies have repeatedly shown that audiences tolerate this sanitized violence, but when the portrayal is unusually graphic, it interrupts viewers' flow of enjoyment, and viewers experience strong negative emotions (British Broadcasting Corporation, 1972; Diener & De Four, 1978; Diener & Woody, 1981).

Another key element in the public's definition of violence is that humor is a camouflage. It appears that when humor blankets violence, the public does not see the violence. This is taken for granted by all kinds of people. An anecdote will illustrate this. A few years ago, I was meeting with the staff of the Viacom Standards and Practices Department in New York City. These seven women are charged with previewing the content to be aired on Viacom's cable channels of MTV, VH1, and Nickelodeon. I was watching a music video while the seven women in the room explained how they screened music videos to determine if those videos met their standards or, if in their judgment, there were things in the portrayals that would offend viewers. For an hour, the women showed parts of music videos and explained how they asked the various music groups to remove or tone down certain images that they felt were demeaning to women. Finally, when I was given a chance to ask a question, I said, "What about violence in the music videos?" Several women were eager to answer that they were sensitive to that issue and that the videos did not have any direct scenes of violence, although violence was implied in certain lyrics. Then I asked about violence on Nickelodeon. There was a rather long pause as the women looked at me as if I were a third grader who had just claimed that two plus two equals seven. One of the women looked very puzzled and said, "But there is no violence on Nickelodeon." I returned the puzzled face. She then flashed a big smile and said, "But those are not violent. Those are cartoons!" Were these women naive? No, they had a highly sophisticated

© Moviestore collection Ltd / Alamy

▶ The public may be less sensitive to violence in cartoons like *Teenage Mutant Ninja Turtles* when it is depicted with humor.

understanding of violence—as defined by the general viewing public. These women knew that the public was not concerned by the actions—even the most brutal— portrayed in cartoons.

What is the reason for humor camouflaging the violence? It appears that humor tends to remove the threat of violence. For viewers to consider something violent, they need to feel a degree of personal threat. This insight can be found in the work of Barrie Gunter in Great Britain. He reported that viewers' ratings of the seriousness of violent acts were higher as the fictional settings were closer to everyday reality in terms of time and location. In contrast, "Violence depicted in clearly fantastic settings such as cartoons or science-fiction were perceived as essentially non-violent, non-frightening and nondisturbing" (Gunter, 1985, p. 245).

The public is also not concerned much about acts of aggression and violence that result in nonphysical harm, such as verbal aggression where characters inflict emotional, psychological, and social harm to their victims. Studies have shown the occurrence of verbal violence is far more prevalent—up to three times more frequent—than physical forms of violence (Greenberg, Edison, Korzenny, Fernandez-Collado, & Atkin, 1980; Martins & Wilson, 2012; Potter & Vaughan, 1997). For example, Martins and Wilson (2012) conducted a content analysis of the portrayal of social aggression in the 50 most popular TV programs among 2- to 11-year-old children. Results revealed that 92% of the programs in the sample contained some social aggression. On average, there were 14 different incidents of social aggression per hour in these shows, or one every 4 minutes.

In summary, viewers who watch an average amount of TV are likely to see one act of violence per week that is highly graphic in its depiction of serious physical harm. And this is the basis for their criticism that there is too much violence in the media. However, the average person is likely to view over 100 acts of physical violence per week—almost all of it sanitized or camouflaged with humor. Add to that another 200 to 300 acts of nonphysical aggression in the form of hate speech, harsh insults, put-downs, and the like. Indeed, there is a great deal of violence throughout the TV landscape—far more than the average person perceives.

The public underestimates the amount of violence in the media because of a narrow conception of what constitutes violence. When we take a broader conception of violence—one that shows how exposure to media violence can lead to a wide range of negative effects—we can understand that the public's narrow conception of violence is truly faulty.

Filtering Out and Harm

The irony is that the acts that people filter out by using their narrow conception are the acts that are likely to lead to greater harm. As you saw previously, people filter out acts that are not graphic, acts that are considered fantasy or humorous, and acts that are nonphysical.

People filter out acts that are not graphic because they do not offend them. The irony is that people should be offended by producers who present violence in a non-offensive manner. Violence should be offensive. When violence is presented in a non-offensive manner, people are not upset by it, and they are likely to think it is no big deal. Repeated exposure to violence that does not show blood and gore and where victims are not shown as suffering is precisely the kind of portrayal that leads to people becoming desensitized to violence and to the suffering of others. Thus, these portrayals exert a negative influence on the public over time.

People filter out acts of violence when they are presented as humorous and/or fantasy. They discount humorous portrayals (like the *The Three Stooges* and cartoon characters) through their laughter. But this trivializes the violence and the seriousness of the consequences to the victims. For example, cartoon characters get stabbed, burned, shot, and blown up, yet they appear completely unharmed in the next scene. The public also discounts fantasy portrayals as not being realistic, leading them to reason that the chances of people imitating those fantasy portrayals as negligible. But if you've ever observed young children watching Saturday morning cartoons with fantasy characters, you will see those children imitating those characters. This fantasy play is typically harmless, but it does increase the danger of those children getting hurt.

People filter out acts of violence when they are nonphysical. Granted that acts of physical violence are likely to result in the most serious harm to victims, acts of nonphysical aggression (such as verbal bullying, taunting, threatening, insulting, embarrassing, etc.) are much more likely to be imitated. For example, if you watch portrayals of daring criminals robbing high-security banks and blowing up the cars and helicopters that chase them, you are not likely to imitate this pattern of violent behavior. But if you watch portrayals of characters insulting, verbally abusing, and embarrassing other characters in highly witty attractive ways, the probability of you trying to imitate such behavior is much higher. When we consider verbal violence in addition to physical violence, we can see that even a presumably rarely occurring effect such as imitation is likely to be occurring with much more frequency than we had originally thought. What makes this opinion possible is a narrow conception of what effects are possible from exposure to media violence. Compared to physical aggression, social aggression is more imitatable so we should expect portrayals of social aggression to lead to more negative effects than portrayals of physical aggression, and these effects are not just imitations of behavior, they can be negative emotional effects. For example, Mares, Braun, and Hernandez (2012) conducted an experiment on middle school children by showing them programs popular with tweens (8 to 14 years old) where there were depictions of serious social conflicts. They found that habitual exposure was associated with expectations of encountering specific crowds in middle school (person schemata), with expectations of less friendliness and more bullying (behavioral scripts), and with greater anxiety about attending their future school. Similarly, those who saw high-conflict episodes anticipated more hostility and less friendliness in their future school and felt more anxious and less positive about going there than those who saw low-conflict episodes.

Finally, the acts of verbal aggression are far more numerous on TV than acts of physical aggression. Given the much higher number of portrayals and the greater likelihood of verbal aggression being imitated, it is a serious mistake to ignore their influence.

SOME PEOPLE ARE MORE VULNERABLE THAN OTHERS

Vulnerable Groups

When people complain about the amount of violence in the media, they usually fear the effect that the portrayals will have on criminals and children. As for criminals, the public worries that constant portrayals of violence will teach these people how to behave violently and motivate them to behave that way.

As for children, many adults believe that children have not yet developed sufficient inhibitions for behaving in a violent manner. Adults are concerned that when children watch violent TV shows like wrestling, children will be compelled to imitate the violent actions they see, and this could result in harm to those children.

Criminals and children are vulnerable to negative effects from exposure to media violence. However, vulnerability is not limited to these two groups. Everyone is vulnerable. Having a false sense that only other people are affected by vulnerability is a belief that has been called the **third-person effect.**

Third-Person Effect

If you ask the typical person, "Does violence in the media have any effect?" most people will say yes—recalling a horrible instance when someone copied a violent criminal act that was in a movie or in the news. However, if you were to ask those same people if violence in the media has had an effect on them, most would say no. Thus, most people believe that other people are at risk but think they are free from risk. This difference in perception between one's self and others has been labeled the third person-effect.

The reason for this third-person effect with media violence can be traced to the public's narrow view that the negative effect from exposure to media violence is limited to aggressive behavior. Given this narrow view, most people reason that since they cannot remember behaving aggressively after watching media violence, they are not harmed by such exposures. However, this is faulty thinking because we are all vulnerable.

▶ What violent media content has shocked you recently? Have you become desensitized to certain kinds of violence in movies or on TV?

We Are All Vulnerable

In order to understand the widespread nature of vulnerability from exposure to media violence, we need to expand our perspective on media effects. Recall from Chapter 8 that I showed you how to broaden your perspective on media effects in general. Now let's focus on broadening your perspective in the specific area of media violence.

Table D.1 shows you that there are many different types of effects of media violence, and all of them can happen to you. Each of these has been well documented by research. Notice that some are immediate effects (meaning that they occur during exposure to the media violence), whereas others are long-term effects (which take many exposures over a long period of time to build up to a manifestation). Notice also that although there are behavioral effects, there are also effects that are more physiological, attitudinal, emotional, and cognitive.

Let's examine one of these effects that people rarely perceive. This is the cultivation of fear effect that shapes your emotions concerning your personal risk about being a victim of violence. Of course, real-world violence and crime do exist, but they do not exist to the levels that the general public has been conditioned to believe. The crime rate in the United States increased from 1960 to 1990 then began falling. Now the crime rate is the lowest in 40 years, and the murder rate the lowest in 50 years (Good news is no news, 2011, June 4). While the crime rate was falling throughout the 1990s, a poll taken in 1996 found that only 7% of Americans believed that violent crime had declined in the previous 5-year period (Whitman & Loftus, 1996). Also, from March 1992 to August 1994, public perceptions of crime as the most important problem in the United States jumped from 5% to 52% (Lowry, Nio, & Leitner, 2003).

Table D.1 What Are the Effects?

The Immediate Effects

Behavioral Effect

1. Imitation of behaviors: People watch a violent sequence and copy those behaviors.
2. Triggering novel behavior: Exposure to media violence stimulates people to act in a violent manner without actually imitating the behaviors they see in the media.
3. Disinhibition: Exposure to media violence can reduce viewers' normal inhibitions that prevent them from behaving in a violent manner.
4. Attraction: People seek out violence in the media because violent stories are exciting, arousing, and suspenseful.

Physiological Effect

5. Fight/flight: Exposure to violence can temporarily arouse people physiologically by causing their heart rate and blood pressure to increase as the body prepares to fight off a threat or flee from it.
6. Excitation transfer: Violence presented in the media tends to arouse and energize audiences. People then use this energy to behave in all sorts of ways, not necessarily in a violent or aggressive manner. This energy from the arousal is short-lived and usually dissipates within several minutes after exposure.

Emotional Effect

7. Temporary fear: Violence in films and on TV can produce intense fear. This fear reaction typically lasts for only a short period of time, but it could endure for several hours, days, or even longer.

Attitudinal Effect

8. Immediate creation/change of attitudes: A person's attitude can be created or changed with as little as a single exposure. For example, researchers have shown that when people are exposed to a violent TV program, they will show an immediate drop in sympathetic attitude.

Cognitive Effect

9. Learning specific acts and lessons: People can learn behavior patterns by watching characters perform in the media. For example, children watching cartoon characters bash each other over the head without harm can learn how to perform a particular pattern of aggression without performing those behaviors.

Long-Term Effects

Behavioral Effect

10. Training behavior: Repeated engagement with violence in violent video games over time gradually teaches people the techniques of using violence in a successful way and helps them get better at performing those violent actions.

Physiological Effect

11. Physiological habituation: This is building up or increasing physiological tolerance over the long term. With repeated fight-or-flight responses, the human body gradually builds up a resistance to the exposure to media violence.

12. Narcoticizing: Not only does habitual viewing of violence over time dull our reactions but some people also continue to crave the strong "arousal jag" they used to get from violent exposures. But to experience the same degree of arousal, they search out more graphic and stronger forms of violence.

Emotional Effect

13. Desensitization: Some violent portrayals are presented so often that our natural response of horror or disgust erodes, and our emotional reactions are reduced over time.

14. Cultivation of fear: After watching portrayals of violence and crime over the long term, people develop an unrealistically high fear of being victimized in their everyday lives.

Attitudinal Effect

15. Long-term reinforcement of attitudes/beliefs: Because the media provide so many messages of violence and because those messages are usually presented with the same cluster of contextual factors, viewers' existing attitudes about violence are reinforced over time.

Cognitive Effect

16. Learning social norms: Long-term exposure to characters using violence and aggression to solve problems teaches people that society not only permits such action but even encourages it.

Effects on Society

17. Changing institutions: When violence permeates the media year after year in all kinds of programming, it puts pressure on institutions—such as the criminal justice system, the educational system, religion, and the family—to change.

Where do people get the idea that crime is a problem when they don't experience any in real life? From the media. The media constantly present stories about crime. There are cable TV channels, such as Court TV, that present one high-profile crime after another. Also, the media, through the news, present a constant stream of crime news that reinforces this impression that there is a great deal of terrible crime and this has been found to create an irrationally high fear of victimization (Romer, Jamieson, & Aday, 2003).

When we take into consideration the full range of effects that are possible from exposure to media violence, it should become more apparent that you, too, are at risk.

This, however, does not mean that you are actually experiencing all these effects. There are many things that you can do to reduce the probability that any of these would actually occur. But it is important that you take a media literacy approach to avoid these negative effects. Ignoring them will not protect you.

Reducing the Amount of Violence

If the probable harm in the exposure to media violence is attributable primarily to frequency of exposure, then it is reasonable to argue that we need to reduce the frequency of those portrayals. However, we know from generations of storytelling that it is the way the story is told that delivers the lessons and establishes meaning— not how many times the story is told. This is also a clear finding in the large research literature on media effects. It is the way violence is portrayed in the media that signals to audiences what the meaning of violence is and that meaning is very influential in bringing about effects. Therefore, the concern over frequency should be secondary to the concern about context.

To illustrate this point, consider the following two scenarios. In the first scenario, there are two brothers who are selfish, petty, and physically ugly. Although they are weak, they each have a gun, which they use to extort money from hardworking "mom and pop" store owners in the neighborhood by pistol-whipping them. At night, they mug people and beat them up for fun. The victims of their violence are shown suffering all kinds of harm—fear, financial hardships, and physical pain. Eventually, the brothers are arrested and put in jail where they are beat up by larger, stronger criminals. Their punishment is shown in detail as they work their way through the criminal justice system and are sentenced to long prison terms.

In the second scenario, the two brothers are young studs who are witty and highly intelligent. They spend their days hacking into private databases to find medical doctors who overcharge for their services and insurance investigators who cheat people out of their rightful benefits. At night, they capture their targets and take them to their secret laboratory where they torture them with high-tech devices and cutting-edge pharmaceuticals to get them to confess to their criminal behavior. While it is obvious that the targets are being tortured, the audience never sees any blood or gore. Afterward, it is implied that they kill their targets and carefully dispose of their bodies. However, they are eventually arrested and brought to trial, but the police are not able to find much evidence of their crimes so a jury finds them not guilty.

The first scenario is closer to what happens in real life. The actions of the brothers are disgusting and are likely to offend audiences. There is little chance that audience members will identify with the brothers or be motivated to imitate their actions. Furthermore, audiences are likely to believe that other people who watch these portrayals will also be less likely to want to commit violence. So increasing this type of portrayal will likely send a prosocial message—don't behave this way because it is disgusting and you will be severely punished. But because this type of portrayal will likely offend audiences, there is little chance that this type of portrayal will increase.

In contrast, the second scenario follows more closely the typical patterns of violent portrayals found in the media—that is, the perpetrators are glamorized and the violence is sanitized. People who watch these kinds of portrayals are more likely to believe that violence is often a good way to solve problems, that it is justified, and that only bad people experience harm. Thus, the increase in this type of portrayal would be a bad thing for society. As you can see from this argument, the increasing of media violence can have either a prosocial or antisocial effect; it depends on how the violence is presented. They key is context more so than frequency.

The context in the way the violence is portrayed increases the probability of all sorts of negative effects. The sanitization of the violence leads viewers to become desensitized to the suffering of victims. The glamorization of violence leads viewers to become attracted to the violence and over time have their socialized inhibitions to performing violent acts eroded. The trivialization of violence with humor leads viewers to believe the risk to them of being punished is slight. If instead of being presented the way it currently is across the TV landscape, violence were presented in the context of a morality play, then the repetitive exposure to media violence would be a positive thing for society because it would teach people that violence is not acceptable, that perpetrators are punished in all sorts of ways, that it is rarely if ever justified, and that it causes serious long-term harm to victims and their loved ones.

CONCLUSIONS

The public complains that there is too much violence in the media. Their complaint, however, is too narrow because it is not based on a recognition that the violent portrayals can negatively affect them and not just other people. Also, the public greatly underestimates the number of violent portrayals—especially the types of portrayals that could harm them most.

How can we best proceed toward a better situation with media violence? The easy answer is to reduce the number of violent portrayals. But this type of answer is too superficial because it ignores many important factors in the dynamic of media effects. It ignores the fact that the risk of a negative effect is determined much more by the way the violence is portrayed than the frequency of portrayals. It ignores the fact that we are all vulnerable to a wide variety of negative effects. And it ignores the fact that much of the violence we are exposed to in the media is not perceived by us as violence, so we are underestimating the amount of violence in the media. We are also underestimating the range of harm, and underestimating the scope of people who are constantly being influenced by these portrayals.

When constructing your informed opinion about media violence, check your definition of media violence and your conception of harm. If these are faulty, then it follows that your opinion will also be faulty. When you have a broader conception of violence, you will see much more violence in the media than you have in the past. When you realize that the continual presentation of violence in the media has been constructing negative effects in you, then you will become much more concerned about this issue; harm has not been happening only to other people. And when you realize that the degree to which these violent portrayals are putting you and others at risk for negative effects is traceable more to context than to frequency, then you will be able to take control of the process of influence.

Once you have constructed an informed opinion about media violence, you are likely to see this issue in a very different way. And more importantly, you are likely to be thinking that the problem requires solutions that are very different than have been suggested in the past.

FURTHER READING

Bushman, B. J., Huesmann, L. R., & Whitaker, J. L. (2009). Violent media effects. In R. L. Nabi & M. B. Oliver (Eds.), *Media processes and effects* (pp. 361–376). Thousand Oaks, CA: Sage.

This chapter presents a relatively current review of the empirical literature on the effects of exposure to violence in the media. The authors focus on studies that take a strong psychological perspective and use the methods of experiment and survey.

Cantor, J. (2009). Fright reactions to mass media. In J. Bryant & M. B. Oliver (Eds.), *Media effects: Advances in theory and research* (3rd ed., pp. 287–303). New York, NY: Routledge.

This chapter reviews the literature on how violence and related media content have been found to trigger fear reactions in audiences, especially children.

Potter, W. J. (2003). *The 11 myths of media violence.* Thousand Oaks, CA: Sage. (259 pages with index)

This book begins with a chapter illuminating the current state of public debate over media violence and ends with a chapter reflecting on the prognosis for change. In between are 11 chapters, each dealing with a faulty belief about media violence. Taken together, these myths lock people (the general public, people in the media industries, media regulators, and media researchers) into a maze of unproductive thinking. These myths include the following faulty beliefs: There is too much violence on TV, the media are only responding to market desires, and reducing the amount of violence in the media will solve the problem.

Sparks, G. G., Sparks, C. W., & Sparks, E. A. (2009). Media violence. In J. Bryant & M. B. Oliver (Eds.),

Media effects: Advances in theory and research (3rd ed., pp. 269–286). New York, NY: Routledge.

This chapter presents a brief history of the media violence controversy then moves on to review the research and theoretical work that tries to explain the phenomenon of violence in the media and how it affects audiences.

Analyzing Criticism of Media Violence

The Situation:

We can abstract the issue by expressing it in three statements:

A. There is a great deal of violence in the media.

B. Certain types of people are vulnerable to media influence.

C. Therefore, reducing the amount of violence in the media would decrease the influence on these vulnerable people and make society safer.

Notice that these three statements illustrate the skill of deduction. The first two of these are premises that can be tested. The third statement is a conclusion that is reasoned from the first two premises. Thus, this is an example of the skill of deduction.

In order for the conclusion of a deduction to avoid being faulty, it needs to meet two criteria:

* First, the two premises themselves cannot be faulty.

* Second, the conclusion must be reasoned logically from the premises.

Examining the Argument:

Let's systematically evaluate the conclusion in this deduction using the following three-step procedure.

1. Evaluate the accuracy of the first premise: *There is a great deal of violence in the media.* Is there a credible, factual basis for the premise, or is it an opinion that is uninformed?

   a. Analyze the scholarly definitions of violence. Go to the scholarly literature and look at some content analyses of media violence.

   How do scholars define media violence?

   How much violence did they find in the media?

   b. Evaluate those scholarly definitions of violence.

   Which definition do you like best? Why?

   How much violence was found using that definition?

(Continued)

(Continued)

   c. Analyze how the public defines violence. (Find this in the appendix.)

   d. Evaluate the public's definition of violence.

      Is the public's definition of violence better or worse than the scholarly definition you selected?

   e. Select either the public's definition or the scholarly definition, and determine how much violence is in the media using that definition of violence.

2. Evaluate the accuracy of the second premise: *Certain types of people are vulnerable to media influence.* Is there a credible, factual basis for the premise, or is it an opinion that is uninformed?

   a. Pick one particular effect of exposure to media violence (see Table D.1).

      Do you think everyone is at risk for this effect, or is there a particular group of people who is likely to be especially vulnerable?

   b. Pick a second effect of exposure to media violence (see Table D.1).

      Do you think everyone is at risk for this effect, or is there a particular group of people who is likely to be especially vulnerable?

   c. Do you think vulnerability changes across effects?

      If you think that different groups of people are vulnerable for different kinds of effects, then what is the implication on what you ask the industry to do concerning media violence?

   d. Pick one effect that you think is the most harmful to people and or society. What factors of influence do you think are most responsible for causing such an effect?

      Are these factors of influence characteristics of how much violence is presented, the way in which the violence is portrayed, or characteristics about the audience members?

3. Examine how the two premises are used to arrive at the conclusion: *Therefore, reducing the amount of violence in the media would decrease the influence on these vulnerable people and make society safer.*

   a. Threshold problem: Can you select a number to express the degree to which he amount of violence should be reduced?

      Is there an acceptable level of media violence? If so, what is that level?

   b. Logical reasoning: Does the conclusion automatically follow from the two premises?

   c. Thinking outside the box: Can you think of other conclusions besides reducing the amount of violence?

TEST YOUR KNOWLEDGE ANSWERS

Chapter 1
1. F, 2. F, 3. F, 4. F

Chapter 2
1. T, 2. F, 3. T, 4. F

Chapter 3
1. T, 2. F, 3. F, 4. F

Chapter 4
1. T, 2. F, 3. F, 4. T

Chapter 5
1. F, 2. F, 3. T, 4. T

Chapter 6
1. F, 2. F, 3. T, 4. F

Chapter 7
1. T, 2. T, 3. T, 4. F

Chapter 8
1. F, 2. T, 3. T, 4. F

Chapter 9
1. F, 2. T, 3. T, 4. F

GLOSSARY

Above-the-line employees: People who are hired for their specific creative talents to make media messages (actors, directors, writers, composers, etc.)

Abstracting: The skill of creating a brief, clear, and accurate description capturing the essence of a message in a smaller number of words (or images, sounds, etc.) than the message itself

Adaptation: The fifth and last phase in the life cycle pattern of the development of a mass medium where the medium redefines itself in the media marketplace and provides different messages or services not provided by the other media

Analog coding: Information that is stored in a form special to each medium, unlike digital coding, which is uniform across all media; with analog coding, musical information was stored as fluctuations in the grooves of a vinyl record and film information was stored as a series of still pictures on an acetate strip of film.

Analysis: The skill of breaking down a message into meaningful elements

App: Computer-based application program that can be downloaded from the Internet to a person's computer or mobile device

Attention: Exposure to a media message that takes place in the attentional state; conscious awareness of the media message

Attentional state: The experience of being aware of a media message and actively processing its information while being exposed to the message

Attitudinal-type effect: The media-influenced effect that is manifested as the acquisition of a new attitude or the triggering, alteration, or reinforcement of existing attitudes

Audience conditioning: A strategy used by media organizations to make their existing audience members want to continually expose themselves to their subsequent messages

Automatic routines: Sequences of behaviors or thoughts that we learn from experience then apply again and again with little effort; think of these as computer programs that run in the back of our minds without us consciously paying attention to them.

Automatic state: The experience of being exposed to a media message without being aware of the message

Automaticity: An exposure state where we put our minds on "automatic pilot" and filter out almost all message options.

Behavioral-type effect: A type of media-influenced effect that is manifested as the triggering of actions in a person or over time of altering as well as reinforcing patterns of action

Belief-type effect: A type of media-influenced effect that is manifested as the acquiring of a belief or the long-term alteration as well as reinforcing of an existing belief

Beliefs: Faith in the existence or truth of things

Below-the-line employees: People who work in the media industries and exhibit skills that are not especially unique—that is, the skills required to do their jobs are widespread in the population

Blog: Short for web log; Internet sites set up by individuals, businesses, and news organizations that are designed to attract the attention of as many visitors as possible with text, audio, and video

Cognitive-type effect: A type of media influenced effect that is manifested as the acquisition of information (factual or social) as well as the triggering, alteration, or reinforcement of a mental process

Competencies: The ability to accomplish a task successfully, such as match the meaning of a media message element; in contrast to skills, competencies are categorical—that is, either you can perform the task successfully or you cannot.

Conceptual differentiation: The ability to classify objects into a large number of mutually exclusive categories

Conglomerates: Very large companies that own and operate many businesses across different industries

Content analysis: A social scientific research method that focuses on certain characteristics of media messages (such as the demographics of characters or the portrayals of violence) and counts how frequently those characteristics occur

Convergence: The moving together over time of things that were separated into a common group; this is a powerful force on the mass media that has three manifestations: technological, business, and psychological

Cross-media promotion: Advertising your media message in another medium so as to attract people in that medium to try exposing themselves to your message

Cross-vehicle promotion: Advertising your media message in another vehicle so as to attract people in that medium to try exposing themselves to your message

Decline: The fourth phase in the life cycle pattern of the development of a mass medium where the medium loses audience members and revenue due to competition from a newer medium that provides better messages or the same messages in a better way

Deduction: The skill of using general principles to explain particulars

Demographic segmentation: Identifying a niche audience by their enduring characteristics, such as gender, ethnicity, etc.

Denoted meanings: Standard meanings for symbols that are shared by all people; these are the dictionary-type meanings we memorize for words and symbols when we are in elementary school.

Desensitization: A long-term emotional effect where the continual exposure to a certain kind of media message erodes the intensity of our emotional reaction—for example, repeated exposure to acts of aggression leads us to reduce our sympathy for victims of aggression

Developing news events: Newsworthy occurrences that change over the course of days or weeks; journalists continue to file updated stories realizing that each story is only partial and may contain inaccurate information

Digital coding: Information that is stored a binary code so that it can be transported across all channels of distribution

Economies of scale: The high costs of making the first copy of a media message are spread out over many copies; as additional copies are produced, the high cost of making the initial copy is averaged over a greater number of copies and the cost per copy is reduced

Economies of scope: The high costs of making a media message spread out over different messages; when an original message is translated into similar messages and distributed through different media

Electromagnetic spectrum: A range of frequencies that are used for broadcasting messages without wires; in the United States, the Federal Communications Commission (FCC) is in charge of assigning frequencies to individuals and businesses for transmission of radio, TV, and cell phone signals.

Electronic games: Platforms offering competitive experiences using electronic devices (video, computer, smartphone, etc.)

Emotional intelligence: The ability to understand and control one's emotions

Emotional-type effect: The type of media-influenced effect that is manifested as the triggering of an emotional reaction or the altering of emotional patterns over time

Evaluation: The skill of judging the value of an element; the judgment is made by comparing a message element to a standard

Exposure: The condition of being in proximity (place and time) to a message as well as having the message occur within our perceptual abilities and leave some impression (however slight) in our minds. Thus, there are three hurdles for exposure: physical, perceptual, and psychological.

Exposure states: Four qualitatively distinct psychological states people can be in when experiencing a media message; these four states are automatic, attentional, transported, and self-reflexive.

Factual information: Discrete bits of information that can be confirmed by objective sources; examples include names (of people, places, characters, etc.), dates, titles, definitions of terms, formula, lists, and the like.

Federal Communications Commission (FCC): Agency established by the U.S. Congress in the 1920s to regulate the new broadcasting industry and later the developing telecommunication industry; focuses primarily on establishing national standards for developing information technologies as well as regulating ownership of broadcasting and telecommunication businesses

Field independency: A natural ability to distinguish between the signal and the noise in any message where the noise is the chaos of symbols and images, while the signal is the information that emerges from the chaos

Filtering decisions: The information processing task where we continually make decisions about filtering out media messages (ignore them) or filtering them in (pay attention to them)

Flow: When playing video games, the experience of being so focused on playing the game and achieving one's goals that the player loses track of time and place

Frame: A set of experiences we use to interpret media messages; frames are composed of our beliefs, preferences, emotions, etc.

General entertainment story formula: The generic structure of all entertainment-type stories

begins with a conflict or a problem, the conflict is heightened throughout the story as the main characters try to solve the problem, and the story is resolved in a climactic scene.

Genres: This refers to kinds of message and suggests that there are categories within which media messages can be organized; the most general genres of media messages are entertainment, news/information, and persuasive messages (such as commercial messages and public service announcements [PSAs]).

Geographic segmentation: Identifying a niche audience by where its members live and shop

Grouping: The skill of determining which elements are alike in some way; determining how a group of elements are different from other groups of elements

Induction: The skill of inferring a pattern across a small set of elements, then generalizing the pattern to all elements in the set

Information processing tasks: A sequence of tasks of filtering media messages, then matching meaning and meaning construction

Innovation: The first phase in the life cycle pattern of development of a mass medium; it is characterized by technological and marketing innovations

Interactive media: Media platforms allow—and typically require—their audiences to create the content either by themselves, in interaction with other audience members, or in interaction with employees of mass media organizations. Audience members are not paid for creating any of this content; to the contrary, audience members not only create the content for free but they often pay the interactive mass media companies for access to the content either through subscription fees (as with many games) or by agreeing to be exposed to advertising.

Internet service provider (ISP): Media company that offers users a way to connect to the Internet through wires or Wi-Fi

Knowledge structures: Sets of organized information stored in a person's memory

Life cycle pattern: A sequence of five stages of development typically followed by all mass media; the five stages are innovation, penetration, peak, decline, and adaptation

Long tail marketing: A strategy of identifying smaller niche audiences that have been ignored by other media companies; the "long tail" refers to the extreme ends on the bell curve and ignoring the fat middle where the majority is represented.

Lowest common denominator (LCD): A programming principle where a media company (especially TV) tries to attract the largest audience possible by creating messages that will not offend anyone and thus appeal to a wide range of people

Macro-type effects: Types of media-influenced effects that are manifested as the gradual altering or reinforcing of processes in aggregates of individuals such as organizations, institutions, and society

Manifested media effects: Media-influenced effects that can be observed and can be easily attributed to media influence

Marketing concept: A practice among marketers that begins with research to identify audience needs, then creates the types of messages that can satisfy those particular needs

Marketing convergence: Using the advantages of technological convergence across channels of media to attract niche audiences for a particular message with as many platforms as possible

Marketing innovations: Essential characteristics of the innovation stage in the development of a mass medium where marketers attract new users to its medium and convince them that the new medium is a superior way for those users to access media messages

Marketing orientation: A belief among managers of media companies that it is their job to identify existing needs in various niche audiences then develop media messages to satisfy those needs

Mass audience: The outdated conceptualization of the media audience as being a very large mass with no social organization or interaction among audience members, who are heterogeneous, anonymous, and interchangeable

Mass communication: The outdated conceptualization that media send messages to a mass audience in a one-way flow with no feedback

Massively multiplayer online role-playing games (MMORPGs): Internet-based platforms that attract thousands of game players from all over the world who want to create personas in a fantasy world and compete for virtual rewards in those worlds

Meaning construction decisions: The information processing task where we engage in a process of creating our own meaning for a media message; this process is usually engaged when we have no denoted meaning already residing in our memory or when the denoted meaning does not satisfy our current needs.

Meaning matching decisions: The information processing task where we engage in a process of recognizing elements (referents) in a media message and then automatically access our memory to find the meanings we have memorized for those elements

Media literacy: A set of perspectives that we actively use to expose ourselves to the mass media to interpret the meaning of the messages we encounter; media literacy is multidimensional, consisting of cognitive, emotional, aesthetic, and moral dimensions; and media literacy is a continuum, not a category.

Mental codes: Rules for decision making that we have learned through exposure to media messages; these codes are stored in our memory and are automatically activated when we engage in information processing tasks of filtering and meaning matching.

Messages: The instruments that deliver information to us from the media

Net loser: People and organizations who complete economic exchanges with resources of less value compared to the resources they gave up in the exchange

Net winner: People and organizations who complete economic exchanges with resources of greater value compared to the resources they gave up in the exchange

Next-step reality: The idea that media messages must be based on real-world elements (recognizable characters, situations, etc.) so that audiences can relate to what happens in those messages but then the messages must also take a step away from pure reality by adding fantasy elements in order to capture and hold the audience's attention

Niche audience: A relatively small audience that is defined by a shared interest or need

Peak: The third phase in the life cycle pattern of development of a mass medium where the medium commands the most attention from the public and generates the most revenue compared to other media

Penetration: The second phase in the life cycle pattern of development of a mass medium where it continues to attract larger numbers of audience members of all kinds

Perceptual exposure: The media message falls within human's bandwidth of visual and/or auditory perception

Personal locus: A person's plan for building knowledge structures about the media along with the psychic energy needed to execute the plan

Physical exposure: The message and the person occupy the same physical space for some period of time

Physiological-type effect: The media-influenced effect is manifested as the triggering of an automatic bodily function, such as increasing blood pressure or heart rate

Process effects: Media-influenced effects that are continually occurring without being easily observed

Professional responsibility orientation: A belief among some journalists that it is their responsibility to inform the public about the most important and significant events of the day so that people can use the information to make better decisions as citizens of that society

Profit: The positive difference between a company's revenue and expenses; often used mistakenly as a synonym for revenue

Psychographic segmentation: Identifying a niche audience by their psychological and lifestyle characteristics

Psychological convergence: The breaking down of barriers between audiences and mass media organizations as well as the barriers separating audience members from one another due to geography or other social constraints

Puffery: A technique used by advertisers to use words in a way that it appears they are making claims for the superiority of their products when in fact they are not making any product claims that can be tested

Revenue streams: Sources of income for a business

Self-reflexive state: The experience of being exposed to a media message with a high degree of awareness of the media message as well as a high awareness of standing apart from the message while analyzing it

Simplified extended conflict (SEC): A news story formula that tells journalists to look for some angle of conflict that appears very simple, then structure their stories to emphasize the simple conflict between two people or two points of view

Skills: Tools we use to build strong knowledge structures; the seven fundamental skills necessary with media literacy are analysis, evaluation, grouping, induction, deduction, abstraction, and synthesis

Social information: A type of information that is characterized by rules and patterns about how individuals behave around other people; this information, which cannot be verified by authorities in the same way factual information can be, is typically inferred as individuals observing how people behave in social interactions and the consequences of those behaviors.

Social networking sites (SNSs): A platform for individuals and businesses to create an identity on the Internet and provide information to friends and the public about themselves (e.g., Facebook, LinkedIn)

Socialization: Long-term effect where we use media messages to form our beliefs about how society works in the real world

Story formula: A guideline that producers of media messages use to attract audiences, hold their attention throughout the message, and condition them for repeat exposures; audiences use these guidelines to follow messages and make sense of them.

Synthesis: The skill of assembling information elements into a new structure to reveal new relationships among the elements

Talent: An economic resource of above-the-line media employees that refers to their ability to attract and condition audiences for repeat exposures

Technological convergence: The breaking down of barriers that separated the different media channels of communication (such as print media, broadcast TV, film, computers, etc.) primarily due to the digitization of information so that a message could move seamlessly across all media channels of communication

Technological innovations: Characteristics of the innovation stage in the development of a mass medium where inventors develop a new form of transmitting information

Telescoping: The way electronic game players keep the big picture of the overall game in mind while focusing on the immediate objectives that face them at any one point in the game

Third-person effect: The widespread belief in the public that exposure to media can harm other people (the third person) but not themselves personally

Timing of effects: Focuses on when a media influenced effect is manifested; it has two values of immediate (where the manifestation occurs during the media exposure or shortly after) and long term (where the manifestation does not occur until the person has experienced many exposures to media messages)

Tolerance for ambiguity: The willingness to follow situations into unfamiliar territory that goes beyond our preconceptions and takes us out of our comfort zone

Transported state: The experience of being exposed to a media message and being swept away by it into a different place and time such that you lose sense of your current physical surroundings and current point in time

Type of effect: Refers to the form of the manifestation of the effect in individuals (cognitive, attitudinal, emotional, physiological, or behavioral) and in larger aggregates (macro-type effect)

Valence of effects: Refers to whether an effect is positive or negative

Vehicles: The means by which a media company sends its messages to audiences; for example, with TV, the vehicles are the programs.

Adams, D., & Hamm, M. (2001). *Literacy in a multimedia age.* Norwood, MA: Christopher-Gordon.

Ader, D. R. (1995). A longitudinal study of agenda setting for the issue of environmental pollution. *Journalism & Mass Communication Quarterly, 72,* 300–311.

Albarran, A. B. (2010). *The media economy.* New York, NY: Taylor & Francis.

Altheide, D. L. (1976). *Creating reality: How TV news distorts events.* Beverly Hills, CA: Sage.

Anderson, C. (2006). *The long tail: Why the future of business is selling less of more.* New York, NY: Hyperion.

Badenhausen, K., Ozanian, M. K., & Settimi, C. (Eds.). (2013, January 23). The NBA's most valuable teams. Retrieved April 19, 2013, from http://www.forbes.com/nba-valuations

Bagdikian, B. (1992). *The media monopoly* (4th ed.). Boston, MA: Beacon.

Bagdikian, B. (2004). *The new media monopoly.* Boston, MA: Beacon.

Baker, C. (2003, August). Cracking the box office genome. *Wired,* p. 52.

Bartholomew, D. (2002, May 4). Bill would outlaw soda sales at schools. *Santa Barbara News-Press,* p. A3.

Baseball Player Salaries. (n.d.). Retrieved April 19, 2013, from http://baseballplayersalaries.com

Bauder, D. (2000, March 14). CBS to air two reality TV shows. *Tallahassee Democrat,* p. B1.

Bauer, R. A., & Bauer, A. (1960). America, mass society and mass media. *Journal of Social Issues, 10*(3), 3–66.

Beal, T. K. (2011). *The rise and fall of the Bible: The unexpected history of an accidental book.* New York, NY: Houghton Mifflin Harcourt.

Beam, R. A. (2003). Content difference between daily newspapers with strong and weak market orientations. *Journalism & Mass Communication Quarterly, 80,* 368–390.

Becker, L. B., Kosicki, G. M., & Jones, F. (1992). Racial differences in evaluation of the mass media. *Journalism Quarterly, 69,* 124–134.

Bellamy, R. V., Jr. (1998). The evolving television sports marketplace. In L. A. Wenner (Ed.), *MediaSport* (pp. 73–87). New York, NY: Routledge.

Bennett, W. L. (2003). *News: The politics of illusion* (5th ed.). New York, NY: Longman.

Bollier, D. (2008). *Viral spiral: How the commoners built a digital republic of their own.* New York, NY: The New Press.

British Broadcasting Corporation. (1972). *Violence on television: Programme content and viewer perceptions.* London, England: Author.

Brooks, D. (2011). *The social animal: The hidden sources of love, character, and achievement.* New York, NY: Random House.

Bruner, J. S., Goodnow, J., & Austin, G. A. (1956). *A study of thinking.* New York, NY: John Wiley.

BtoBonline. (2013, January 2). Media M&A activity in 2012 doubled. Retrieved April 17, 2013, from http://www.btobonline.com/article/20130102/MEDIABUSINESS10/301029996/media-m-a-activity-in-2012-doubled

Bushman, B. J., Huesmann, L. R., & Whitaker, J. L. (2009). Violent media effects. In R. L. Nabi & M. B. Oliver (Eds.), *Media processes and effects* (pp. 361–376). Thousand Oaks, CA: Sage.

Cantor, J. (2009). Fright reactions to mass media. In J. Bryant & M. B. Oliver (Eds.), *Media effects: Advances in theory and research* (3rd ed., pp. 287–303). New York, NY: Routledge.

Cantril, H. (1947). The invasion from Mars. In T. Newcomb & E. Hartley (Eds.), *Readings in social psychology* (pp. 619–628). New York, NY: Holt.

Castronova, E. (2005). *Synthetic worlds.* Chicago, IL: University of Chicago Press.

Chew, F., & Palmer, S. (1994). Interest, the knowledge gap, and television programming. *Journal of Broadcasting & Electronic Media, 38,* 271–287.

Chock, T. M. (2011). Is it seeing or believing? Exposure, perceived realism, and emerging adults' perceptions of their own and others' attitudes about relationships. *Media Psychology, 14,* 355–386.

Cloud, J. (2012, August 27). Gadgets go to class. *Time*, pp. 48–50.

Crider, D. (2012). A public sphere in decline: The state of localism in talk radio. *Journal of Broadcasting & Electronic Media, 56*, 225–244.

Csikszentmihalyi, M. (1988). The flow experience and its significance for human psychology. In M. Csikszentmihalyi & I. S. Csikszentmihalyi (Eds.), *Optimal experience: Psychological studies of flow in consciousness* (pp. 15–35). New York, NY: Cambridge University Press.

D'Alessio, D., & Allen, M. (2000). Media bias in presidential elections: A meta-analysis. *Journal of Communication, 50*, 133–156.

Davenport, T. H., & Beck, J. C. (2001). *The attention economy: Understanding the new currency of business*. Boston, MA: Harvard Business School Press.

de Kunder, M. (2013, February 2). The size of the World Wide Web (Internet). Retrieved from www.worldwidewebsize.com

Diener, E., & De Four, D. (1978). Does television violence enhance programme popularity? *Journal of Personality and Social Psychology, 36*, 333–341.

Diener, E., & Woody, L. W. (1981). TV violence and viewer liking. *Communication Research, 8*, 281–306.

Dill, K. E. (2009). *How fantasy becomes reality: Seeing through media influence*. New York, NY: Oxford University Press.

Doyle, G. (2002). *Understanding media economics*. Thousand Oaks, CA: Sage.

Eichelberger, C. (2013, January 30). NFL sees modes revenue growth as sponsors stay shy on economy. Retrieved April 20, 2013, from http://www.bloomberg.com/news/2013-01-30/nfl-sees-modest-revenue-growth-as-sponsors-stay-shaky-on-economy.html

Einstein, M. (2004). *Media diversity: Economics, ownership, and the FCC*. Mahwah, NJ: Lawrence Erlbaum.

Essany, M. (2008). *Reality check: The business and art of producing reality TV*. Burlington, MA: Focal Press.

Ferguson, D. A. (1992). Channel repertoire in the presence of remote control devices, VCRs, and cable television. *Journal of Broadcasting & Electronic Media, 36*, 83–91.

Fico, F., & Soffin, S. (1995). Fairness and balance of selected newspaper coverage of controversial national, state, and local issues. *Journalism & Mass Communication Quarterly, 72*, 621–633.

Fishman, J. M., & Marvin, C. (2003). Portrayals of violence and group difference in newspaper photographs: Nationalism and media. *Journal of Communication, 53*, 32–44.

Flanigan, J. (1999, July 30). There's no defense for NFL expecting more L.A. funds. *Los Angeles Times*, pp. C1, C2.

Flint, J. (2009, August 29). Appeals court sides with Comcast in market-share battle with FCC. *Los Angeles Times*, p. B2.

Foreman, J. (2009, June 6). Drug labels, ads at center of battle. *Los Angeles Times*, pp. E1, E5.

Frechette, J. D. (2002). *Developing media literacy in cyberspace: Pedagogy and critical learning for the twenty-first-century classroom*. New York, NY: Praeger.

Friedman, T. (1995). Making sense of software: Computer games and interactive textuality. In S. G. Jones (Ed.) *CyberSociety: Computer Mediated Communication and Community* (pp. 73–89). Thousand Oaks, CA: Sage.

Friedson, E. (1953). The relation of the social situation of contact to the media in mass communication. *Public Opinion Quarterly, 17*, 230–238.

Frosch, D. L. Krueger, P. M., Hornik, R. C., Cronholm, P. F., & Barg, F. K. (2007, March–April). Creating demand for prescription drugs: A content analysis of television direct-to-consumer advertising. *Annals of Family Medicine, 5*, 179.

Gardner, R. W. (1968). *Personality development at preadolescence*. Seattle: University of Washington Press.

Gibbs, N. (2012, August 27). Your life is fully mobile. *Time*, pp. 32–39.

Giddings, S., & Kennedy. H. W. (2006). Digital games as new media. In J. Rutter & J. Bryce (Eds.), *Understanding digital games* (pp. 129–147). Thousand Oaks, CA: Sage.

Good news is no news. (2011, June 4). *The Economist*, p. 36.

Greenberg, B. S., Edison, N., Korzenny, F., Fernandez-Collado, C., & Atkin, C. K. (1980). In B. S. Greenberg (Ed.), *Life on television: Content analysis of U.S. TV drama* (pp. 99–128). Norwood, NJ: Ablex.

Gunter, B. (1985). *Dimensions of television violence*. Aldershot, England: Gower.

Henry, N. (2007). *American carnival: Journalism under siege in an age of new media*. Berkeley: University of California Press.

Hofmeister, S. (2005, September 8). Study ties indecency to consolidation of media. *Los Angeles Times*, pp. C1, C11.

Ito, M., et al. (2009). *Living and learning with new media: Summary of findings from the Digital Youth Project*. Cambridge, MA: The MIT Press.

James, M. (2011, May 29). Redstone & Co. stand out. *Los Angeles Times*, pp. B1, B10–B11.

Jamieson, K. H., & Waldman, P. (2003). *The press effect: Politicians, journalists, and the stories that shape the political world*. New York, NY: Oxford University Press.

Jeffres, L. W. (1994). *Mass media processes* (2nd ed.). Prospect Heights, IL: Waveland.

Jenkins, H. (2006). *Convergence culture: Where old and new media collide*. New York: New York University Press.

Jenkins, H., Purushotma, R., Weigel, M., & Clinton, K. (2006). *Confronting the challenges of participatory culture: Media education for the 21st century*. Cambridge, MA: MIT Press.

Jensen, C. (1995). *Censored: The news that didn't make the news— and why*. New York, NY: Four Walls Eight Windows.

Jensen, C. (1997). *20 years of censored news*. New York, NY: Seven Stories Press.

Jensen, T. (2013, February 6). 4th annual TV news trust poll. Retrieved May 5, 2013, from http://www.publicpolicypolling.com/main/2013/02/4th-annual-tv-news-trust-poll.html

Johnson, S. (2006). *Everything bad is good for you*. New York, NY: Riverhead Books.

Jones, J. P. (2004). *Fables, fashions, and facts about advertising: A study of 28 enduring myths*. Thousand Oaks, CA: Sage.

Kaniss, P. (1996, December 19). Bad news: How electronic media muddle the message. *Philadelphia Inquirer*, p. A35.

Kepplinger, H. M., Geiss, S., & Siebert, S. (2012). Framing scandals: Cognitive and emotional media effects. *Journal of Communication, 62*, 659–681. doi: 10.1111/j.1460-2466.2012.01653

Kerr, A. (2006). The business of making digital games. In J. Rutter & J. Bryce (Eds.), *Understanding digital games* (pp. 36–57). Thousand Oaks, CA: Sage.

Kinkema, K. M., & Harris, J. C. (1998). MediaSport studies: Key research and emerging issues. In L. A. Wenner (Ed.), *MediaSport* (pp. 27–54). New York, NY: Routledge.

Lacy, S., & Riffe, D. (1994). The impact of competition and group ownership on radio news. *Journalism & Mass Communication Quarterly, 71*, 583–593.

Lee, M., & Solomon, N. (1990). *Unreliable sources: A guide to detecting bias in news media*. New York, NY: Carol.

Lewis, M. (2004). *Moneyball: The art of winning an unfair game*. New York, NY: Norton.

Li, S. (2011, May 18). Maybe mister right is right over there. *Los Angeles Times*, pp. A1, A11.

Lih, A. (2009). *The Wikipedia revolution: How a bunch of nobodies created the world's greatest encyclopedia*. New York, NY: Hyperion.

Linthicum, K. (2009, June 5). Wikipedia limits Scientology access: The encyclopedia site shuts out computers from the church's Los Angeles headquarters. *Los Angeles Times*, p. B2.

Lowry, D. T., Nio, R. C. J., & Leitner, D. W. (2003). Setting the public fear agenda: A longitudinal analysis of network TV crime reporting, public perceptions of crime, and FBI crime statistics. *Journal of Communication, 53*, 61–73.

Luntz, F. (2000, March). Public to press: Cool it. *Brill's Content*, pp. 74–79.

Lussier, G. (2011, February 11). 2011 will break the all time record for movie sequels. Retrieved July 15, 2011, from http://www.slashfilm.com/2011-break-time-record-movie-sequels

Macedo, D. P., & Steinberg, S. R. (Eds.). (2007). *Media literacy: A reader*. New York, NY: Peter Lang.

Mackey, M. (2007). *Literacies across media* (2nd ed.). New York, NY: Routledge.

Maney, K. (1995). *Megamedia shakeout: The inside story of the leaders and the losers in the exploding communications industry*. New York, NY: John Wiley.

Mares, M-L., Braun, M. T., & Hernandez, P. (2012). Pessimism and anxiety: Effects of tween sitcoms on expectations and feelings about peer relationships in school. *Media Psychology 15*, 121–147.

Martins, N., & Wilson, B. J. (2012). Mean on the screen: Social aggression in programs popular with children. *Journal of Communication, 62*, 991–1009. doi:10.1111/j.1460-2466 .2012.01599

McChesney, R. W., Newman, R., & Scott, B. (Eds.). (2005). *The future of media: Resistance and reform in the 21st century*. New York, NY: Seven Stories Press.

McKnight, M. (2012). *The 50 highest-earning American athletes*. Retrieved April 19, 2013, from http://sportsillustrated.cnn.com/specials/fortunate50-2012

Medrich, E. A., Roizen, J. A., Rubin, V., & Buckley, S. (1982). *The serious business of growing up: A study of children's lives outside school*. Berkeley: University of California Press.

Metallinos, N. (1996). *Television aesthetics: Perceptual, cognitive, and compositional bases*. Mahwah, NJ: Lawrence Erlbaum.

Metropolitan Sports Facilities Commission. (n.d.). Next generation of sports facilities. Retrieved May 7, 2004, from http://www.msfc.com/nextgen.cfm

Mindich, T. Z. (2005). *Tuned out: Why Americans under 40 don't follow the news*. New York, NY: Oxford University Press.

Mitchell, A. (1983). *The nine American lifestyles: Who we are and where we're going*. New York, NY: Macmillan.

Mnookin, S. (2002, August 19). The tobacco sham. *Newsweek*, p. 33.

Nabi, R. L., & Oliver, M. B. (Eds.) (2009). *Media processes and effects*. Thousand Oaks, CA: Sage.

Napoli, P. M. (2011). *Audience evolution: New technologies and the transformation of media audiences*. New York, NY: Columbia University Press.

National Center for Educational Statistics. (2012). *Program for international student assessment*. Retrieved February 5, 2009, from http://nces.ed.gov/surveys/pisa/index.asp

National Football League 1999 salaries. (2000, May 23). *USA Today*, pp. 14C–15C.

NBA player salaries 2012–2013. Retrieved April 19, 2013, from http://espn.go.com/nba/salaries

Neuman, W. R. (1991). *The future of the mass audience*. New York, NY: Cambridge University Press.

Neuman, W. R. (Ed.). (2010). *Media, technology, and society: Theories of media evolution*. Ann Arbor: University of Michigan Press.

NFL teams dodge salary cap. (1996, January 2). *Santa Barbara News-Press*, p. B5.

Nielsenwire. (2012, December 3). The state of the media: The social media report 2012. Retrieved from http://blog .nielsen.com/nielsenwire/global/social-media-report-2012-social-media-comes-of-age

Ocasio, A. (2013). *Reality TV by the numbers*. Retrieved March 20, 2013, from http://screenrant.com/reality-tv-statistics-infographic-aco-149257

Ozanich, G. W., & Wirth, M. O. (1993). Media mergers and acquisitions: An overview. In A. Alexander, J. Owers, & R. Carveth (Eds.), *Media economics: Theory and practice* (pp. 115–133). Hillsdale, NJ: Lawrence Erlbaum.

Parenti, M. (1986). *Inventing reality: The politics of the mass media*. New York, NY: St. Martin's.

Pariser, E. (2011). *The filter bubble: How the new personalized web is changing what we read and how we think*. New York, NY: Penguin Books.

Paul, R. P., & Elder, L. (2006). *How to detect media bias & propaganda* (3rd ed.). Dillon Beach, CA: Foundation for Critical Thinking.

Petty, R. E., & Cacioppo, J. T. (1986). *Communication and persuasion: Central and peripheral routes to attitude change*. New York, NY: Springer-Verlag.

Picard, R. G., Winter, J. P., McCombs, M., & Lacy, S. (Eds.). (1988). *Press concentration and monopoly: New perspectives on newspaper ownership and operation*. Norwood, NJ: Ablex.

Pingdom (2014). Internet in numbers. Retrieved June 4, 2014, from http://royal.pingdom .com/2014/06/14/ internet-2014-in-numbers

Pipher, M. (1996). *The shelter of each other.* New York, NY: Putnam.

Plack, C. J. (2005). Auditory perception. In K. Lamberts & R. I. Goldstone (Eds.), *Handbook of cognition* (pp. 71–104). Thousand Oaks, CA: Sage.

Plunkett Research. (2013). Entertainment & media industry market research. Retrieved April 20, 2013, from http://www .plunkettresearch.com/ entertainment-media-publishing-market-research/ industry-trends

Poniewozik, J. (2012, September 24). Check, please. Fact-checking has been good news in 2012, but it's only a start. *Time*, p. 68.

Postman, N., & Powers, S. (1992). *How to watch TV news.* New York, NY: Penguin.

Potter, W. J. (1987a). Does television viewing hinder academic achievement among adolescents? *Human Communication Research, 14,* 27–46.

Potter, W. J. (1999). *On media violence.* Thousand Oaks, CA: Sage.

Potter, W. J. (2003). *The 11 myths of media violence.* Thousand Oaks, CA: Sage.

Potter, W. J. (2005). *Becoming a strategic thinker: Developing skills for success.* Upper Saddle River, NJ: Prentice Hall.

Potter, W. J. (2012). *Media effects.* Thousand Oaks, CA: Sage.

Potter, W. J. (2013a). *Media literacy* (7th ed.). Thousand Oaks, CA: Sage.

Potter, W. J. (2013b). *The skills of media literacy.* Las Vegas, NV: Knowledge Assets, Inc.

Potter, W. J., & Vaughan, M. (1997). Aggression in television entertainment: Profiles and trends. *Communication Research Reports, 14,* 116–124.

Pozner, J. L. (2010). *Reality bites back: The troubling truth about guilty pleasure TV.* New York: Seal Press.

Pritchard, D. A. (1975). Leveling-sharpening revised. *Perceptual and Motor Skills, 40,* 111–117.

Raney, A. A. (2009). The effects of viewing televised sports. In R. L. Nabi & M. B. Oliver (Eds.), *Media processes and effects* (pp. 439–453). Thousand Oaks, CA: Sage.

Raney, A. A., & Bryant, J. (Eds.). (2006). *Handbook of sports and media.* Mahwah, NJ: Lawrence Erlbaum.

Rhodes, S., & Reibstein, L. (1996, July 1). Let him walk! *Newsweek*, pp. 44–45.

Roberts, D. F., & Foehr, U. G. (2008). Trends in media use. *Children and Electronic Media, 18.* Retrieved May 4, 2011, from http://futureofchildren.org/ futureofchildren/publications/ journals/article/index .xml?journalid=32&article id=55&sectionid=233&submit

Robertson, L. (2001, March). Ethically challenged. *American Journalism Review*, pp. 20–29.

Romer, D., Jamieson, K. H., & Aday, S. (2003). Television news and the cultivation of fear of crime. *Journal of Communication, 53,* 88–104.

The Roper Organization. (1981). *Sex, profanity and violence: An opinion survey about seventeen television programs.* New York, NY: Information Office.

Sammy, S. (2012, July 18). The financial web of the Spiderman films. Retrieved May 3, 2013, from http://www.therichest.org/ entertainment/financial-web-of-the-spider-man-films

Saporito, B. (2012, November 5). What's in a name? *Time*, pp. 54–55.

Schudson, M. (2003). *The sociology of news.* New York, NY: Norton.

Schumpeter, J. (2011, April 16). Fail often, fail well. *The Economist, 399,* p. 74.

Schwartz, B. (2004). *The paradox of choice: Why more is less.* New York, NY: HarperCollins.

Screenwerk. (2014). Local Online Ads Grow to $24.5B in 2013. Retrieved June 24, 2014, from http://screenwerk .com/2013/01/11/local-online-ads-grow-to-24-5b-in-2013

Second Life. (n.d.). What is second life? Retrieved June 29, 2011, from http://secondlife .com/whatis/?lang=en-US

Second Life Grid Survey. (2013, May 5). Retrieved May 5, 2013, from http://www.gridsurvey.com

Seguin, J., & Culver, S. H. (2012). *Media career guide: Preparing for jobs in the 21st century* (6th ed.). Boston, MA: Bedford/St. Martin's.

Shoemaker, P. J., & Reese, S. D. (1996). *Mediating the message: Theories of influences on mass media content* (2nd ed.). White Plains, NY: Longman.

Silver, N. (2012). *The signal and the noise: Why so many predictions* fail—but some don't. New York, NY: Penguin Press.

Smith, C. (2013, March 23). How many people use the top social media, apps & services. Retrieved April 1, 2013, from http://expandedramblings.com/index.php/resource-how-many-people-use-the-top-social-media

Sparks, G. G., Sparks, C. W., & Sparks, E. A. (2009). Media violence. In J. Bryant & M. B. Oliver (Eds.), *Media effects: Advances in theory and research* (3rd ed., pp. 269–286). New York, NY: Routledge.

Sponder, M. (2012). *Social media analytics: Effective tools for building, interpreting, and using metrics.* New York, NY: McGraw-Hill.

Spotrac.com. (2012). NFL salaries. Retrieved April 19, 2013, from http://www.sportscity.com/nfl/salaries

Stampler, L. (2013, February 4). Here are all the super bowl 2013 ads in order. Retrieved April 20, 2013, from http://www.businessinsider.com/all-the-super-bowl-2013-ads-in-order-2013-2?op=1

Statista. (2014). Social media usage. Retrieved June 28, 2014, from http://www.statista.com/statistics/270229/usage-duration-of-social-networks-by-country

Steele, J. E. (1995). Experts and the operational bias of television news: The case of the Persian Gulf War. *Journalism & Mass Communication Quarterly, 72,* 799–812.

Stewart, L. (2004, March 24). Study criticizes school over diversity, graduation rates. *Los Angeles Times,* p. D5.

Sunstein, C. R. (2006). *Infotopia: How many minds produce knowledge.* New York, NY: Oxford University Press.

Sykes, J. (2006). A player-centred approach to digital game design. In J. Rutter & J. Bryce (Eds.), *Understanding digital games* (pp. 75–92). Thousand Oaks, CA: Sage.

The highest paid celebrities. (2012, August 27). Retrieved April 14, 2013, from www.forbes.com/pictures/mfl45lhfj/oprah-winfrey-21

Thompson, C. (2009, September). The new literacy. *Wired,* p. 48.

Top 15 most popular political websites. (2015, February). Retrieved February 14, 2015, from www.ebizmba.com/articles/political-websites

Tyner, K. Ed. (2010). *Media literacy: New agendas in communication.* New York, NY: Routledge.

Tyre, P. (2002, August 5). Fighting "big fat." *Newsweek,* pp. 38, 40.

Unkind unwind. (2011, March 19). *The Economist,* pp. 76–78.

USA Today salaries databases. (2013). *USA Today online.* Retrieved April 19, 2013, from http://content.usatoday.com/sportsdata

U.S. Bureau of the Census. (2012). *Country business patterns.* Retrieved from http://censtats.census.gov/cgi-bin/cbpnaic/cbpdetl.pl

U.S. Bureau of the Census. (2013). *Statistical abstract of the United States: 2012.* Washington, DC: Department of Commerce.

U.S. Bureau of Labor Statistics. (2011). *Occupational outlook handbook, 2010–11 edition.* Retrieved July 22, 2011, from http://www.bls.gov/oco/ocos320.htm#emply

U.S. Bureau of Labor Statistics. (2013a, January). *Media and information: Average wages, selected media-related occupation, May 2011.* Retrieved February 5, 2015, from http://www.bls.gov/spotlight/2013/media

U.S. Bureau of Labor Statistics. (2013b, January). *Media and information: Numeric and percent changes in projected employment, selected media-related occupations, 2010–2020.* Retrieved February 5, 2015, from http://www.bls.gov/spotlight/2013/media

Vogel, H. L. (2011). *Entertainment industry economics: A guide for financial analysis* (8th ed.). New York, NY: Cambridge University Press.

Wang, Z., & Tcherney, J. M. (2012). The "myth" of media multitasking: Reciprocal dynamics of media multitasking, personal needs, and gratifications. *Journal of Communication, 62,* 493–513. doi: 10.1111/j.1460-2466.2012.01641

Wenner, L. A. (Ed.). (1998). *MediaSport.* New York, NY: Routledge.

Whitman, D. (1996, December 16). I'm OK, you're not. *U.S. News & World Report,* pp. 24–30.

Whitman, D., & Loftus, M. (1996, December 16). Things are getting better? Who knew? *U.S. News & World Report,* pp. 30, 32.

Wikipedia Statistics. (2014). Retrieved June 28, 2014, from http://en.wikipedia.org/wiki/Wikipedia:Statistics

Witkin, H. A., & Goodenough, D. R. (1977). Field dependence and interpersonal behavior.

Psychological Bulletin, 84, 661–689.

Wolff, M. (2003, May 26). Troubled times. *New York Magazine,* pp.18–21.

Wright, A. (2007). *Glut: Mastering information through the ages.* Washington, DC: Joseph Henry Press.

YouTube. (2009). Statistics. Retrieved from http://www.youtube.com/t/press_statistics

YouTube. (2014). Retrieved June 28, 2014, from www.youtube.com/yt/press/statistics.html

Zillmann, D. (1991). Television viewing and physiological arousal. In J. Bryant & Zillmann, D. (Eds.), *Responding to the screen: Reception and reaction processes* (pp. 103–133). Hillsdale, NJ: Lawrence Erlbaum.

INDEX